560-52

THROUGH RUSSIAN EYES:

AMERICAN-CHINESE RELATIONS

THROUGH RUSSIAN EYES:

AMERICAN-CHINESE RELATIONS

By

S. SERGEICHUK

international library

book | publishers

ARLINGTON, VIRGINIA

1975

ORIGINAL RUSSIAN TITLE:

SShA I KITAI

(THE U.S.A. & CHINA)

Published in Moscow,

1968 (1st ed.), 1973 (2nd ed.)

Authorized Translation
by
Elizabeth Cody-Rutter

Edited by
Philip A. Garon

Library of Congress Catalogue Card Number: 74-75134
ISBN 0-914250-03-5

Printed in the United States of America

CONTENTS

PREFACE

Many specialists in international affairs consider the intricacies of American-Chinese relations to be among the most complex problems facing the modern world. "Ping-pong diplomacy" and the subsequent personal contacts between high-ranking government officials of the United States and the People's Republic of China—events which, in a sense, greatly surprised many international observers—engendered in various countries widespread public interest in American-Chinese relations, and prompted a number of perplexing questions as well.

It should be noted in this regard that even during the years which preceded the "ping-pong diplomacy," scholars and journalists throughout the world closely followed the development of American-Chinese relations and published a number of interesting works on the topic. American readers, in particular, could turn for information to such books as *The American People and China* (1966) by Archibald T. Steele, *Recognition of Communist China?* (1961) by Robert Newman, *The United States and China in World Affairs* (1966) by Robert Blum, and numerous others.

The U.S.A. and China, written by the Soviet Sinologist S. Sergeichuk and published in Moscow in 1969 (a second, revised edition was published in 1973),* ranks among the serious studies of contemporary American-Chinese relations. The author, in his own words, "does not pretend to offer a comprehensive analysis and interpretation of the relations between the United States and the People's Republic of China," but attempts instead to provide a "concise historical outline of American policy with regard to China." The book was written amid the

Through Russian Eyes: American-Chinese Relations is a translation of the second, enlarged edition. (*Editor's note*)

flurry of onrushing events, and is therefore based more on newspaper and magazine reports, eyewitness accounts, and current documents, than on archival research.

This kind of approach to the study and interpretation of major international problems demands, of course, solid erudition, as well as a certain degree of courage. It fully raises the possibility that an author's book will become outdated even before it comes off the printing-press. Sergeichuk's work, however, has withstood the tests of both time and rapidly changing circumstances. Written in 1967 and early 1968, *The U.S.A. and China* has not been rendered obsolete by the dramatic changes which have occurred in American policy toward the People's Republic of China during the past four-to-five years. Indeed, the book sounds particularly timely today. The reason for its continuing relevance, in our opinion, is the author's skill in perceiving, amid the artful design of facts and contradictory actions discussed in the book, a *definite trend*, which he carefully delineates throughout his narrative.

Even a casual reading of the book's table of contents gives the reader a clearly drawn sketch of the development of American-Chinese relations during the last quarter-century. And Sergeichuk simultaneously has succeeded in demonstrating the manner in which the foreign policy issue of relations with China affected the internal political struggle within the United States, the way in which the demagogue Senator Joseph McCarthy exploited the issue for his own purposes, and the changes which occurred in the "China lobby" during those years. These features, in our judgment, make the book of considerable interest to the American reader. We know of only one work by an American author with a scope of events that compares with Sergeichuk's book: the late Foster Rhea Dulles' *American Policy toward Communist China: The Historical Record, 1949-1969*, which was published in 1972. Without intending to draw a parallel between these two works, we would suggest only that a comparison between the views of the Soviet scholar and the American specialist in this field will inevitably arouse the interest of all those who are closely observing current international affairs.

From conversations with Sergeichuk, we gather that he has not ruled out the possibility of returning to this subject at some later date, to continue the analysis of events—visible and invisible—which are transpiring in the sphere of American-Chinese relations. Sergeichuk, in response to our question concerning his assessment of the recent development of American-Chinese relations, pointed out that contacts between the two nations are now taking place in an international atmosphere which totally differs from that which prevailed prior to 1972. The relaxation of international tension which has occurred since that date cannot fail to exert a marked influence upon future U.S. policy toward China. However, even given these circumstances, Peking's tendency to turn back the clock of history, to return mankind to the sad memory of the "cold war" era, remains clearly apparent. The question thus arises: Which does the United States prefer—further progress along the path of detente, or connivance with Peking's Great Power aspirations?

Such a question may seem, at first glance, much over-simplified and even a bit naive. Naturally, history has a tendency to develop in ways other than a straight line. It should nonetheless be recognized that the entire foreign policy of the leadership of the People's Republic of China is presently directed *against* the further relaxation of international tension, and toward the fomenting of misunderstanding and conflict. This means that the success of a nation's efforts to develop relations with Peking depends not so much upon that nation's good will as upon its determination to stand firm in adherence to the basic principles of its own foreign policy. One would like to think that the appointment of such an experienced and skillful diplomat as George Bush to head the U.S. Liaison Office in Peking reflects America's recognition of these very considerations.

It is absolutely clear that the policy of anti-Communism and anti-Sovietism has yielded no dividends for the architects of American foreign policy, neither generally nor in the specific case of relations with China. To conduct a truly effective foreign policy, the United States must understand the increasing influence of the Soviet Union and other socialist countries, respect the aspirations for peace held by the broad masses of people in all countries, and recognize the significance of the national liberation movements and other positive factors in the current world development. American policy toward China will thus depend primarily upon the course which the United States will adopt in international relations as a whole.

In recommending S. Sergeichuk's book to the American reader, we hope that it will enhance the understanding in the United States of the Soviet community's attitude toward one of the most important aspects of U.S. foreign policy, and thereby promote mutual understanding between our peoples.

N. MOLCHANOV
Doctor of Historical Sciences
September 1974   *Professor, U.S.S.R. Ministry of Foreign Affairs*

AUTHOR'S INTRODUCTION

The major directions and goals of the current foreign policy of the Soviet government were defined by the XXIVth Congress of the Communist Party of the Soviet Union. Comrade Leonid I. Brezhnev, General Secretary of the Central Committee of the Soviet Communist Party, stated in March 1972: "The program adopted by the Congress, which became known as the Soviet Peace Program, is being practiced consistently and has become an effective factor in world politics. Our principal course is the active defense of peace, freedom and the security of nations."

The Plenum of the Central Committee of the Soviet Communist Party, which convened in May 1972, stated with great satisfaction that "the Leninist foreign policy of the Communist Party and government of the Soviet Union enjoys the unanimous support of the entire party and the Soviet people. The principled, consistent foreign policy of the U.S.S.R. responds to the basic interests of the Soviet Union, world socialism, and the national liberation movement. It actively furthers the strengthening of principles of peaceful coexistence among nations with differing social systems, and the rejection of the aggressive policy of imperialism."

The cooperation of the socialist states, successes of the fraternal countries in economic development, and close coordination of their foreign policy actions strengthen the position and international prestige of socialism. Socialism is exerting an increasing influence upon the course of world events. The truly significant results of the Soviet government's efforts to strengthen peace and security throughout the world are well known to all mankind. Prominent Soviet leaders, including General Secretary Brezhnev, A. N. Kosygin, Chairman of the U.S.S.R. Council of Ministers, and N. V. Podgorny, Chairman of the

Presidium of the Supreme Soviet of the U.S.S.R., have visited a number of countries in Asia, Africa and America; their visits played an important role in the achievement of these goals. The ratification in Paris in October 1971 of such important documents as the Principles of Cooperation between the U.S.S.R. and France, the Soviet-French Declaration and others constituted the true realization of the Leninist principles of peaceful coexistence, and raised Franco-Russian cooperation to a new and loftier level, extending to the political sphere.

Important and positive changes are also occurring in the Soviet Union's relations with the Federal Republic of Germany. The treaty concluded between the U.S.S.R. and the Federal Republic of Germany responds to the established territorial and political realities in Europe and lays the foundation for the development of good neighborly relations between the two nations. Soviet relations are also developing successfully with other European states—Finland, the Scandinavian countries, Austria, Italy and a number of other nations. The Soviet Union, actively implementing the Peace Program, has continually risen to support resolutely the safeguarding of a durable peace and security, not only on the European continent, but in all corners of the globe, including Asia, Africa and America.

It is well known that broadened perspectives for normalizing the international situation were unveiled as a result of the Soviet-American summit talks (May 1972). A foundation was laid for further improvement of relations between both countries, and a number of bilateral agreements in various areas were concluded. It is especially noteworthy that mutual understanding was not achieved to the detriment of any other nation's best interests. The understanding which was reached fully concurs not only with the interests of the peoples of the U.S.S.R. and the United States of America, but also with the necessity for international security.

It should simultaneously be noted that Western reactionary circles— above all, the bosses of the American military-industrial complex and the NATO militarists—are opposing with all their strength the process of relaxation of international tension, and are promoting the acceleration of the arms race. This compels the Soviet people to maintain continual vigilance, always keeping alert to the adventures of reactionaries of every stripe. Our country has been, and remains, the main bulwark in the struggles against the imperialists' intrigues. The Soviet people resolutely oppose acts of aggression and any moves to suppress the struggle for national liberation, to interfere in other nations' affairs, or to violate other nations' rights.

The Soviet government and Communist Party, while actively seeking the relaxation of international tension, are realistically evaluating the existing world situation and reacting in a timely manner to all changes. The Soviet Union is thus endeavoring to improve relations with the People's Republic of China. Characteristically, the Peking leadership, in an effort to break out from its known isolation in the international arena, is currently revamping China's foreign policy. The Hong Kong journal *China News Analysis* portrayed these revisions as nothing more than a "big game of good will and polite smiles." It must be said, however, that Peking's policy, as in the past, continues to be based upon anti-Sovietism, the provocation of schisms which are detrimental to world socialism and the international Communist movement, and dissociation from the anti-imperialist forces. Under these conditions, the Soviet state, although resolutely repulsing the intrigues of the Peking leadership, is nonetheless full of good feeling toward the People's Republic of China and, as before, favors normalization of relations. This policy course, the principal one of our party, takes into consideration the long-range socialist interests of both the Soviet and Chinese peoples.

The fundamental reorientation of China's foreign policy toward and economic relations with the imperialist powers, especially the United States, has in recent years attracted significant interest in the world community. In this regard, public awareness of the problems of American-Chinese relations has also risen sharply. This author does not pretend to offer a comprehensive analysis and interpretation of the relations between the United States and the People's Republic of China. His task is significantly more modest: to present a concise historical outline of American policy with regard to China, on the basis of available documents, publications and materials from periodicals.

In preparing the second edition of this work, the author has added additional chapters, as well as new material which updates the narrative to the end of 1972.

CHAPTER I

AMERICAN - CHINESE
RELATIONS: A NEW FACTOR

It is well known that foreign political conditions at the time of the Chinese revolutionary victory led the masses of the Chinese people and the cadre of the Chinese Communist Party to understand that successful advancement along the path of basic social transformation was impossible without guidance from, and lessons taught by, the experience of the Soviet Union and other socialist countries. It later became clear, however, that while the workers then predominant in the party recognized this state of affairs as the key to socialist reconstruction of Chinese society, Mao Tse-tung and his supporters were governed primarily by nationalist considerations. Mao understood, of course, that without economic, military and other aid from the Soviet Union, China could not become an independent state and bolster its prestige in the international arena. However, Mao and his group meant to utilize the overwhelming progress achieved by China during its socialist development, which was advanced by the U.S.S.R. and other fraternal countries, for the realization of their own Great Power, hegemonic ambitions. The Maoist group's Great Power ambitions became significantly clear only much later, for during the first years of its existence the People's Republic of China established bonds of brotherhood and international unity with the socialist countries.

The position of the People's Republic of China as an integral part of the world socialist system also determined the direction of American policy with regard to China during this period (1949-57). The White House pursued a policy toward Peking which was a component of such political and military stratagems of American imperialism as the "doctrine of containment" and the "doctrine of liberation," both aiming at the liquidation of the Chinese people's achievements. It is also significant that the Pentagon's military plans during that period automatically envisaged a simultaneous strike against the U.S.S.R. and the People's Republic of China. In Washington, no distinction was made in this regard between the Soviet Union and the Chinese people's young state. Even then, there were two trends—nationalist and internationalist— in the leadership of the Chinese People's Republic. Yet, the official declaration of policy for socialist construction inevitably fostered the strengthening of the internationalist tendencies in the party and people. Huge successes in China's economic and cultural development, its population's heightened standard of living, and the growth in prestige of the Chinese People's Republic in the international arena inspired confidence that China was headed in the right direction. This assurance was confirmed by the resolutions adopted in 1956 by the VIIIth Congress of the Chinese Communist Party, which met under the banner of consolidation and growth of the Marxist-Leninist forces in the party ranks. The Congress reaffirmed the Chinese Communist Party's general policy on the construction of socialism.

The aid of the fraternal socialist countries and the strenuous efforts of the Chinese workers achieved most appreciable results. Thus, the output of industrial production in the Chinese People's Republic grew more than five-fold between 1949 and 1957. Within ten years after the formation of the People's Republic of China, the proportion of the country's total industrial output produced solely with the aid of equipment provided by the Soviet Union was 35-40 percent of the iron, steel and rolled metal; 100 percent of the aluminum; 85 percent of the trucks and tractors; 40 percent of the electrical energy; 45 percent of the electrical equipment; and 35 percent of heavy machine production.

All these facts were well known in Washington during that period, but certain circles nevertheless pinned serious hopes on the growth of nationalist sentiments in China and the consolidation of the "good will tendencies" toward the United States which still existed in "certain circles of the Chinese leadership." Later developments demonstrated that these hopes were not without foundation.

The Communist Party of China, as is generally known, originated and developed in a semicolonial, semifeudal country, which was extremely backward economically, socially and culturally. The words of V. I. Lenin automatically leap to mind: "The more backward a country, the stronger its small-scale agricultural production, its patriarchal character and its remoteness, all of which inevitably leads to that particular strength and firmness of the deepest petit-bourgeois prejudices, namely, prejudices of national egotism and national narrowmindedness."

The structure of Chinese society had reflected this backwardness even before the revolutionary victory. Of note, above all, was the small size of the working class. In 1925, industrial workers in China numbered approximately 1.8 to 2.5 million, which means that they comprised only about 0.5 percent of the population. Furthermore, the workers were dispersed among small enterprises. In 1935, for example, only 5 percent of all industrial enterprises in the eleven main provinces of the Chinese interior and the four main cities (Shanghai, Nanking, Hangchow, and Peking) employed more than 500 workers each, whereas the great bulk (48.7 percent) consisted of small enterprises, each with 30-50 workers. For comparison, we point out that in Russia on the eve of the October Revolution, 54 percent of all industrial enterprises employed at least 500 workers. Along with the peasantry, which constituted the predominant mass of the population, there was in China another large social class: the petit-bourgeoisie, consisting of small merchants and artisans.

All these factors were destined to leave an imprint upon the Chinese Communist Party's formation and development, which, under these conditions, occurred with major difficulties. The Plenum of the Central Committee of the Chinese Communist Party noted in November 1927 that "the Chinese Communist Party had already begun to be formed as a political current and as a party during that period when the Chinese proletariat had not yet constituted itself as a class, and when the class movement of workers and peasants was still in the embryonic stage. . . . During that period, the most radical elements of the petit-bourgeoisie rushed into the ranks of our party and occupied the far left-wing of the national liberation movement front. These elements also constituted the original nucleus of the Chinese Communist Party."

Of course, the ideas of the Great October Revolution and the support of the Comintern—the collective organ of the international Communist movement—had a beneficial influence upon the situation within the Communist Party of China. "On this basis," noted the journal *Kommunist*, "a nucleus of Communist-internationalists, who were oriented toward Marxism-Leninism and endeavored to apply that philosophy to conditions in their own country, was formed within the Communist Party of China. From the very outset, two trends within the Communist Party of China were struggling with each other: the Marxist-Leninist internationalist trend, and the petit-bourgeois nationalist trend."

It is significant that the diverse factions of the nationalist trend within the leadership of the Chinese Communist Party during various periods of China's history linked the realization of their own plans with the involvement of the Soviet Union in an armed conflict with the forces of imperialism. So it was, for example, in 1930, when leftist-inclined elements within the leadership of the Chinese Communist

Party, which refused to face reality, launched a campaign—contrary to the advice of the Comintern—for an armed seizure of the cities, calculating that these uprisings in China would simultaneously draw the U.S.S.R. into battle with imperialism. This policy, which Mao Tse-tung embraced, had adherents who thought that as a result of the world war which would then erupt, the international proletariat would rise in a world revolution and, by this very fact, assure the victory of socialism in China. Since the end of the Thirties, the nationalism of the Mao Tse-tung group, which seized the leadership of the party, has become evident in the efforts to isolate the Communist Party of China from the influence of the international proletariat, and to set the so-called "thoughts of Mao Tse-tung" in opposition to Marxist-Leninist teachings and the entire experience of the international working class.

At the 1957 Moscow Conference of the Communist and Workers' Party, Mao Tse-tung advocated the anti-Marxist thesis that world imperialism can be defeated only through nuclear war, and attempted to push the nations of the world onto a path of atomic catastrophe. Furthermore, Mao and his group regarded, and continue to regard, as inconsequential the innumerable casualties, calamities and worldwide suffering which would result. "Let's try force first," Mao advised the socialist countries in 1957, "and then we shall return to construction."

While trying to push the U.S.S.R. and the United States into nuclear conflict, Mao's group simultaneously favored a tactic of passive restraint and, thus, did not hasten to fulfill the international obligation of the Communist Party of China toward the world Communist movement. This situation prevailed during the Second World War, when all revolutionary and progressive forces of the world, including the Chinese people, engaged in a bloody struggle against German fascism and Japanese militarism. Under these circumstances, Mao Tse-tung did not merely attempt to foist upon the Communist Party of China the tactic of passive restraint, but actually denied the Comintern's direct request in the fall of 1941 to intensify China's war against Japan in order to avert a Japanese attack against the Soviet Union from the rear. The Maoist group adheres to this tactic even now, when the breach caused by the Communist Party of China in the united front of the socialist states has allowed the United States to launch its larcenous aggression against the Democratic Republic of Vietnam. It was thus characteristic of Mao as early as the Thirties to underestimate existing objective situations, to think unrealistically, and to exaggerate facts excessively.

The nationalism of the Mao Tse-tung group which had seized the leadership of the party subsequently began to manifest itself in an attempt to isolate the Communist Party of China from the influence of the international proletariat. Furthermore, Mao's supporters cultivated nationalist sentiments in the party and warred against the Communist-internationalists under the demagogic slogan of overcoming "foreign clichés." It is interesting to note in this connection that the American General Hurley, visiting Yenan in 1944 to meet with leaders of the Communist Party of China, was so amazed by their views that he later claimed that the Chinese Communists could be distinguished from Oklahoma farmers only in so far as the Chinese were armed.

The leadership of the Chinese Communist Party took the first steps toward adjustment of official and unofficial relations with Washington in the mid-Forties. A number of Washington figures at that time viewed the Chinese Communists as a real force capable of resisting the Japanese war machine, and were quite willing to use the Chinese people's armed forces and bases, which were under Communist Party leadership, in the struggle against Japan. American diplomatic and military observers appeared in the center of the liberated regions—at Yenan, and among units of the people's armed forces. Secret and even super-secret reports and memoranda on the internal situation in China, the role and significance of the Communist Party of China, and the positions which its leadership occupied were drawn up in the quiet of Washington offices.

American Sinologists note with regret that the bulk of these materials is still classified and sealed in steel vaults in the National Archives. One report, however, happened to be published because of an internal political struggle among various groups of congressmen. This document, titled "The Chinese Communist Movement," was prepared in July 1945 by the U.S. War Department Office of Intelligence. Ninety-two copies were distributed to various American military and intelligence agencies, fifteen to the White House, and three to the Department of State. According to its authors, the data in this report were gathered from more than 2,500 official and unofficial sources, and constituted an effort not only to describe the economic and political situation in the liberated regions, but also to analyze the possible course of action which the leaders of the Communist Party of China might take. The authors of the report thus endeavored to answer the question of whether the United States had—to use their own phrase—"bet on the right horse" in China.

It is not the intention herein to analyze in detail this report of approximately 400 typewritten pages. We shall dwell only upon those parts which enable us to shed additional light on the position of the nationalist circles within the leadership of the Communist Party of China, and upon the reasons for Peking's subsequent contacts with Washington.

American intelligence deemed it necessary above all to point out that, in the opinion of the majority of Western observers, the "Chinese

Communists* are not at all Communists," since the Chinese had repudiated socialist and revolutionary ideals and become simple "reformists," who could in no sense be compared with the Russian bolsheviks. One of these observers–Brooks Atkinson of *The New York Times*–stated that the leaders of the Communist Party of China had "concluded that China was not ready for socialism and would not be ready for at least a half-century." Another American observer reported from Chungking that it was simply "unfortunate that the present-day Communist Party [in China] bears the name. . . . The [Chinese] Communists adhere more closely to the basic . . . fundamentals of Sun Yat-sen's 'Three Principles'–Nationalism, Democracy, and the People's Livelihood–than does the Kuomintang."

It is evident that American observers in China even then judged the true nature of the nationalist leadership of the Communist Party of China not by its bombastic phrases, but by its concrete actions. They also received reliable information from confidential talks with Mao Tse-tung and his associates. Thus, at the end of 1944 American observers in Yenan were frankly informed that the leadership of the Communist Party of China would not object to placing its forces under a single commander of all armed forces in China, on condition that he would be "an American whom the American government will firmly support."

From July 1944 on, a group of American military observers began to function officially in Yenan. On March 13 and April 1, 1945, Mao Tse-tung held lengthy conversations with John Stewart Service, one member of this group, during which, according to the authors of the report, Mao allegedly gave a "detailed outline of the policy and attitude of the Chinese Communists toward the United States and the implications of American support of the Chungking government."** Mao stressed, in particular, five points: (1) China needed American aid both during and after the war; (2) the Chinese Communists would extend cooperation to the United States regardless of American action; (3) the Kuomintang could not develop China into a stabilizing force in the Far East; (4) the Kuomintang was unable to maintain friendly relations with "Soviet Russia and other neighbors"; (5) the Communist Party of China represented the interests of the Chinese people, and it would thus be to the best interest of the United States to support the Chinese Communists, for only under Communist leadership could democracy be established in China.

---

*Here and elsewhere, this term refers to the nationalist leadership of the Communist Party of China. (*Author's note*)

**i.e., the Chiang Kai-shek government (*Author's note*)

According to notes of the conversations between Mao Tse-tung and Service, Mao's exact words to Service were: "Between the people of China and the people of the United States there are strong ties of sympathy, understanding and mutual interests. . . . China's greatest post-war need is economic development. . . . America is not only the most suitable country to assist this economic development of China: she is the only country fully able to participate. For all these reasons, there must not and cannot be any conflict, estrangement or misunderstanding between the Chinese people and America.

"Communist [Chinese] policy toward the United States is, and will remain, to seek friendly American support of democracy in China and cooperation in fighting Japan. But regardless of American action, whether or not they receive a single gun or bullet [from the Americans], the Communists will continue to offer [to the Americans] and practice cooperation in any manner possible. . . . The Communists will continue to seek American friendship and understanding, because it will be needed by China in the post-war period of reconstruction.

"Whether or not America extends cooperation to the Communists is, of course, a matter for only America to decide. But the Communists see only advantages for the United States. . . .

"America does not realize her influence in China and her ability to shape events there. . . .

"There is no such thing as America not intervening in China!

"You are here as China's greatest ally. The fact of your presence is tremendous. America's intentions have been good."

The authors of the report noted that Mao Tse-tung's statement concerning cooperation with the United States, regardless of whether the Americans supported the Communists, "may have been more diplomatic than realistic." But at this point they emphasized that other American observers in China, who had close contacts with the Communist Party of China, confirmed that Mao and his associates preferred to have America as their friend. These very same observers, however, warned that continuation of American aid to Chiang Kai-shek and refusal to support Mao Tse-tung would compel Mao and his group to begin viewing America as their enemy. The United States was the "greatest hope and greatest fear" for the nationalist leadership of the Communist Party of China, but China preferred to have the United States as a friend—such was the conclusion which these observers reached in November 1944.

On April 2, 1945, Major General Patrick J. Hurley, the U.S. Ambassador to China, announced at a Washington press conference that the Chinese Communist Party leadership had asked the United States at the beginning of 1945 to supply its troops with arms. It is well known, however, that the American ruling circles shifted during the second half of the Forties from a policy of advances toward the nationalist elements in the leadership of the Communist Party of China to one of unconditional support for Chiang Kai-shek's Kuomintang regime, thereby seriously limiting the possibilities for American initiatives in relations with China. The policy of alliance with the Kuomintang appeared to be part of that reactionary course in international affairs which the American ruling circles began to pursue after the Second World War, when they shifted from cooperation with the U.S.S.R. to "cold war." Washington's support of Chiang Kai-shek appeared to be one of the concrete manifestations of the so-called "doctrine of the containment of Communism," the predominant foreign policy dictum of American imperialism during that period. Washington's alliance with the Kuomintang was strengthened by the conclusion of the so-called Five Year Treaty of Friendship, Commerce and Navigation, in Nanking on November 4, 1946.

The Soviet Army's destruction of Hitler's Germany and Russia's decisive role in the defeat of imperialist Japan were the most important international factors in the victory of the Chinese revolution. This victory resulted not only in the strengthening of the positions of internationalist circles within the leadership of the Communist Party of China, but also in the striking of a powerful blow against the nationalist aspirations of Mao Tse-tung and his group. Manchuria, liberated by Soviet troops, simultaneously became a powerful military-strategic base for the Communist Party of China's armed forces—an advantage which, in the end, was a decisive factor in the defeat of the Kuomintang regime, armed by American imperialism.

The Maoist group began its sharp departure from the general policy of the international Communist movement at the end of the Fifties, when the leadership of the Communist Party of China issued a public statement of views which was at variance with Marxism-Leninism. The Chinese leadership advocated its erroneous policy on many questions of world development at the Moscow Conference of Communist and Workers' Parties (1957), a session of the World Federation of Trade Unions in Peking (1960), the Bucharest Conference of Representatives of the Communist and Workers' Parties (1960), and the Conference of Representatives of 81 Communist and Workers' Parties in Moscow (1960).

It is common knowledge that the attempts of the Chinese leadership to impose its particular policy upon the world Communist movement were rejected by the participants in the Conference of Representatives of 81 Communist and Workers' Parties. After they hypocritically put their signatures to the "Declaration and Appeal to the Peoples of the

World," the Chinese Communist Party leaders actually embarked upon a political struggle against the Communist movement and began to pursue a typical Great Power policy, completely ignoring the true interests of the world revolutionary movement. Mao and his group simultaneously did everything possible to aggravate international tension, where this seemed advantageous to them, and to pour oil on the flames of simmering conflicts.

It is significant that the positions of the Maoist group often coincide with those of the ruling circles of imperialist powers. It is generally known that the Peking leaders embarked upon the unprincipled formation of alliances "on an anti-Soviet basis with any forces, even the most reactionary, be they the most zealous anti-Soviets among the English Tories or revanchist elements in the Federal Republic of Germany, the Portuguese colonialists or the racists from South Africa." The Maoist positions coincide, in essence, with the position of the revanchist circles and of the NATO militarists on such questions as anti-Sovietism, the convocation of an all-European conference on the problems of formulating a system of security and cooperation in Europe, the drive for nuclear weapons, the aggravation of tension in Europe, and the revision of state borders. Peking's representatives also take a negative position on questions of disarmament, the permanent ban on the use of nuclear weapons, and the non-application of force in international relations. All this notwithstanding, efforts are being made in Peking to cover up its policy with pseudo-revolutionary slogans and ultra-left phrases, which were particularly noticeable at the XXVIIth Session of the United Nations General Assembly, held at the end of 1972.

From approximately 1957 onward, the statements and actions of the United States ruling circles concerning the People's Republic of China must be considered in light of that policy in international relations which Mao Tse-tung and his group began to pursue. In December 1972, L. I. Brezhnev, General Secretary of the Soviet Communist Party's Central Committee, noted: "It is already more than ten years since the leaders of the Chinese People's Republic adopted a policy of struggle against the U.S.S.R., and actually against the entire socialist alliance, which they continue to view as the main obstacle in the path of their Great Power plans." If this policy is not taken into consideration, it is impossible to understand the true character and aims of American policy toward Peking, for the latter has to a significant degree been determined by the main thrust of Mao's foreign policy, which is directed not against imperialism, but against the socialist countries, and primarily the Soviet Union.

By its vividly expressed anti-Sovietism, Peking gives Washington the impression that the Maoists consider the primary task not the struggle against imperialism, but against the Soviet Union and other socialist countries—the fundamental opponents of imperialism. This reactionary platform was specifically reaffirmed once again at the XIIth Plenum of the Central Committee of the Communist Party of China which, according to a report of the Hsin Hua agency, convened in October 1968. Thus, notwithstanding all the "anti-imperialist" slogans of the Maoist group, its opposition to the aggressive policy of the United States actually amounts only to high-sounding phrases—to which Washington long ago stopped paying attention.

The facts indicate that the "anti-Americanism" of Mao Tse-tung and his group has in reality already lost its anti-imperialist substance and turned into a nationalist doctrine, under which the United States is regarded primarily as a rival to Peking's aspirations to hegemony in the world arena. The United States ruling circles are endeavoring to exploit for their own aims both the anti-Sovietism and the superficial "anti-Americanism" of the leadership of the People's Republic of China, while intensively propagandizing the idea of "building bridges" to Peking. Since 1968, United States trade with the People's Republic of China has been expanding through intermediary third parties in Hong Kong.

Reactionary circles are simultaneously attempting to exploit the anti-Sovietism of Mao Tse-tung and his group so as to intensify China's struggle against the socialist bloc countries, and primarily against the Soviet Union. But the "ultra-revolutionary" and adventurist side of Peking's policy leads certain American circles to justify their aggressive actions, to thrust China's neighbors into the embrace of American imperialism, and to force them to receive American military "aid." This is exactly the way the "Nixon Doctrine," which is aimed specifically at the establishment of a new "balance of power" in Asia, has manifested itself in recent years. Such policies make it possible to create a new, innately nationalist basis for relations between the chauvinistic Maoist group and the ruling circles of imperialist America.

The Great Power aspirations which have become the foundation for the entire political course of the present Chinese Communist Party leadership are simultaneously becoming important factors in American-Chinese relations. Based upon certain aspects of these aspirations— primarily anti-Sovietism—some American circles are persistently attempting to "build bridges" to Peking. It is common knowledge that anti-Sovietism has become the fundamental policy orientation of the Mao Tse-tung group. Mao's anti-Soviet course is, by admission of the well-known American political figure Averell Harriman, a factor which has "vitally important" significance for world imperialism. Other figures in the United States, especially Senator Henry Jackson, have also expressed the same thought. The policy of "building bridges" to Peking on an anti-Soviet foundation has received the support of such distinguished American statesmen as former Vice President Hubert Humphrey, and former Assistant Secretaries of State Nicholas Katzenbach and Eugene Rostow.

Soviet Sinologists note in this connection that at the base of all Peking's foreign policy doctrines lies a traditional "China-centrism," which may be the source of China's hostility not only toward the U.S.S.R., but toward any country or group of countries. At present, the leaders of the Chinese People's Republic have embarked upon an energetic rapprochement with countries of the imperialist camp.

Thus, in examining American policy toward the People's Republic of China, one must not forget that nationalism and the Great Power designs of the Mao Tse-tung group are important factors in American-Chinese relations, greatly influencing the development of those relations and exerting a pronounced influence upon the entire complex White House approach to the problem of China.

CHAPTER II

BLIND ALLEY

1. *"CHINA WHITE PAPER"*

Momentous events sometimes have as startling an impact as a sudden bolt of lightning. This statement, however read, rather accurately conveys the reaction of the average American and, to a certain extent, the American ruling circles to the defeat of Chiang Kai-shek and his expulsion from mainland China. The failure of the Kuomintang regime, in the words of Robert Newman, author of the book *Recognition of Communist China?*, "left America gasping."

Indeed, the ordinary American had reason for consternation. For years the merits of Generalissimo Chiang Kai-shek's regime had been drummed into him, and every effort had been made to convince him of the necessity to render to this regime vast aid, the cost of which exceeded the astronomical sum of $6 billion just during the three-and-a-half year period from the day of Japan's surrender to March 1949. And the ordinary American, with the aid of official propaganda, naively believed that Chiang Kai-shek was a "hero of the Chinese nation" and the "saviour of China." One of the people subsequently involved in this propaganda campaign, who wished to remain anonymous, acknowledged that during the Forties, Chiang Kai-shek's prestige in the United States was "built up to outlandish proportions."

Of course, material which portrayed Chiang Kai-shek and his associates in a true light occasionally surfaced in the pages of the American press. This was the case, for example, in 1944, when a scandal broke in connection with the recall from China, at Chiang Kai-shek's insistence, of the American General Joseph W. Stilwell, Chiang Kai-shek's Chief of Staff and Commander of the American Forces in China, who attempted to press the Kuomintang army into combat operations against the Japanese forces, an effort not completely attuned to Chiang Kai-shek's personal plans. Newspapers were compelled to publish Stilwell's denunciation of the whole Kuomintang regime, which he characterized as inefficient, thoroughly corrupt, and "on the brink of disaster." But the storm subsided, Stilwell's denunciations were quickly forgotten, and the American press continued, as before, to burn incense at the shrine of the newly created Chinese Messiah.

From official reports of its representatives in China, the American government could piece together a fairly accurate picture of Chiang Kai-shek's regime. The White House, however, was conducting a policy of double-dealing. On the one hand, Washington realized that the Kuomintang government neither expressed the will of the Chinese people nor commanded the people's respect and support. On the other hand, Washington was not only supporting by every possible means the Kuomintang's attempt to impose its will upon the Chinese people, but was also assiduously promoting the Chiang Kai-shek group, as though it were the only spokesman for China's interests.

Characterizing the policy of the American government during the years preceding the defeat of the Chiang Kai-shek regime in mainland China, Gabriel Almond, an expert on American public opinion, wrote in 1956: "The Administration in 1947-49 chose not only to be inactive, but also largely silent about the collapse of Nationalist China and its consequences. . . ." Almond, however, "is mistaken" in citing an absence of initiatives on the part of the White House, for America's intervention in China was one of the concrete manifestations of the so-called "doctrine of containment," then the dominant foreign policy goal of American imperialism. According to the Soviet historian N. Inozemtsev, "Under the guise of containment of Communist expansion, American imperialism undertook direct armed intervention in China's internal affairs; under the guise of concern for the cessation of civil war, it was in reality the initiator of such a war, which it fanned in every way, rendering maximum possible aid to the reactionary forces."

By mid-1949, almost all regions of China which were most important economically and politically had been occupied by units of the People's Liberation Army of China. The Kuomintang government, which was being supported by the United States with all its might, was spending its last days on mainland China's territory. Washington understood that an urgent review of the Far East policy was imperative. Under these circumstances, the American government began to take steps to explain somehow to Americans what was happening in China, and to justify in some way the failure of the U.S. Far East policy. On instructions of the President, the Department of State prepared a voluminous "China White Paper," officially called "United States Relations with China, with Special Reference to the Period 1944-1949."

As early as February 1948, U.S. Secretary of State George Marshall confidentially acquainted the members of the Committees on Foreign Relations of the U.S. Senate and House of Representatives with the true state of affairs in China and the conclusions which the government had reached. The American government, however, feared that public disclosure at that time of the entire series of facts unfavorable to the Chiang Kai-shek regime could only—in the words of Harry Truman—"hasten the development of events in China," *i.e.*, hasten the fall of Chiang Kai-shek. In any event, it had become clear by the end of 1948 that the collapse of the Kuomintang regime was inevitable. The American military attaché to the Chiang Kai-shek army, General David G. Barr, reported on December 28, 1948, to his Washington command: "It is extremely doubtful that the Nationalist government,* marked with the stamp of failure and having lost face as a result of the forced evacuation of the part of China located to the north of the Yangtze, could secure the necessary popular support to mobilize the masses in this region [Southern China] and to renew its forces, even if it had time for that.... Complete defeat ... is inevitable." The United States ruling circles were thus forced to devise hastily some means for explaining to Americans the reasons for the collapse of the Chiang Kai-shek regime.

According to American sources, President Truman and his Secretary of State, General Marshall, in November 1948 rejected the idea of publishing a collection of documents on China. Dean Acheson, however, who replaced Marshall as Secretary of State in January 1949, secured the President's consent for the publication of what was called the "China White Paper." In the spring of 1949, approximately 80 government officials were busily preparing this volume under the leadership of W. W. Butterworth, the Director of the State Department's Far East Section. The editing was assigned to the distinguished diplomat Philip C. Jessup.

It is interesting to note that, along with the top State Department officials, the former president of the Rockefeller Foundation, Raymond B. Fosdick, and the president of Colgate University, Everett N. Case, were also enlisted for work on the volume. The participation of big business representatives in the drafting of important foreign policy statements of the American government is, of course, no secret to anyone. But the fact that, in this instance, Acheson considered it necessary to make special note even of the date when the new State Department consultants would enter upon their duties, only confirms that at that moment the American government particularly needed the strong support of big business.

---

i.e., the Chiang Kai-shek government (*Author's note*)

The American government was attempting to achieve several goals with the publication of the "China White Paper." First, an effort was made to dispose of America's entire antiquated policy in China, which had failed disastrously. Second, the White House wanted to prepare American public opinion for the inevitable fall of the Kuomintang government. Third, Washington was trying to justify its China policy and thereby avert the accusation that it had provided inadequate assistance to Chiang Kai-shek. Fourth, and finally, it can now be said with great certitude that the American ruling circles were endeavoring through publication of the "White Paper" to make the now well-known political overtures to the nationalist elements in the leadership of the Communist Party of China.

The 230 documents collected in the "White Paper" encompass a century of American policy in China, from the inequitable treaties of 1844, 1858 and 1868, to the agreement of July 9, 1948, concerning American economic aid to China. The collection includes, as well, statements by prominent American and Chinese figures, diplomatic correspondence between the Department of State and the American Embassy in China, and reports to the President of the United States. The documentation is prefaced by an extensive survey of American policy in China, prepared by State Department officials.

Acheson believed that this unwieldy volume (1,096 pages!) would silence the numerous critics of the government's policy. However, events failed to materialize as he had anticipated. The "White Paper" was unexpectedly subjected to severe criticism by both the proponents of armed American intervention in China and the advocates of a more realistic policy. On the very day the "White Paper" was published, Senator William Knowland and Congressman Walter H. Judd declared in the Congress that the documents assembled in the "White Paper" only confirmed the need to reprimand the government for its China policies. And Judd again rose in the Congress on August 19, 1949, to blame the Department of State for its deliberate omission of 16 documents from the volume which would have strengthened the position of the government's critics. The criticism reached such proportions that Acheson was forced to come forward on August 24 with a special statement defending both the "White Paper" and American policy as a whole.

The publication of the "White Paper" only served to confirm the duplicitous policy of the United States government. With words, it had tried to create the impression that it was dissociating itself from the crumbling Kuomintang regime, despised by the Chinese people, while, in fact, not a day passed that it did not render considerable economic and military aid to that regime. During the period when the American government was attempting, through publication of the "White Paper," to create the false impression among certain observers that because of its defeat in China, the United States would not impose its will upon the Asian countries, the foundations of a so-called "new" Asian policy were being laid in State Department offices. This new policy was designed to serve as the future basis for the anti-Communism with which the Asian people had long since become fed up, and to continue the pursuit of the long-standing goal to suppress the liberation movements.

The tactics had changed, but the strategic aims remained as before. This is clearly discernible from a top secret memorandum sent on July 18, 1949, by Acheson to Jessup, who, as is well known, headed the group of consultants charged with the formulation of the principles of the "new American Far East policy." Here is the text of Acheson's memorandum:

"You will please take as your assumption that it is a fundamental decision of American policy that the United States does not intend to permit further extension of Communist domination on the Continent of Asia. . . . Will you please draw up for me possible programs of action relating to various specific areas not now under Communist control in Asia, under which the United States would have the best chance of achieving this purpose? These programs should contain proposed courses of action, steps to be taken in implementing such programs, estimates of cost to the U.S., and the extent to which U.S. forces would or would not be involved. I fully realize that when these proposals are received, it may be obvious that certain parts thereof would not be within our capabilities to put into effect, but what I desire is the examination of the problem on the general assumptions indicated above, in order to make absolutely certain that we are neglecting no opportunity that would be within our capabilities to achieve the purpose of halting the spread of . . . Communism in Asia."

Acheson's memorandum leaves no doubt as to the basis of the so-called "new" White House policy. Acheson, speaking in blunt terms (there was, after all, no reason to feel restrained, since the memorandum was top secret), demanded that the traditional doctrine of "containment of Communism" remain the basis of this new policy, and suggested that Jessup work out a course of action for the achievement of these aims. Jessup, incidentally, replying to the accusation that he had allegedly proceeded from the possibility of recognizing the government of the People's Republic of China while drafting the "new" U.S. Far East policy, was later compelled to read this document before a special subcommittee of the Senate Committee on Foreign Relations.

True, the White House had made efforts to find ways which would have allowed it to establish contacts with the new government of China.

This may clarify the contradictory situation wherein the United States, while rendering political economic and military aid to the Kuomintang people and maintaining friendly diplomatic relations with that government, was simultaneously in no hurry to recall its diplomatic representatives from cities which the People's Liberation Army had freed. According to official State Department data, 3,851 Americans, including 422 official representatives, were on mainland China's territory by July 22, 1949.

American consulates continued to function in cities occupied by units of the People's Liberation Army, specifically in Peking (Consul-General O. Edmund Clubb), Shanghai (Acting Consul-General Walter P. McConaughy), and Mukden (Consul-General Angus Ward). Official United States representatives were present in Talien, Hangchow, Tientsin and Nanking. Angus Ward wrote that the Communist mayor of Mukden paid him an official visit and that Communist Party representatives always referred to him in correspondence by the official title "Consul-General of the United States of America." It is significant that when the United States information centers in Shanghai, Hangchow, Peking, Tientsin and Nanking were closed on orders of the government of the People's Liberation Army in July 1949, the Department of State reacted to this decision with a short statement issued by a minor official.

At first glance, it seems striking that the American Ambassador to China, John L. Stuart, did not leave Nanking prior to the occupation of the city by units of the People's Liberation Army, but remained there in order to discuss with the representatives of the People's Liberation Army (in his words) "their relations with the United States." In fact, Stuart had unofficial meetings with representatives of the People's Liberation Army, one of whom, Huang Hua, is the present Ambassador of the People's Republic of China to Canada. At these meetings the question of possible American recognition of the future new Chinese government was discussed. Secret initiatives by the United States government met with a positive response among a certain segment of the leadership of the People's Liberation Army. It is significant that in September 1949, Chou En-lai invited Stuart to visit the Yenching University in Peking, where Stuart had once been president, and that the Department of State reacted favorably to the idea of such a trip. True, the trip did not take place, but this was due to circumstances beyond Stuart's control.

The Department of State, attempting to preserve for itself the diplomatic initiative, took steps simultaneously to prevent the immediate recognition by other governments of China's new government, which, according to Washington's prognosis, was to be organized by

October 10, 1949. On May 6, 1949, the Department of State had already instructed its ambassadors "in the principal non-Communist countries with interests in the Far East" to try to convince the governments of these countries of "the disadvantage of initiating any moves toward recognition, or giving the impression, through statements by their officials, that any approach by the Chinese Communists seeking recognition would be welcomed; and the desirability for concerned Western Powers to adopt a common front in this regard." In order to appease the "rightists," who may not have known of these measures, Acheson simultaneously gave written assurances that the American government would not make any decisions on the question of recognition without prior consultations with the congressional committees on foreign relations.

The proclamation of the People's Republic of China (October 1, 1949), and its subsequent recognition, first by the Soviet Union and then a number of other primarily socialist countries, compelled the United States government to define its formal relations with both the young national state, the People's Republic of China, and the Kuomintang regime, which then continued to hold a number of regions in southern China.

On October 3, a State Department representative announced that the American government had no intention to recognize the Chinese Communist government without consultations with the Congress. On October 6, 1949, a secret conference was called in the Department of State to discuss the problems surrounding United States policy in China. The Department of State was represented by Acting Secretary of State James Webb; Assistant Secretary of State for Far Eastern Affairs W. W. Butterworth; George Kennan, the Director of the Office of Planning and Policy; Philip Jessup; Counselor Raymond Fosdick; the United States Ambassador to China, John L. Stuart; and a number of other high-ranking officials. In addition, 25 public figures, including big business representatives and professors who were China specialists, were also invited to the conference. This group included former Secretary of State George Marshall, John Rockefeller III, the banker J. Morden Murphy, William R. Herod (General Electric Company), William S. Robertson (American and Foreign Power Company), Harold Stassen, Ernest B. MacNaughton (First National Bank of Portland), Owen Lattimore, Edwin O. Reischauer, Joseph W. Ballantine and others.

Opening the conference, the State Department representative announced that the minutes of meetings would be available only to State Department staff members, and that other conferees would not have the opportunity to review these. If the press should learn of the conference, it was recommended not to answer the newsmen's questions, but to cite the strictly secret nature of the discussions.

The conference, it must be emphasized, was not designed to establish the principles of United States policy in the Far East and, specifically, in China, or even to formulate any new proposals. As Webb announced at the opening session, the Department of State did "not expect any dramatic announcement that can be put out to the world at the end of these conferences, saying that our policy in China has been reversed or changed or even slightly altered. The formulation of basic policy in such a problem as this is a very long and time-consuming process." Webb further asserted that "our broad policy in the Department remains the same for China" as before. Thus, the conference was not designed to elaborate a new policy as such, but only to advise on the question of a new tactical line within the framework of the doctrine of "containment of Communism."

Kennan, Butterworth and other State Department officials, as well as a representative of the CIA, Colonel McCann, appeared before the participants. In analyzing America's policy toward the People's Republic of China, Assistant Secretary of State for Far Eastern Affairs Butterworth considered it necessary to dwell in his speech on those steps which the United States government had taken to isolate the young republic. He recounted a series of diplomatic maneuvers by American representatives in various countries, aimed at delaying official recognition of the People's Republic of China by these countries, and he told of the pressure exerted upon England to cease its trade with China. Butterworth simultaneously emphasized that the United States would retain its consulates in Peking, Tientsin and Shanghai and "has no intention of closing them," but would endeavor to use these as centers for gathering intelligence data. Butterworth understood that such a position scarcely conformed with a policy of non-recognition of the People's Republic of China, and explained that the United States had hitherto succeeded in following this course only in Latin American countries, where Washington retained its consulates even when it did not establish official diplomatic relations with the fast-ripening generals' regimes. He expressed doubt that the United States could successfully maintain a similar policy with regard to the People's Republic of China.

It was repeatedly noted at the conference that the United States had not for one minute ceased to aid the Kuomintang regime, notwithstanding that this assistance was equivalent to flushing money down the drain. The banker Murphy pointed out in his remarks that only just before the conference, the sum of $12 million was transferred to the Chiang Kai-shek regime. Members of the American Chamber of Commerce in Shanghai who learned of this transaction felt compelled to wire Washington and remind it that the Kuomintang regime was already finished; they demanded that no more money be turned over to it. In case anyone still doubted the final defeat of the Chiang Kai-shek regime, Murphy felt compelled to state flatly that the United States had already "lost the capability to make China completely an instrument of our policy."

The conference reached the unanimous conclusion that the days of the Chiang Kai-shek regime on the mainland were already numbered. The question arose, in this connection, whether the Kuomintang could conceivably hold out on Taiwan. The CIA representative pointed out that, in the opinion of American military circles, Chiang Kai-shek had adequate forces to "defend . . . Taiwan indefinitely." This statement by a military representative at a secret conference deserves the most serious attention, for it sheds a completely new light on America's further diplomatic and military initiatives in the Taiwan area.

At the conference, Harold Stassen expressed the views of those advocating the "policy of non-recognition," which is generally known to have reigned supreme in the United States for many years. "I think," he said, "that there is every indication that if we have a basic policy of opposition to the Communist advance, and opposition to the Communist consolidation of Asia, we should then play out every card of opposition. That, of course, means that it would be unthinkable to recognize the Communist government in China and to withdraw recognition from the Nationalist government."* In his speech Stassen dwelt further on the problem of Taiwan, pointing out that he considered that island an "important strategic area" which the United States must take under its military protection. Stassen was not alone in this opinion. The conference gave serious consideration to a plan for strangling China in a vise of hunger, by completely severing trade relations. Rockefeller, in particular, favored a sharp limitation on trade with China.

Other voices were also heard at the conference. It was pointed out that the policy of "containment of Communism" offered "extremely limited opportunities for a satisfactory American policy in China," and that the United States was continuing its deliveries to the Kuomintang regime, now in Taiwan, thereby limiting the flexibility of American diplomatic actions. Some suggested that aid to the "remnants of the Chinese Nationalists" should be terminated as soon as possible, thus preparing American public opinion for the possible recognition of the People's Republic of China.

A number of conference participants voiced, in one form or another, the desirability of recognizing the Chinese People's Republic. True,

---

*i.e., the Chiang Kai-shek regime (*Author's note*)

many simultaneously suggested the avoidance of undue haste in this matter, and they qualified their support of recognition with various conditions. Specifically, there was the further suggestion that the recognition of the People's Republic of China be stipulated upon the condition that the "open door" principle in China must be maintained. Some conference participants pointed out the importance of maintaining business and trade ties between the United States and China. Thus, the California representative acquainted the conferees with the resolution on the question of American-Chinese relations which had been adopted by the San Francisco Chamber of Commerce, and which proposed: (1) continuation for as long as possible of private business ties with the People's Republic of China; (2) rendering all possible aid to American enterprises in China; (3) maintenance of the American Embassy and consulates in China; and (4) readiness to recognize the Communist government of China, regardless of "whether we like it or not."

According to the evidence of American specialists, the conference not only reflected the embarrassment caused by the defeat of the aggressive American policy in China, but also attested to the feverish attempts by the leaders and authors of United States foreign policy to enlist the support of big business and the elite of the intelligentsia for their future policy. The government representatives got what they wanted—principally, support for the continuation of the "containment of Communism" policy in the Far East. The differences were only in small details. As regards the voices in favor of recognition of the People's Republic of China, those were too timid, indecisive, uncoordinated and constrained by numerous reservations.

On October 12, 1949, four days after conclusion of the conference, Secretary of State Acheson pointed out at a press conference the three basic criteria to which the United States government adhered in recognizing the new government of any country. Under these conditions, the new government would need to: (1) control the territory of the entire country that it claimed to control; (2) recognize international obligations; and (3) govern the country with the consent of the people.

American historians report that during the next two months Washington exchanged views with the British government concerning the question of recognition of the People's Republic of China. The United States tried in every way possible to influence Great Britain and to convince Downing Street of the undesirability of recognition. However, the British point of view in this instance differed with the interests of the North Americans. First, England had significantly greater long-standing economic interests in China than the United States. Second, it had no close ties to the Kuomintang regime. Third,

England was worried about the fate of Hong Kong, and although the United States received secret assurances that the British government intended, if necessary, to defend Hong Kong with all available means, England was, of course, not at all attracted by the prospect of being dragged into a war with China. Fourth, England was well aware that two members of the British Commonwealth–India and Australia–believed that the new government should be recognized as soon as possible. And fifth, England was not averse to exploiting the failure of United States policy in China for furtherance of its own interests. As a result, on December 16, 1949, the British government officially notified Washington of its decision to recognize the government of the People's Republic of China.

During the Sixties and thereafter, the assertion that Washington had apparently given serious consideration at the end of 1949 to the possible recognition of the People's Republic of China was highly exaggerated in the American press. Specifically, the former U.S. Consul-General in Peking, O. E. Clubb, subsequently a professor at Columbia University, wrote that Washington gave "serious attention" at the end of 1949 to the problem of recognition of the People's Republic of China. Robert Blum, in his book *The United States and China in World Affairs*, also subscribed to this viewpoint. Blum thought–and not, seemingly, without reason–that the question of American recognition of the Chinese People's Republic depended to a considerable extent upon the possible occupation of Taiwan by units of the People's Liberation Army. In Blum's opinion, recognition of the People's Republic of China could be expected in the event of an early seizure of Taiwan by People's Liberation Army troops. Naturally, the opinions of such informed specialists as Blum and Clubb deserve the most serious attention. This evidence, however, undoubtedly requires confirmation.

One can say, nevertheless, with a certain degree of assurance, that both the publication of the "White Paper" and a number of extremely guarded statements made by the Truman Administration about Taiwan, coupled with Washington's desperate attempts to sour relations between the Communist Party of China and the Soviet Union by blatant slander about Russia's supposed "expansionist" plans in northeastern China, Sinkiang and Inner Mongolia–all these were conceivably dictated by the efforts of certain American circles to find a basis for agreement with the nationalist elements within the leadership of the Communist Party of China.

The end of 1949 brought new defeats for the Kuomintang. At the beginning of December, under pressure from units of the People's Liberation Army, the Kuomintang was forced to move its "capital" from mainland China to Taipei on the island of Taiwan where, on

March 1, 1950, Chiang Kai-shek declared himself "President of the Republic of China."

2. SUPPORT FOR CHIANG KAI-SHEK

During late 1949 and early 1950, a whole group of nations, including Burma, India, Pakistan, Great Britain, Ceylon, Norway, Denmark, Israel, Afghanistan, Finland, Sweden, Switzerland, Indonesia and the Netherlands, followed the example of the Soviet Union and other socialist countries and officially recognized the government of the People's Republic of China. Meanwhile, in the United States the question of how to save the Kuomintang regime on Taiwan from final defeat was being extensively debated. The situation for Washington was becoming more complicated, not only because the Kuomintang had been completely defeated on the mainland, but also because the young government of the Chinese people had considerably strengthened its international position, having concluded a Treaty of Friendship, Alliance and Mutual Assistance with the U.S.S.R. (February 14, 1950). The United States was also compelled to deal with the fact that the Chinese People's Republic had received wide international recognition. For this very reason, the White House followed a policy which Acheson characterized as one of "waiting 'til the dust settles."

The well-known American journalist Archibald T. Steele described the state of American public opinion during that period as follows: "The Communist victory on the mainland of China in 1949—dazzling in its speed and decisiveness—set off a furious war of words in the United States. Anger was mixed with confusion and frustration. We had liberated China from the Japanese. We had expended more than two billion dollars since V-J day to keep her afloat. Now all we stood for had gone down the drain. Who was to blame? Could we have prevented it? Where do we go from here? What to do about Taiwan?"

The question concerning American policy with regard to Taiwan hit the newspaper front pages in early 1950. Senator William Knowland made public the text of a letter which he received from former President Hoover, who believed that America's policy in the Far East must be based upon the following premises: the need for a "wall against Communism" in the Pacific; the defense of Japan and the Philippines; the necessity to place Taiwan, the Penghu islands and the island of Hainan under the protection of the U.S. Navy to preserve Taiwan, even if only as a "symbol" to sustain hope for the return of the Kuomintang to the mainland.

The New York Times gave front page coverage to the report of Hoover's letter. Within a day after its publication, on January 5, 1950, President Truman issued a special statement concerning the American position: "The United States has no predatory designs on Formosa or any other Chinese territory. The United States has no desire to obtain special rights or privileges or to establish military bases on Formosa at this time. Nor does it have any intention of utilizing its armed forces to interfere in the present situation. The United States government will not pursue a course which will lead to involvement in the civil conflict in China.

"Similarly, the United States government will not provide military aid or advice to the Chinese forces on Formosa. In the view of the United States government, the resources on Formosa are adequate to enable them* to obtain the items which they might consider necessary for the defense of the Island."

Thus, the President let it clearly be understood that Washington considered Chiang Kai-shek fully capable to defend the island with his own armed forces. If anyone still had doubts on this score, Secretary of State Acheson bluntly stated at a press conference that same day that there could be no talk of the Kuomintang running short of military equipment, for it had the means to purchase everything needed.

American official circles have recently attempted to prove that the supposed "sudden and rash" statement by Truman on January 5, 1950, was prompted by "domestic political considerations," designed to protect the government from attacks by the Republicans and aimed at the termination of support for the defeated Kuomintang regime. It is, however, difficult to agree with such an interpretation of events. Washington was, in fact, subjected at that time to intensified attacks by the Republicans, but the President's statement not only failed to decrease these, but actually poured oil on the flame of Republican criticism. Moreover, the government understood perfectly well that such a statement, prior to consultation with the Congress, would inevitably result in still harsher criticism. It follows that the White House took this step deliberately, and it is thus clear that such haste was dictated primarily by foreign rather than domestic policy considerations. And this is corroborated by several facts.

It is well known that the first country to recognize the Chinese People's Republic was the Soviet Union, whose example was followed by the other socialist countries. The first non-socialist country to

---

**i.e.*, the Chiang Kai-shek regime (*Author's note*)

recognize the Chinese People's Republic was Burma (December 16, 1949). India announced its recognition on December 30, 1949, and on January 5, 1950, the British government announced its termination of diplomatic relations with the Kuomintang regime. Washington understood that the hour was near when England would recognize the government of the Chinese People's Republic, and that a whole series of capitalist countries would follow its example. These steps were bound to exert a strong influence on American public opinion. Furthermore, they would constitute a great blow to America's international prestige and would at the same time seriously undermine the position of the Kuomintang regime.

American inaction under these circumstances could have been misinterpreted, and for this very reason the White House timed its statement for January 5, *i.e.*, it hastened to issue the statement before England announced its recognition of the Chinese People's Republic. Washington thereby pursued several aims. First, it was attempting to take the initiative into its own hands and minimize the significance of the step which England was contemplating. Second, the statement concerning continuation of economic aid to Chiang Kai-shek expressed Washington's desire to support the Kuomintang, showing the whole world that the United States not only did not intend to sever relations, but planned to give the Kuomintang significant aid in the future. Third, this was a last-minute attempt to influence the final decision of the countries which intended to recognize the Chinese People's Republic. And fourth, the U.S. government was trying to convince the American people that it firmly held the diplomatic initiative in the Far East.

These conclusions may be based specifically upon the almost simultaneous admissions made by Ambassador Philip Jessup and the State Department representative, Michael J. McDermott. Jessup's remarks were made in October 1951, during his testimony before a special subcommittee of the Senate Committee on Foreign Relations. Jessup pointed out that Dean Acheson had replied to a communiqué of December 16, 1949, from British Foreign Affairs Minister Ernest Bevin, which concerned England's impending recognition of the government of the Chinese People's Republic, with a personal message. In his reply, Acheson not only expressed regret over England's decision, but stressed that the United States might consider it necessary to issue its own special statement on the matter of recognition, coinciding with England's announcement of its decision. And the United States proceeded to do just that, with the issuance of President Truman's statement on January 5, 1950, exactly on the eve of the British announcement of recognition of the People's Republic of China. Jessup's testimony thus clearly refutes the story about the "sudden and rash" nature of the President's announcement. In this instance, there can be no talk of haste! On the contrary, the President's announcement was planned beforehand and, no doubt, prepared much in advance. Washington issued the statement at a precisely calculated moment.

The Department of State was compelled to make a second admission on October 2, 1951, in answer to Stassen's criticism. Michael J. McDermott, the Special Assistant for Press Relations to the Secretary of State, explaining United States policy toward China during the late Forties and early Fifties, said, verbatim: "The policy of the government was to prevent the fall of Formosa to the Chinese Reds. The decision of the Joint Chiefs of Staff, however, was that no U.S. forces should be used in this undertaking, and that, therefore, the implementation of this policy must rest upon energetic diplomatic and economic means."

Now it is perfectly clear that Truman's statement of January 5, 1950, was one of those "energetic" diplomatic means. And it is well known that this statement did not achieve the desired results. England's announced recognition of the Chinese People's Republic was followed by Ceylon, Norway, Denmark, Israel, Afghanistan, Finland, Sweden, Switzerland, Holland and Indonesia.

It is interesting that on that same day (January 5, 1950), Ambassador Jessup arrived in Tokyo for talks with General MacArthur, and only a few days later went to Taiwan for additional discussions. For this meeting with the Generalissimo-in-exile from mainland China, the White House sent a man who, to everyone's knowledge, had formulated the new Far East policy. Thus, intentionally or not (but most likely intentionally), Washington aroused much speculation as to whether the policy's principles would be elaborated with Chiang Kai-shek's direct participation, or whether Washington—notwithstanding the "White Paper" publication—might be intending to deny assistance to its "old friend."

This U.S. government policy was not widely supported in American public circles. As evidence, one may cite an investigation on the subject of "American Policy Toward China," conducted in January-February 1959 by the Council on Foreign Relations. It is worth noting that Allen Dulles, a man whom not even the most ardent American reactionaries dared accuse of being a Communist sympathizer, was then president of the Council. In conducting the investigation, the Council expressed no interest in the opinion of ordinary citizens, but sought instead the opinion of the influential elite of American society. Summing up the investigation, the majority of the Council reached the conclusion that it was already "too late" for the United States even to think about increasing aid to the Kuomintang regime, which "does not enjoy the support of the Chinese people," and that an increase of U.S. aid would, therefore, only harm American interests as a whole. As regards its attitude on recognition of the Chinese government, the Council spoke very cautiously, stressing its belief that the best policy must be one of "waiting," but pointing out at the same time that official American recognition of the Chinese People's Republic would be quite possible in the future.

The ruling circles, however, had no desire to consider even these very cautious suggestions of the "influential citizens," and they continued the old policy of providing all possible support for Chiang Kai-shek—a policy which was directed against the Chinese people.

3. *McCARTHY AND THE "CHINA LOBBY"*

President Truman's statement of January 5, 1950, was immediately subjected to harsh criticism by those forces who advocated more active aid to Chiang Kai-shek and direct U.S. military intervention in China's internal affairs. Increasing numbers of new people entered the controversy. As later became clear, this campaign was directed and supported by a large group subsequently called the "China lobby," or "China pushers."

During the Second World War, a number of organizations were already active in the United States, whose purpose was to aid Chiang Kai-shek both in the war against Japan and in the struggle against the Communists. The largest of these was "United China Relief," whose founder was the millionaire Henry Luce. These organizations were initially engaged in the collection of money for Chiang Kai-shek; subsequently, some of them, at the direct request of the Chiang Kai-shek regime, began to devote their main attention to pushing laws and measures through the Administration and Congress aimed at assuring increased aid for Chiang Kai-shek and his army. It turned out later that many Americans who were active in this campaign were supported by the Chiang Kai-shek regime, *i.e.*, they were paid out of those funds which the American government appropriated for aid to the Kuomintang. The pro-Chiang Kai-shek groups were generally called the "China lobby."

"What is the China lobby?" asked one American, Felix Greene. "Essentially," he said, "it is a partnership between agents of the Chiang Kai-shek government and Americans who share the belief that Chiang should be given full support of the United States, and who, collectively and individually, have exerted political pressure to gain their ends."

The "China lobbyists," according to the evidence of *The Reporter* magazine, were the products of "fear, ambition and greed," and were either fanatics "possessed by the nightmare of a Communist conspiracy" in the American government or "politicians who will stop at nothing in their hunt of power." These individuals had in 1945 already formed an organization called the "American China Policy Association," whose leadership was soon assumed by the millionaire textile manufacturer Alfred Kohlberg, a man who, according to the testimony of his closest acquaintances, was "intellectually limited" and "possessed by the obsession to fight Communism."

True, Kohlberg's actions were prompted not so much by an "obsession" as by extremely prosaic mercantile interests—the fear of losing a large part of his fortune. According to *The Reporter*'s evidence, hundreds of thousands of Chinese women and children were working for Kohlberg during the Forties, and his millions were essentially accumulated through their cheap labor. Since Kohlberg repeatedly broke American laws, his devious affairs were twice the subject of investigations by the Federal Trade Commission, which ruled against him in both instances. This, however, did not embarrass the Chiang Kai-shekists; they supported Kohlberg in every possible way, issued export licenses to him without delays, and even decorated him twice with their medals, which he proudly showed off to his friends in his office on 37th Street in New York. Kohlberg was well acquainted with Chiang Kai-shek and many of his representatives in America, including Archbishop Paul Yu-pin and numerous Kuomintang generals.

It was no coincidence that Kohlberg and his confederates named their group the "American China Policy Association." From the first day of its existence, this organization endeavored to the utmost to steer the development of United States policy toward China in the direction desired by Kohlberg. It demanded broad U.S. military intervention in the civil war in China, and exerted pressure upon the Administration and the Congress with every means available to it, including bribery, threats and blackmail. All dissenters were promptly labeled Communists by Kohlberg and his friends. At first, Kohlberg maintained that the American Embassy in Chungking was nothing more than the center of a conspiracy to discredit the Chiang Kai-shek government. Subsequently, the textile manufacturer dedicated himself to the "expulsion of Communists" from the Institute of Pacific Relations, of which he was then a member. He began his attacks upon the Institute with a small brochure in which he maintained that a number of the Institute's works advocated the very same ideas as the publications of the Communist Party of China. Shortly thereafter, Kohlberg demanded an "investigation of the entire policy of the Institute toward China." This proposal, however, was rejected.

Upon leaving the Institute, Kohlberg began the publication of a magazine called *Plain Talk*. The first issue attacked the Department of State, which allegedly conducted a "pro-Soviet" policy in the Far East, and Generals Marshall and Stilwell. The article containing these attacks was titled "The State Department Espionage Case" and bore the by-line of a well-known American journalist. After a while, however, an extremely curious situation came to light. As it happened, two former FBI agents, then employed by Kohlberg, appeared one day in Florida and induced this journalist to travel with them to New York. There, Kohlberg persuaded him to write an article for the first issue of the new magazine. However, Kohlberg and his closest associates were dissatisfied with the article and completely rewrote it, giving it, moreover, a new title.

It was not just coincidental that the American press was compelled to recognize that the "China lobbyists" proceeded in their practical activities on the Jesuit principle that "the end justifies the means." And there was only one end—to prevent, by all means, the Chinese people's establishment of their own state. The lobbyists spared no effort to support Chiang Kai-shek and keep the American people in ignorance about the true nature of events in China. The "big lie" propaganda method—borrowed from Hitler's arsenal—was set in motion, and for a long time successfully fooled many trusting Americans.

Another active "China lobby" organization was the "Committee to Defend America by Aiding Anti-Communism in China," formed in 1949 by Frederick McKee, a Pittsburgh industrialist, who, incidentally, specialized in the manufacturing of coffins. Matthew Woll and David Dubinsky, the leaders of the American Federation of Labor, were members of the Committee's board of directors which, in May and July 1949, advocated an immediate increase in military and economic aid to the Kuomintang regime.

At one time the names of 17 organizations and private companies registered in the United States as paid agents of the Chiang Kai-shek regime were made public. The "Universal Trading Corporation," whose capital resources were estimated at more than $21 million in 1950, was extremely active on behalf of Chiang Kai-shek. The "China Institute of America," of which Henry Luce was a trustee, also played a considerable role. Serious propaganda activity was also conducted by the "Chinese News Service" and the "Central News" agency, which were totally managed by official representatives of Chiang Kai-shek. The "Central News" agency officially announced that during the 1945-51 period, it spent more than one million dollars on propaganda activity. Altogether the astronomical sum of $654 million was spent during the 1946-49 period in the United States.

Where, then, did these enormous sums come from? They came, as Senator Wayne Morse frankly pointed out in the Congress, from the pockets of American taxpayers. There was, he noted, a "vicious circle" in which American dollars flowed: Money was first transferred as foreign aid to the account of Chiang Kai-shek, with the consent of the American government and Congress, and then was returned to the United States to finance the "China lobby." The lobby's activities assumed such proportions that *The Washington Post* was compelled to acknowledge: "Not one person among those who know the slightest thing about how affairs are conducted doubts that the powerful China lobby exerts extraordinary influence on Congress and the President. It is difficult to find a parallel in the history of diplomacy when agents and diplomatic representatives of a foreign power wielded such influence, . . . [and] used the technique of direct intervention to such unprecedented proportions."

The "embassy" in the United States, as well as a number of the closest Chiang Kai-shek supporters who had moved there at one time or another, played a special role in the entire pro-Chiang Kai-shek activity. Madame Chiang Kai-shek, who spent months and even years in America, also actively participated in this effort. Equally active in the United States were such prominent representatives of Chinese bureaucratic capital as T. V. Soong, H. H. Kung and Chen Li-fu. "Ambassador" Wellington Koo and one of his closest advisers, Chen Chih-mai, personally directed the entire propaganda campaign in the United States.

The following facts convey an idea of the manner in which the Chiang Kai-shek diplomats directed the activity of the "China lobby," and how they themselves took an active part therein:

In March 1949 the Chiang Kai-shek regime hired for $30,000 a certain William J. Goodwin as a "public relations adviser," or, speaking plainly, as their own paid lobbyist. Goodwin's selection was not accidental. He gained notoriety in Washington circles as the man who in 1941 had maintained that civil war would break out in the United States if America were to render aid to England in her fight against Hitler's Germany. Now he transferred his sympathies to and began to serve Chiang Kai-shek, since this paid well. Goodwin later tried to maintain, however, that he allegedly worked selflessly, regarding these activities as part of his personal "struggle against Communism."

Goodwin's main task was to "cultivate" in congressmen favorable attitudes toward Chiang Kai-shek. This cultivation occurred during lunches and dinners which Goodwin arranged for congressmen at fashionable restaurants and private clubs in Washington and New York. Ambassador Koo and his counselor Chen often appeared at these dinners, where they conversed privately and at length with the congressmen, explaining to them the needs of the Chiang Kai-shek regime. Goodwin later acknowledged that, with Chiang Kai-shek money, he spent no less than $23,000 for these purposes in the first year alone. During that period, approximately 100 congressmen were, in Goodwin's words, "entertained," and half of these became active supporters of Chiang Kai-shek.

Chen Chih-mai had every reason to be satisfied with Goodwin. In one of his telegrams, the counselor Chen reported to Chiang Kai-shek: "Goodwin has already begun his activity and is developing it feverishly. The leaders of both parties are supporting him." In another telegram, dated August 1, 1949, Chen Chih-mai wrote: "Goodwin is working —trying to destroy the illusions of the Democratic party leaders with regard to the Chinese Communists."

Goodwin's connections with the congressmen as well as with the Chiang Kai-shek regime could not, of course, escape being noticed by the sensation-hungry American press. An article appeared in *The Washington Post* in September 1949, revealing just whose money Goodwin was using to "entertain" the lawmakers, and pointing out openly that the Chiang Kai-shek representatives in the United States were trying to exert pressure upon the Congress for increased American aid. The article caused alarm in the recesses of the Chiang Kai-shek "embassy." These events were reported directly to Chiang Kai-shek in a secret telegram, and Goodwin was ordered to register officially as a "lobbyist for a foreign country," thereby providing a "legal basis" for his activity.

Another aspect of the work of the Chiang Kai-shek diplomats in Washington was tied to the name of Kuomintang Air Force Major Louis Kung, who was attached as "technical adviser" to the staff of the Kuomintang Air Force attaché in Washington. The American press ascertained that Louis Kung was closely connected to a certain David Charnay, the founder and, at that time, director of the American firm "Allied Syndicates." Charnay had connections within top government circles and counted among his friends such personages as U.S. presidential counselor Clark Clifford, Assistant Secretary of Defense Paul Griffith, former Secretary of the Navy John Sullivan, presidential assistant John Steelman and a number of other influential Americans. It was, therefore, no coincidence that the Chiang Kai-shek regime concentrated its attention upon "Allied Syndicates," and supplied more than $75,000 per year for the firm's "services." Charnay subsequently confessed, without the slightest embarrassment, that it was his job, among other things, to prevent United States recognition of the Communist government of China and to assure that the assets of the

Chinese Bank in the United States, which the press estimated at $300 million, were not frozen.

One very important fact should be noted here. The Chiang Kai-shek diplomats always endeavored to pressure American lawmakers and the U.S. government, but up to a certain time this activity was conducted within "legal" limits—although the definition of "legal" was rather broadly construed. By the end of 1948, however, when the position of the Chiang Kai-shek armies on mainland China had sharply deteriorated, it became difficult to achieve the desired results within the limits of the old "legal" framework. Thus, an important decision was made during the winter of 1948-49 in the offices of the Chiang Kai-shek "embassy": to shift from "legal" methods to "demagoguery, slander, intimidation, and outright interference in American domestic politics."

And thus, Allied Syndicates went to work. In 1949 a new employee joined the firm. All that was known about him was his name, Happenie, and his family background—"from somewhere around Boston." Happenie, of course, did not talk about himself, particularly the fact that he had once been sentenced in South Carolina to five years imprisonment for blackmail. It was also strange that Happenie, as it turned out, who received no salary from the firm, soon moved from a modest apartment on the outskirts of New York into a luxury apartment on Park Avenue, one of the most expensive parts of the city. The explanation is quite simple: Happenie was sent to H. H. Kung's firm, where he received $25,000 a year "for services." Allied Syndicates was only a cover for the improper activities in which Happenie was engaged on the orders of Major Louis Kung. In his work, Happenie utilized the staff of the firm in every way possible for interference in America's domestic political life.

In the fall of 1950, Allied Syndicates was in the forefront of the senatorial election campaigns of several Republicans. Charnay and Leo Casey, a fellow worker in the firm, developed a campaign strategy jointly with the Republicans, and the American press reported that Major Louis Kung also worked with them during these days. There is every reason to assert that it was no coincidence that the Chiang Kai-shek regime was counting on the Republicans. For a simple explanation, one may cite the statement made in January 1947 by the not unknown John Foster Dulles, who was then the chief foreign policy adviser of the Republican party: "A Democratic President and his Secretary of State can propose, but a Republican Congress can dispose." And, in fact, the Republicans in Congress at that time supported Chiang Kai-shek.

In 1948 the Chiang Kai-shek regime pinned great hopes on the Republican presidential candidate, Thomas Dewey, but, as is well known, he was defeated and Harry Truman was re-elected as President. Chiang Kai-shek's representatives in the United States, however, did not change their old attachments and continued to give direct support to the Republicans in their bid for the votes of the American electorate. Thus, Chiang Kai-shek's interference in America's domestic political life constantly increased during the 1948-50 period. Furthermore, the Chiang Kai-shek regime showed no restraint in its selection of methods.

Chen Chih-mai, in one of his telegrams to Chiang Kai-shek, wrote: "Concerning our work in the United States, we must occupy ourselves with both the Administration and the legislative branch; in this regard, special efforts should be made to establish closer ties with the latter." And the Chiang Kai-shek regime exerted considerable efforts to this end, even to the extent of promoting particular measures in the congressional committees. Thus, at the end of 1948 an "idea arose," over cocktails in the Chinese embassy, to send former Senator Clark to China with a group of advisers. As later became clear, the greater part of the Clark group's travel expenses were borne by the Chiang Kai-shek government. Clark did not long remain in its debt; in his report, he recommended an immediate increase of military and financial aid to the Chiang Kai-shek regime.

In September 1949, the aluminum magnate Louis Reynolds offered, in Chiang Kai-shek's name, a five million dollar job with the Chiang Kai-shek regime to the American General Albert C. Wedemeyer. The General declined the offer, and told Chen Chih-mai that Chiang Kai-shek's situation on the mainland was, in fact, already hopeless. But Wedemeyer's refusal failed to discourage Chen Chih-mai, who began to sound out other high-ranking military officials and soon came to an agreement with the recently retired Admiral Charles Cook, the Commander of the U.S. Seventh Fleet from 1947-48. Furthermore, Cook not only agreed to go personally to Taiwan, but also planned to take with him a group of experienced military specialists. Thus, at the beginning of 1950 a group of American technical and military specialists arrived in Taiwan, including, in addition to Cook, sixteen "retired" high-ranking U.S. military officers. Even the necessary formal consent of the President appeared to be no obstacle; nobody requested it, and the group was made to appear as employees of a "private American concern." They forgot to explain, of course, in this connection that this "private concern" had received $750,000 from the Chiang Kai-shek regime.

Notwithstanding the indefatigable activity of the "China lobby," the prestige of Chiang Kai-shek and his supporters fell catastrophically in the eyes of the American people. The proclamation of the People's Republic of China and the subsequent recognition of the new government by the socialist and numerous other countries struck an especially severe blow against the Kuomintang forces. The ceaseless flow of phrases from the mouths of Kohlberg, McKee and others like them about a Communist conspiracy in the Department of State found no fertile soil and even failed to make the pages of the yellow, gutter press.

But fate sent the "China lobby" a man who, in Kohlberg's words, had "guts enough and [was] dumb enough" to thrust these accusations onto the pre-election campaign platform. This man turned out to be Joseph McCarthy, the theretofore little known Senator from the state of Wisconsin. McCarthy was constantly looking for a "suitable theme" with which he could make a big name for himself and be re-elected to the Congress. The country's "most successful demagogue" (according to the American press) found such a theme in the writings and verbiage of Kohlberg, who had returned to the United States in the summer of 1949 from a trip to Taiwan and had renewed his charges against the Department of State and the Institute of Pacific Relations.

It should be noted that charges of alleged "pro-Communist sympathies" among State Department officials had been heard before. In 1945, General P. J. Hurley, who had resigned as U.S. Ambassador to China, publicly stated that a "significant part of the Department of State is trying to support Communism in general, and specifically in China." According to the American press, the hearings of the Senate Foreign Relations Committee, at which Hurley's accusations were investigated, more closely resembled a farce than a serious discussion. In the end, the government officially announced that all of Hurley's accusations were unfounded.

And now, at the beginning of 1950, Senator McCarthy decided to pick up all the old charges and give them a new coat of paint. This he did initially on February 9, 1950, in a speech at Wheeling, West Virginia. McCarthy's accusations immediately landed on the front pages of the American newspapers. The failures of the American Far East policy in general, and particularly in China, demanded explanation. The "White Paper" was not convincing for Republican critics of the government, and wide circles of the American public were simply not aware of this document. But then McCarthy appeared, and explained everything fairly simply: "Communists and spies" sown throughout the government—especially in the Department of State—were to blame for everything. Furthermore, McCarthy claimed that he had in his possession a complete list of more than 200 such "Communists." The most reactionary-minded Republicans immediately voiced their solidarity with the Senator; the well-known Senator Taft advised his younger colleague to press his accusations firmly. As McCarthy continued to inveigh against the "Communists" from the platform of Congress, he was supported by an increasing number of prominent Republicans.

In his speeches, McCarthy, after a personal meeting with Kohlberg, directed the entire fire of his criticism against the China specialists, and his accusations were soon supported by the most reactionary forces in the country. "To right-wingers of all shades all over the country," wrote *The Reporter*, "China suddenly became, under Senator Mc-Carthy's impetus, the magic issue that might finally provide the road to power." These "obsessed" persons longed for power, and McCarthy now showed them the means in the form of the old, well-tested bugaboo of anti-Communism. No matter that countless defeats lay along that road—this time they might be lucky!

People who had no willingness whatsoever to recognize that the defeat of American policy in China was dictated, above all, by the anti-popular, anti-Communist, imperialist and predatory nature of U.S. policy itself, happily seized upon McCarthy's theory of an imagined Communist infiltration of the American government. And even the government itself did not oppose this theory very strongly, since it provided grist for the anti-Communist mill of Truman and Acheson. McCarthy's demagoguery was advantageous to the U.S. government because: (1) it distracted the attention of wide circles of the American public from the serious foreign policy problems and true reasons for the failure of America's policy in China; (2) it created an anti-Communist atmosphere in the country which allowed the government to pursue more confidently, and in disregard of domestic criticism, the policy of "containment of Communism"; and (3) it provided excellent grounds for getting rid of all those who opposed, even in the slightest degree, the policy pursued by the government.

The authorities did not fail to avail themselves of the opportunity offered. Using McCarthy's charges as a pretext, they fired 20 out of 22 specialists employed by the State Department for the formulation of China policy. Furthermore, one employee was "checked" six times, although in every case the State Department Employees' Loyalty Board found nothing incriminating in his activity. Nevertheless, McCarthy secured his dismissal.

McCarthy "raged" in the Congress only as long as the ruling elite permitted. When McCarthy became expendable to them, the President of the United States personally spoke out against the Senator. This was enough for the Senate to censure McCarthy's conduct by an overwhelming majority of votes. But that occurred later—in December 1954. Until then, McCarthy, with the silent consent of the American government, kept himself busy for almost five years searching for supposed Communist infiltrators in government agencies. He created and actively fanned anti-Communist hysteria in the country, and by every conceivable means clouded the minds of millions of ordinary Americans on questions of American foreign policy, especially with regard to China. With McCarthy's active participation, the atmosphere of fear and suspicion created in the country was such that even the slightest criticism of Chiang Kai-shek was regarded as pro-Communist.

The united efforts of the McCarthyites, the "China lobbyists," reactionary Republicans and the extreme right-wing groups resulted in a situation where even a simple statement regarding the desirability to examine objectively the question of recognizing China became tantamount to suicide. The matter reached the point that during confirmation of the U.S. delegation to the regular session of the General Assembly of the United Nations, the senators demanded that each delegate answer the question of where he stood on the recognition of the new government of China. Yet, the senators were well aware that the U.S. government, its diplomatic representatives and the top officials of the Department of State always categorically opposed recognition of the People's Republic of China.

Speaking before a special subcommittee of the Senate Committee on Foreign Relations, Jessup summarized U.S. policy toward China during that period as follows:

1. The United States has never considered the possibility of recognition of Communist China.
2. The United States has exerted its influence to block the recognition of Communist China by other governments.
3. The United States has constantly supported the Chiang Kai-shekists in the United Nations and has in every way possible prevented the admission of the People's Republic of China to the United Nations.
4. The United States has never told other governments that Washington might, under certain circumstances, recognize the People's Republic of China.
5. The United States has never expressed its approval of, or consent to, actions of other governments aimed at the recognition of the People's Republic of China.
6. The Department of State has never recommended the recognition of the new government of China, either to the President or to the U.S. National Security Council.

All this was perfectly well known to the congressmen. And their heart-rending anti-Communist statements, hysterical outcries concerning the clandestine "Communists" in government circles and their fellow-travelers, made it, in fact, easier for the government to pursue an imperialist policy in China. Such statements were designed to mislead wide circles of Americans who were seriously perturbed by the results of their government's Far East policy, and who wrote letters to the Department of State which demanded recognition of the People's Republic of China and pointed out all the advantages of such a step. So numerous were these demands that it was impossible to brush them aside. The State Department offices, to reply to such demands, produced a form letter which said that recognition of Peking on Peking's terms "would have led only to short-term and illusory advantages to the detriment of our long-term interests. For this reason, the government of the United States at the present time is not in a position to actively re-examine the question of recognition of the Chinese Communist regime."

The sentiments of ordinary Americans were, of course, bound to disturb the ruling circles, who therefore welcomed the extensive debates which were under way in the Congress. It was clearly understood in Washington that even among the most severe congressional "critics" of government policy, the White House had genuine allies who were paving the way for an even more aggressive Far East policy. These individuals were trying to manipulate American public opinion and, thus, to promote a whole series of military measures which the U.S. government was taking in the Far East—measures designed, in the final analysis, to strengthen the U.S. position in that region and to increase aid to the Kuomintang.

Reactionary Republican senators spared no effort to portray Chiang Kai-shek as virtually the only friend the American people had in the Far East. And this was done on the direct instructions of the Chiang Kai-shek representatives in Washington. Chen Chih-mai, in one telegram to Chiang Kai-shek, wrote frankly:

"Senator Taft was immensely interested in the problems of Formosa. He at one time even advocated last January to send the U.S. fleet to defend Formosa. Your humble subordinate, Chen Chih-mai, gave Taft the following idea: We ... are willing to share the responsibilities, along with General MacArthur, in a fight against Russia and Communism; however, the economic strength in Formosa is weak and the source of manpower is limited—whereas the mainland of China is teeming with guerrillas and is a practically inexhaustible source of recruits. What they need is a proper leader and a proper organization. Your career in ... anti-Communism is brilliantly reorded in history, and you are the most natural leader of Asia and the United States as well.

"The above idea will be used by Taft in his speech, which will, in turn, sell the same idea to the United States authorities."

It is evident that the "China lobby" received detailed instructions from the Chiang Kai-shek regime, and then tried to convince the American citizens of matters which were beneficial to Chiang Kai-shek and his associates. The American press was compelled, significantly later, to acknowledge that the "lobbyists," McCarthyites and reactionary Republicans had by joint efforts achieved their aims: The ordinary American believed that all-out support of the Chiang Kai-shek regime was the only correct American policy in Asia. Furthermore, this in itself implied that, in the pursuit of such a policy, the United States did not need to take into consideration, even to the slightest degree, either the opinions of the Asian countries or those of America's European allies. No wonder that, under these circumstances, the U.S. government could in 1950 easily shift from a somewhat veiled support of Chiang Kai-shek to direct armed intervention against the People's Republic of China.

CHAPTER III

CHIANG KAI-SHEK IN TAIWAN

1. A BIT OF HISTORY

On December 7, 1941, Japan unleashed war in the Pacific. When the military leaders in Washington learned that the massive raids on the Philippine Islands by the Japanese Air Force had been made from airfields in Taiwan, they demanded immediate intelligence information about the island. Maps dating from 1894 were extracted from the American military intelligence archives, as well as photographs made prior to World War I and a report concerning Japan's attempts to use Taiwan for further expansion into Indochina, which was compiled on the basis of materials published in the French press in 1905. That was all the material that the American military intelligence had at its disposal in December 1941 about the island which in subsequent decades would become the center of America's political, economic and military activities in the Far East.

The United States, attracted by Taiwan's wealth and advantageous geographical location, had become interested in the island long before. As far back as 1854, the American Commodore Perry suggested that the U.S. government seize the island of Taiwan and turn it into a base for the American fleet in the Far East, thus creating a springboard for further infiltration of the Asian continent.

Japan, victorious in the Sino-Japanese War, seized the island in 1895, closed all Chinese schools in Taiwan and made Japanese the official language. Local inhabitants were completely forced out of the island government, and the Japanese took over all important posts. The Taiwan inhabitants, however, did not willingly accept the Japanese occupation. One uprising followed another on the island.

The Great October Socialist Revolution enormously influenced the development of the island's liberation movement, and between 1919 and 1920 resistance to the Japanese invaders spread widely. A fresh upsurge of the Taiwanese liberation movement occurred in connection with the 1925-27 revolution in China. The island's businesses were gripped in a wave of strikes led by the vanguard of the Chinese working class, the Communist Party. The first workers' organizations emerged in Taiwan. During that period the liberation movement on the island, under the leadership of the Communist Party of China, became more widespread and purposeful, and numerous segments of the peasantry were drawn into it. The counterrevolutionary coup which was carried out in China in 1927 by Chiang Kai-shek, with the support of the Anglo-American imperialists, helped the Japanese invaders to weaken somewhat the island population's mass movement to oppose foreign occupation and support reunification with China.

Thanks to the Soviet Union's entrance into World War II, imperialist Japan was forced to surrender in September 1945, and all the conditions were set forth for the return of Taiwan to China. China's sovereign right to Taiwan was recognized in a number of important international documents. The Cairo Conference Declaration of the three Great Powers unequivocally stated that the aim of the signatory countries—China, the United States and Great Britain—was that "all territories which Japan had wrested from the Chinese, as, for example, Manchuria, Formosa and the Pescadores Islands,* should be returned to the Republic of China." The Potsdam Declaration, which stipulated that the territory of Japan be limited to the Japanese islands proper, also called for the return of Taiwan to China.

In 1942, however, the U.S. Department of Defense decided that it was necessary to approach the question of Taiwan's fate primarily from the standpoint of America's "carefully considered interests." The Far East Division of the U.S. Military Intelligence Service prepared a series of materials which proffered the idea that the military importance of the island precluded its return to China. All these considerations were submitted to the Department of State, which was preparing recommendations for Taiwan's occupation by American troops and the establishment of an American military government on the island. It was emphasized that the island would remain under American military control until the conclusion of a peace treaty with Japan, which, according to the thinking of the authors of the proposal, was to determine Taiwan's "future status."

Although these proposals originated within the Department of State,

---

*i.e., the northeastern China provinces, Taiwan and the Penghu islands (*Author's note*)

their most ardent supporters were the U.S. Navy representatives, who had also been entrusted with the necessary preparatory work. Special courses were organized at Columbia University for the training of more than 2,000 officers to staff the military government in Taiwan. Ten special manuals on civil administration, including maps of the several regions and other auxiliary materials, were prepared and issued to the future Taiwan occupation officials. According to the authoritative testimony of Joseph W. Ballantine, who was the Director of the Far East Section in the U.S. Department of State in 1944-45, plans for the establishment of an American military government in Taiwan were not finalized until September 1945, *i.e.*, after Japan's surrender.

At the end of World War II, the American public demanded the swift return of the American soldiers. Under these conditions, the stationing of special occupation troops in Taiwan would have been opposed by the Congress as well as diverse circles of the American public. Washington, of course, had to take into consideration such popular sentiments. It was decided to return the island to China, in accordance with the appropriate provisions of the Cairo and Potsdam Declarations.

After Japan's surrender, when the first facts of the island population's resentment of the pillage by the Kuomintang soldiers became known, a group of officers from the U.S. Office of Strategic Intelligence polled Taiwan's population on whether the island should (a) remain a part of China, (b) be returned again to Japan, or (c) be placed under the trusteeship of the United Nations, with the United States as the trustee country. It was perfectly clear that the poll organizers were openly laying the groundwork for a re-examination of the decisions stated in the Cairo and Potsdam Declarations. Evidence for such a conclusion can be found in the fact that, even in January 1947, the United States did not consent to the recognition of the Taiwanese inhabitants as Chinese citizens, and, in fact, negotiated with China on this question until the formation of the People's Republic.

Works by American Sinologists often emphasize that the United States allegedly began to render military aid to the Chiang Kai-shek troops stationed in Taiwan only after the beginning of the Korean events (1950). The facts, however, indicate something entirely different. The first groups of American officers appeared in Taiwan immediately after Japan's surrender, and even before the Chiang Kai-shek troops landed on the island. Soon thereafter, part of the staff of the U.S. Military Attaché in China (specifically, the Assistant U.S. Naval Attaché G. Kerr) arrived in Taipei. The Americans announced the establishment of their consulate on the island and searched for a building in which to locate. Military representatives from Washington continually visited the island.

The presence of the American military in Taiwan provoked the protests and displeasure not only of wide circles of the population, but also of the Kuomintang officials. Kerr frankly acknowledged that the relations between the U.S. military representatives and the local authorities were "officially polite but strained, and a series of ugly after-hours incidents left no doubt that our presence was most unwelcome." During the first months after Japan's surrender, the local newspapers and magazines published articles criticizing the American presence on the island. Before the Americans had time to open their consulate, several anti-American demonstrations were held nearby. The Americans, however, had no intention to abandon the island. The United States Information Agency soon opened an office in Taiwan to propagandize the American way of life; it sought to compel the local inhabitants "to close their ears and eyes to anything unfavorable to the American image."

The victories of the Chinese People's Liberation Army and its swift advance toward southern China forced the Chiang Kai-shek supporters to seek refuge in Taiwan. Shortly thereafter, approximately 1,600 Kuomintang generals, 200 admirals, thousands of officials, hundreds of thousands of enlisted men and officers turned up on the island. The generals, admirals and top officials soon received rather cushy jobs in the various institutions and local governmental bodies of the so-called "National Government of China."

A cruel military-bureaucratic dictatorship, based on mass terror, was thus established in Taiwan. The head of the Chiang Kai-shek secret police stated later that during the first three-and-a-half years, 550 "conspiracies" (an average of 13 "conspiracies" a month) were uncovered in Taiwan. Chiang Kai-shek made short shrift of everyone who had ever wronged him. A number of top generals were shot, including the Deputy Minister of National Defense, the Infantry Chief of Supply, the Commander of the 70th Division and others.

There are no exact data on the strength of the Chiang Kai-shek army in Taiwan during the early Fifties; its size, according to various sources, was estimated at 500,000-to-800,000 men. General MacArthur, speaking in Congress after his retirement, reported that, according to his figures, by mid-1951 Chiang Kai-shek's military forces totaled approximately 600,000 men (345,000 infantry troops, 45,000 navy, 70,000 air force and 140,000 service and garrison units).

The American press openly admitted that all power on the island was, in fact, concentrated in the hands of "garrison headquarters, the special police and several secret police organizations." The journal *Foreign Affairs* reported that "For the great majority of Chinese on Formosa, the fearful feature of this situation is the lack of legal protection for the ordinary citizen. He can be arrested at night by a squad of military police, tried by a military court-martial and sentenced, with little opportunity for appeal. Once taken into custody, the ordinary Chinese is, in effect, at the mercy of the garrison headquarters. . . . He can be picked up simply because someone who wants his job or property has denounced him to the authorities as a Communist."

One would think that the publication of such evidence was aimed at exposing the Chiang Kai-shek regime's abuses of power. Not at all—the implication of these reports was entirely different. The thought may have occurred to the reader that if there had been an American rather than Chiang Kai-shek administration on the island, the "legal protection" of the population might have been ensured. In short, the idea of transferring Taiwan to an American trusteeship was being cultivated.

General MacArthur visited Taiwan on July 31 and August 1, 1950. Afterwards, the Deputy Chief of Staff of the American Far East Command, Major General Alonzo Fox, arrived on the island. Fox's inspection mission, according to a *New York Times* report of May 5, 1951, reached the conclusion that approximately $500 million was needed to re-arm and re-equip the Chiang Kai-shek army. The White House accepted this advice, and in the first year alone (*i.e.*, by June 30, 1951) Chiang Kai-shek received, according to Secretary of State Acheson, arms and equipment worth $90 million. It was further proposed to spend $300 million for these purposes during the next fiscal year.

Somewhat earlier, in March 1951, the Joint Chiefs of Staff recommended to the government the establishment in Taiwan of a group of advisers for the provision of military aid, and also a special military troop-training mission. On April 20, 1951, the U.S. Department of Defense announced that an American military assistance group headed by Major General William Chase was being dispatched to Taiwan. The staff of this advisory group exceeded 1,250 men. American officers and enlisted men then began to arrive in Taiwan by the hundreds. The British journalist H. Maclear Bate wrote, in his book *Report from Formosa*, that at the beginning of 1951, "Everywhere, or so it seems, you will find American soldiers, not one of them under the rank of top sergeant, attached to the formidable military mission. . . . America has certainly realized the strategic importance of the island, and from her capacious pockets has produced the weapons of war."

Summing up the first months of its activity, the military advisory group reported to Washington in February 1952 that during this initial period its "activities have centered primarily on reorganization of the

Chinese* military forces, and assisting those forces to make the best use of their present equipment and supplies. . . . Further progress may be expected as the flow of U.S. aid increases, on the basis of preparations which are being made at an increasingly rapid rate by the Chinese military establishment** under the guidance of the United States Military Assistance Advisory Group."

American propaganda untiringly reiterated that military aid was being given to Chiang Kai-shek to "support internal security or for legitimate self-defense." Chiang Kai-shek, however, repeatedly pointed out another goal—the return to mainland China. He boasted that "As soon as the necessary arms and equipment are on Formosa . . . we shall need six months to strike a powerful counter-blow." Furthermore, even many American observers frankly stated that the ultimate goal of American military aid to Chiang Kai-shek was to unleash a war against the People's Republic of China. Kerr bluntly confessed that thousands of American military advisers in Taiwan were busily attempting to "prepare for war in China, which could become necessary any day." This is yet one more piece of evidence about the true intentions of the American imperialists and militarists. While they never ceased to profess, in flourishes of rhetoric, their feelings of love for the Chinese people, they were, in fact, equipping the Chiang Kai-shek army, which had been driven by this same people beyond the borders of mainland China to its shelter in Taiwan, where it was protected by the American artillery.

2. *ON THE BEATEN PATH*

On June 27, 1950, President Harry S. Truman specifically told the press that "The occupation of Formosa by Communist forces would be a direct threat to the security of the Pacific area, and to the United States forces performing their lawful and necessary functions in that area. Accordingly, I have ordered the Seventh Fleet to prevent any attack upon Formosa." Thus, the United States, tossing aside all diplomatic stipulations, decided to place the remnants of the Chiang Kai-shek army under its protection. The President's statement of January 5, 1950, which had solemnly promised non-interference in the course of events in China, was now forgotten.

---

*i.e., Chiang Kai-shekist (*Author's note*)

**i.e., Chiang Kai-shekist units (*Author's note*)

Serious preparation had preceded this decision. The ships of the Seventh Fleet, deployed in the Philippine Islands area, were significantly reinforced. Brigadier General Louis J. Fortier, Chief of Intelligence for the U.S. Troop Command in the Far East, flew to Taiwan at the end of May in order to acquaint himself with the state of affairs on the island. He later met with Secretary of Defense Johnson and General Bradley, the Chairman of the Joint Chiefs of Staff of the U.S. Armed Forces, in Tokyo, where they had arrived from Washington. A series of top secret meetings were held with General MacArthur. Upon their return to Washington, Johnson, Bradley and Fortier submitted to the President a special memorandum on the Taiwan situation prepared by MacArthur.

In October 1949, Department of Defense representatives had firmly expressed the opinion that Chiang Kai-shek could hold the island with his own forces; by the summer of 1950, this confidence had been significantly shaken. By May, the U.S. Army, Air Force and Navy attachés who were stationed on the island considered it fully possible that the People's Liberation Army could occupy the island during the coming summer. This conclusion was also prompted by the fact that units of the People's Liberation Army had liberated the island of Hainan on May 2, 1950, and within a few days had expelled the Chiang Kai-shekists from the Chu Shan archipelago, located between the Yangtze delta and Taiwan.

The journey to the island by General Fortier, an experienced intelligence officer, was undoubtedly related to the apprehensions of top U.S. military representatives. It became known soon thereafter that MacArthur's memorandum had emphasized Taiwan's strategic importance to the United States. Considerably later, President Eisenhower plainly stated that "ever since World War II, the United States has recognized the strategic necessity of maintaining the integrity of the Western Pacific chain, including Formosa, as one of its principal links. Our readiness to go to the defense of that island, if it is attacked, has been announced as a government policy." And if the government's policy prior to June 1950 was limited to diplomatic and economic measures, the United States now shifted to military measures, without fear that in so doing it was in gross violation of the United Nations Charter. The American ruling circles, of course, understood all this perfectly well. It was not just coincidental that the President made his statement only after the Seventh Fleet had already moved into its positions in the Taiwan Strait.

President Truman's statement of June 27, 1950, outlined a broad program of expansionist actions in Asia. The American imperialist circles, rifles in hand, made a decisive effort to suppress the liberation struggle of countries in that region of the globe. It is significant that the yearbook published by the American Council on Foreign Relations, *The United States in World Affairs: 1950*, noted that it was difficult for many countries to accept Truman's statement at face value. The yearbook's authors wrote in this context: "The Chinese Communists had not attacked in Korea.... The United States ... was taking advantage of the Korean crisis to lay hands on Formosa for its own purposes. It was notable in this connection that the President did not even reaffirm China's right to the possession of Formosa."

Chiang Kai-shek quickly realized the direction in which the wind was blowing, and immediately offered the Americans his aid for the Korean war. Only yesterday, Chiang himself had been thirsting for United States military aid; today, protected by ships of the Seventh Fleet, he was offering to send 33,000 of "his best" enlisted men and officers to Korea. It is interesting to note that Truman's "first reaction," as he later wrote, "was to accept this offer." Secretary of State Acheson, however, pointed out that it would be "a little inconsistent to spend American money to protect an island while its natural defenders were somewhere else." The military specialists also opposed accepting Chiang Kai-shek's offer because Chiang Kai-shek's troops, in their opinion, "would have very little modern equipment." General MacArthur, in particular, had little respect for the Chiang Kai-shek army.

The National Security Council, at a Washington meeting on July 27, 1950, decided, upon recommendation of the Joint Chiefs of Staff, to render broad military assistance to Chiang Kai-shek. Not only did the Council decide to expand military aid (which, incidentally, had never ceased), but it also suggested that MacArthur's staff should inspect Chiang Kai-shek's troops and that intelligence flights should simultaneously commence along the entire coast of mainland China. The United States Air Force staff was readying proposals for the expansion of such flight zones into the Vladivostok and Kuril islands regions.

Following the decision by the Washington strategists, General MacArthur himself flew to Taiwan for personal discussions with Chiang Kai-shek. These discussions, as noted earlier, were held in Taipei on July 31 and August 1, 1950, and were attended, in addition to MacArthur, by Lieutenant General George E. Stratemeyer, Commander of the U.S. Air Force in the Far East; Vice Admiral Charles T. Joy, Commander of the U.S. Naval forces in that area; and Vice Admiral Arthur D. Struble, Commander of the U.S. Seventh Fleet. After MacArthur's return to Tokyo, the President's representative, Averell Harriman, arrived there for a discussion of the Far East political situation.

Harriman, in a memorandum to the President, reported that

MacArthur had discussed "military problems" with Chiang Kai-shek during his sojourn in Taiwan, and that the latter, in his turn, had suggested MacArthur assume "command of the Chinese National* troops." MacArthur considered this proposal "inappropriate" for himself, but agreed to give Chiang Kai-shek "military advice." Chiang Kai-shek, Harriman reported to the President, had the "burning ambition to use Formosa as a stepping-stone for his re-entry to the mainland. MacArthur recognized that this ambition could not be fulfilled, and yet thought it might be a good idea to let him land and get rid of him that way."

MacArthur, with the simplicity characteristic of him as a soldier, expressed the hidden thought of many American generals: It was absolutely necessary to get rid of Chiang Kai-shek—who had compromised himself—by any means possible. Harriman, however, advised the Commander-in-Chief that the United States still needed Chiang Kai-shek as a cover for the retention of the island, as a screen for pursuing a Far East policy advantageous to the United States, and as an obedient puppet in the United Nations. Harriman "forgot" to add in this regard that only six months earlier the Department of State had seriously weighed the possibility of Chiang Kai-shek's removal and had already been searching for a replacement among local Taiwanese leaders.

On August 1, 1950, General MacArthur stated that as a result of his visit to the island, plans had been formulated for the coordination of operations between the United States and Chiang Kai-shek to resist "any attack" on Taiwan. Chiang Kai-shek simultaneously announced with satisfaction that the negotiations with the General had resulted in an agreement on all problems under discussion, including the island's joint defense and military collaboration with the United States.

The decisions of the President and the National Security Council in June and July, 1950, marked the beginning of a new phase in American-Chinese relations. These decisions, arising from the hostility of the United States ruling circles toward the 600 million Chinese, amounted to naked aggression. They plainly demonstrated to the whole world that America's hypocritical reference to the traditional, allegedly friendly relations with the people of China was only a smoke screen, aimed at concealment of America's true intentions in China. These decisions demonstrated time and again that the United States ruling circles cared neither for the true interests of the Asian people, nor for their fate and aspirations.

*i.e., Chiang Kai-shekist (*Author's note*)

In Korea, the United States attempted to achieve its aims by military means. General MacArthur, as Truman later acknowledged, received a clear order to "destroy the armed forces of North Korea" and to occupy all of Korea. A campaign was then launched in the United States for the expansion of military operations. Secretary of the Navy Francis Matthews, speaking on August 25, 1950, before an audience numbering in the thousands, called on America to become the "first aggressor for the sake of peace" (?!) and to initiate a "preventive war." Matthews' speech constituted a "trial balloon" launched at the direct suggestion of Secretary of Defense Louis Johnson, who in private conversations had advocated the doctrine of preventive war.

On August 29, 1950, *The New York Times* published a letter from General MacArthur to the Veterans of Foreign Wars in which he called Taiwan "an unsinkable aircraft carrier and submarine tender," and emphasized that the U.S. Air Force could threaten from that island "any Asiatic port from Vladivostok to Singapore." Several days later, Major General O. Anderson, Commander of the Air Force Academy, spoke of the "advisability of launching an atomic war against the U.S.S.R."

All these statements could not, of course, have been mere coincidence. They undoubtedly reflected the efforts of certain circles within the country—and extremely influential circles, at that—to exert serious pressure upon the United States government. Trying somehow to save face in the eyes of world public opinion, the American government demanded that General MacArthur "disavow" his letter. In addition, Secretary of Defense Johnson was replaced by General George Marshall.

The ambitions of the Washington politicians and their generals, however, were not realized. First, the Soviet Union came to the defense of the People's Democratic Republic of Korea, whose position was staunchly supported by the other socialist countries. The People's Republic of China issued a subsequent statement to the effect that the Chinese people would remain indifferent neither toward the invasion of the territory of the People's Democratic Republic of Korea by troops of the United States and its allies, nor toward the threat of an expanded war. Under these circumstances, Washington politicians were quickly forced to review the potential consequences of their actions.

The President decided to meet personally with General MacArthur in order to "receive first-hand information." Truman frankly admitted that one of the basic reasons which prompted his hasty journey to Wake Island in the Pacific, where General MacArthur was stationed, was the attempt to clarify how real the possibility that Chinese troops might enter the war actually was. The problem at that time was

America's lack of sufficient military reserves; draftees of the National Guard units would have been unprepared for military action until March 1951.

After the President's conversation with MacArthur, the following group of people convened with Truman and MacArthur in a general meeting: Secretary of the Army Frank Pace; Admiral Arthur W. Radford, the Commander of the U.S. Pacific Fleet; General Omar Bradley, the Chairman of the Joint Chiefs of Staff; Ambassadors Jessup, Muccio and Harriman; and Dean Rusk from the Department of State. Truman later said that at that conference he "gave MacArthur an opportunity to repeat to the larger group some of the things he had said to me in our private meeting." MacArthur boasted about the slim possibility of Chinese intervention, commenting that "if the Chinese tried to get down to Pyongyang, there would be the greatest general slaughter." The General expressed the opinion that he could conclude military operations victoriously within the coming month-and-a-half.

It is common knowledge, however, that everything did not come to pass entirely as the American General had wished. The entry into the war of units of Chinese people's volunteers forced MacArthur to begin talking in a totally different manner. In his message of November 6, 1950, to the Joint Chiefs of Staff, he reported that the situation which had arisen "not only jeopardizes, but threatens the ultimate destruction of the forces under my command."

Washington then became alarmed. When MacArthur requested permission to bomb airfields in northeast China (Manchuria), it was decided to consult America's Korean war allies about the advisability of such a tactic. They categorically opposed this step, and the United States, seriously fearing that the U.S.S.R. might come to the defense of the People's Republic of China, was forced to abandon the idea. Under these circumstances, the Joint Chiefs of Staff submitted to the President for consideration the following proposals:

"1. Every effort should be expended, as a matter of urgency, to settle the problem of Chinese Communist intervention in Korea by political means, preferably through the United Nations, to include reassurances to the Chinese Communists with respect to our intent, direct negotiations through our allies . . . with the Chinese Communist government, and by any other available means.

"2. Pending further clarification as to the military objectives of the Chinese Communists and the extent of their intended commitments, the missions assigned to the Commander-in-Chief, United Nations Command,* should be kept under review, but should not be changed.

*the name given the contingents of aggressors in the United States (*Author's note*)

"3. The United States should develop its plans and make its preparations on the basis that the risk of global war is increased."

This top secret document sheds new light on the state of confusion and alarm which then prevailed in the highest American military and political circles. The President, after a discussion of these proposals at a National Security Council meeting, soon resorted to an attempt at atomic blackmail. At a press conference on November 30, Truman, answering correspondents' questions, said that the United States had always "actively considered" the possibility of using the atomic bomb against China.

This statement evoked protest even from such leaders as Churchill, Eden and Butler; one hundred British Parliament members of the Labor Party expressed their protest in a special letter addressed to Prime Minister Attlee. During the debates in the British Parliament, which the American Embassy characterized in its secret report to Washington as the "most serious, most alarming and most important discussion of international problems in the House of Commons since the Labor Party came to power in 1945," all speakers demanded positive statements from the government that the events in Korea would not develop into a new world war. During these debates, Prime Minister Attlee announced that he would fly to Washington to discuss the problem.

Thus, notwithstanding that some countries supported America's aggressive actions in Korea and even dispatched their troops to that country, there was no unanimity among the allies. Only the United States came out decisively in favor of expanded military operations. The incipient defeats of the American interventionist troops in Korea, who were operating under cover of the United Nations flag, further undermined the prestige of the United States. This was clearly apparent from the instructions issued to General MacArthur by the Joint Chiefs of Staff on November 29, in reply to his recommendation for acceptance of Chiang Kai-shek's offer, submitted several months earlier, to send 33,000 soldiers into Korea. These instructions specifically stated: "Your proposal is being considered. It involves worldwide consequences. We shall have to consider the possibility that it would disrupt the united position of the nations associated with us in the United Nations, and leave us isolated. It may be wholly unacceptable to the Commonwealth countries to have their forces deployed alongside the Nationalist Chinese. It might extend hostilities to Formosa and other areas. Incidentally, our position of leadership in the Far East is being most seriously compromised in the United Nations. The utmost care will be necessary to avoid the disruption of the essential Allied line-up in that organization."

Above all, however, it is necessary to emphasize the undeniable fact that the very steadfast position of the Soviet Union and other socialist countries prevented the American ruling circles from launching broad military operations against the People's Republic of China. This was unequivocally acknowledged by George Marshall, the Secretary of Defense in the Truman Administration. Correspondents once asked Marshall directly: "If you were convinced that Soviet armed forces would not participate in the event of war with China, would you recommend that General MacArthur bomb Manchuria?" Without hesitation, the Secretary answered: "If there were no danger whatsoever of U.S.S.R. intervention, the bombings to which you refer would start without delay."

The United States tried to use the meeting with the Prime Minister of Great Britain (December 4-8, 1950) primarily to strengthen the fragile unity of the allies in Korea and to involve England further in its Far East military adventure. Much of the conference was, of course, devoted to the China problem. Statements made by Truman and Attlee during these discussions are extremely curious. The President of the United States emphasized his hope that, in the end, "the Chinese will understand that their real friends are not in Moscow and Siberia, but in London and Washington." Attlee fully concurred with this point of view, and added that the Western Powers must aim at disrupting the unity of the Russians and the Chinese. "I think," said Attlee, "all of us should try to keep the Chinese from thinking that Russia is their only friend. I want the Chinese to part company with Russia. I want the Chinese to become a counterpoise to Russia in the Far East." It is now appropriate to state that the present leadership of the Chinese Communist Party has followed that very road along which the leaders of the imperialist powers long ago tried to push it.

Truman and Attlee also discussed the Taiwan problem and came to the conclusion that Taiwan could not be returned to China because, in the hands of America's enemies, it could play a dangerous role.

This conference finally developed and formulated the so-called "limited hostility" policy toward the People's Republic of China, which became in succeeding years the official American policy.

Politically, the "limited hostility" policy was expressed in America's categoric refusal to recognize the People's Republic of China, the exertion of pressure on third countries to prevent their establishment of diplomatic relations with the People's Republic of China, the strenuous opposition to allowing the Chinese People's Republic to take its legal seat in the United Nations and other international organizations, and the recognition of the Chiang Kai-shekists sheltered in Taiwan as the "only legal" representatives of China.

Economically, the policy was expressed in the complete embargo on all American trade with mainland China, the demand that other countries refrain from supplying the People's Republic of China with so-called strategic goods, and efforts to prevent other countries from developing normal economic and trade relations with the People's Republic of China.

Militarily, the "limited hostility" policy was expressed primarily in the direct provocations of the People's Republic of China, the effort to encircle the People's Republic with a ring of American military bases, direct military support of Chiang Kai-shek, the creation of aggressive blocs in Asia, rendering of military assistance to a number of states adjacent to the People's Republic, and the unleashing of large military conflicts in China's immediate vicinity.

From 1950 on, the policy of "limited hostility" toward the People's Republic of China became the official policy of the United States. A striking expression thereof was a speech by Dean Rusk, then U.S. Assistant Secretary of State for Far Eastern Affairs, at a dinner given in New York on May 18, 1951, by the so-called China Institute. Rusk plainly stated in his speech that the United States did not "recognize the authorities in Peiping. . . . The Peiping regime . . . is not the government of China. . . . It is not entitled to speak for China."

In addition, Rusk clearly defined U.S. relations with the Chiang Kai-shek regime. "We recognize," he emphasized, "the Nationalist government of the Republic of China,* even though the territory under its control is severely restricted. We believe it more authentically represents the views of the great body of the people of China, particularly their historic demand for independence from foreign control. That government will continue to receive important aid and assistance from the United States." Rusk even stated that the United States "would aid Nationalist China in the seizure . . . of the continent."

It can thus be seen that the leading officials of the Department of State very broadly interpreted the "limited hostility" policy. This policy of the Truman Administration was, in fact, characterized by an unconcealed hostility toward the People's Republic of China and its citizens.

*the term used by the White House to describe the Chiang Kai-shek regime (*Author's note*)

CHAPTER IV

REPUBLICANS IN POWER

1. *FIRST PERIOD*

In July 1952, the National Convention of the Republican party nominated General Dwight D. Eisenhower as its presidential candidate, and Richard M. Nixon, a senator from the state of California, as its vice-presidential candidate. In the elections of November 4, 1952, the Republicans won not only the United States Presidency and Vice Presidency, but also the majority in both Houses of Congress.

The subsequent United States policy toward China is closely linked with the name of John Foster Dulles, who headed the Department of State for more than six years (January 1953-April 1959). Even before Eisenhower appointed him Secretary of State, Dulles was considered the leading Republican expert on foreign policy problems and, as such, was actively utilized by Truman's Democratic Administration. Within American ruling circles Dulles had the reputation of "a realist and experienced statesman." Thus, when he spoke out, in his 1950 book *War or Peace*, in favor of admission of the People's Republic of China to the United Nations, his remarks were bound to attract the attention of influential Republican congressmen who were among the "China lobbyists."

At first glance, it might seem incredible that such an ardent "cold war" apologist could ever advocate the admission of the People's Republic of China to the United Nations. But let Dulles speak for himself: "If the Communist government of China in fact proves its ability to govern China without serious domestic resistance, then it, too, should be admitted to the United Nations. Communist governments today dominate more than 30 percent of the population of the world. We may not like that fact; indeed, we do not like it at all. But if we want to have a world organization, then it should be representative of the world as it is."

After Dulles became Secretary of State, however, he abruptly changed his mind. As the well-informed American journalist Cyrus L. Sulzberger tells it, Dulles first met with General Eisenhower in May 1952 in Paris. Soon afterwards, it became obvious that Dulles was being groomed to head the Department of State in the forthcoming Eisenhower Administration. Certain statements made by Dulles, however, perturbed the Republicans, and consequently, even before Eisenhower officially assumed the office of President, Republican congressmen whose names were closely linked with the "China lobby" plainly told the candidate for Secretary of State that if he did not change his attitude with regard to admitting the People's Republic of China to the United Nations, his appointment would not be confirmed by the American Congress.

Dulles clearly understood that these were not empty threats: The Republicans then enjoyed a majority in both Houses. And it is said that he "privately" assured those present that he had long ago abandoned his old position on this question. Trying in every way possible to reassure and to impress the legislators as favorably as possible, Dulles promised to appoint as his assistant for Far Eastern affairs anyone whom the assembled congressmen would recommend. The congressmen could hardly reject such an opportunity, and proposed for the position Walter S. Robertson, a man closely linked with the American financial oligarchy, who had once served in the American Embassy in China as an adviser on economic affairs and was a well known Chiang Kai-shek sympathizer.

From its first days in power, the Eisenhower Administration made perfectly clear its intention to pursue the old policy of "limited hostility" toward the People's Republic of China. This may be explained primarily by the fact that the People's Republic of China during that period had unconditionally joined the world system of socialism. The leadership of the Communist Party of China realized at that time that without the economic, military and political aid of the U.S.S.R., China could not achieve the status of an independent sovereign state and strengthen its prestige in the international arena. As Soviet commentators have observed, "The existence of the world system of socialism opened exceptionally favorable perspectives for the strengthening of China's independence. The alliance with the socialist states protected the country from imperialist intervention and broke the economic blockade. The socialist countries rendered to the People's Republic of China significant aid in training national cadre and in solving other problems in the construction of a new, socialist China."

Naturally, this course of events did not suit the Washington ruling circles. The policy of "limited hostility" toward the People's Republic of China during that period (1950-1958) was a manifestation of that pathological anti-Communism which so characterized the political course of the Truman and Eisenhower Administrations.

Only a few days after taking office, President Eisenhower, in his "State of the Union" message to the Congress, said that the American Seventh Fleet would not "shield mainland China" in the future. This was bare-faced hypocrisy, for the Seventh Fleet was, in reality, already "shielding" Chiang Kai-shek himself, who, as high officials acknowledged, wanted significantly more than the neutrality protected by the American fleet. Commenting on President Eisenhower's decision, the American press wrote that Chiang Kai-shek had at last been—as they put it—"unleashed." The reactionary newspapers and magazines were full of articles about the Generalissimo's offensive plans. It is common knowledge, however, that the unity and solidarity of the socialist countries and the powerful support which the Soviet people gave to the people of China foiled Chiang Kai-shek's wild plans.

The knowledgeable American commentator Stewart Alsop subsequently wrote that Dulles originated the idea to "unleash" Chiang Kai-shek, which he had first expressed as far back as March 1952 at a joint meeting of Department of State and CIA officials. The President's decision to "unleash" Chiang Kai-shek was not so much to have military as political consequences for, in the opinion of American specialists, "the action, whether intended or not, tended to link the United States more closely to Chiang Kai-shek's ambitions."

Eisenhower later recalled that among the many problems facing him as President in early 1953, "none required more urgent attention than the war in Korea." And although the General had promised the voters in pre-election speeches to bring about a cessation of hostilities, his first action upon becoming President was the formulation and consideration of plans for expansion of the war, including the bombing of China's northeastern provinces, a naval blockade of the entire China coast, and other such measures.

The American ruling circles, forced to agree to a cease-fire in Korea, had no intention at all to abandon their predatory plans in this region. Just ten days after the signing of the armistice on August 7, 1953, Dulles was urgently dispatched to Korea, where he approved a plan for a so-called "mutual defense treaty" with the Syngman Rhee authorities. Article 4 of this treaty granted the United States the right to deploy its land, air and naval forces on the territory of South Korea. Like the earlier treaties America had concluded with Australia, New Zealand, the Philippines and, in early 1954, Japan, the new treaty was primarily intended to strengthen the positions of American imperialism in that region, and its thrust was directed against the People's Republic of China.

The Eisenhower government at the same time took steps to prevent the Western countries from expanding trade with the People's Republic of China. Notwithstanding the enormous pressure exerted by the United States, many of America's Western allies increased their exports to the People's Republic of China in 1953. For example, 1953 exports from the Federal Republic of Germany were nine times greater than those of 1952. Exports from Japan increased more than eight times during that year, and those from France, almost four times.

At a meeting of the foreign ministers of the four Great Powers—the U.S.S.R., the United States, France and England—held in Berlin during January and February of 1954, it was agreed to call a conference in Geneva on April 26, "for the purpose of reaching a peaceful settlement of the Korean question." The four foreign ministers simultaneously agreed that "the problem of restoring peace in Indochina would also be examined at the conference, to which representatives of the U.S.S.R., U.S.A., France, England, the People's Republic of China and other interested governments shall be invited."

The invitation of the People's Republic of China to discuss problems presented to the Geneva Conference was a powerful blow to the interests of American reactionary circles. U.S. Secretary of State Dulles, speaking at the Conference of Ministers of the Four Powers on January 26, 1954, in Berlin, was forced to justify America's policy toward the People's Republic of China. Dulles acknowledged that the United States did not deny the existence, force and authority of the government of the People's Republic of China. "We in the United States well know that it exists, and has power . . . ," he said. "We do not refuse to deal with it where occasion requires. We did deal with it in making the Korean armistice. We deal with it today at Panmunjom."

The inclusion of the question of peace restoration in Indochina as part of the Geneva Conference agenda seriously damaged the plans of American imperialism. As the clandestine Pentagon Papers, which were published by the American press, indicated, the United States government had prepared as early as 1952 a secret policy statement, titled "United States Objectives and Courses of Action with Respect to Southeast Asia." Specifically, that statement set forth the real interests of American imperialism in that region of the globe: "Southeast Asia, especially Malaya and Indonesia, is the principal world source of natural rubber and tin, and a producer of petroleum and other strategically important commodities. The rice exports of Burma and Thailand are critically important . . . to all important areas of . . . Asia." And the basic aim of American imperialism was the seizure of the resources of these regions, rich in strategically important raw materials. For that very reason, Dulles did everything possible in Berlin to wreck the forthcoming conference, while President Eisenhower was considering the possibility of U.S. military intervention in Indochina.

To develop a plan for such intervention, a special committee was formed, consisting of Under Secretary of State Walter B. Smith; Deputy Secretary of Defense Roger M. Kyes; Allen Dulles, the Director of the Central Intelligence Agency; and Admiral A. W. Radford, the Chairman of the Joint Chiefs of Staff. While John Foster Dulles tried in Berlin to wreck the forthcoming Geneva Conference on Indochina, the United States, on the recommendation of the special committee, hurriedly stationed twenty-two B-26 bombers in Indochina and sent there its military personnel, including pilots. This was done by circumvention of existing United States law, with the silent consent of the leaders in both Houses of Congress. Officially, it was said that the military personnel were being sent to Indochina only until mid-July 1954. Lieutenant General John O'Daniel was appointed to head the American advisory group to render military assistance to Vietnam. The United States also offered to undertake the instruction and training of the Bao Dai Army, but this proposal was rejected by France.

All these military measures were carried out in the strictest secrecy, but President Eisenhower, on February 10, 1954, publicly stated: "It is impossible to imagine a greater tragedy for the United States of America than to be drawn into the present war in Indochina. . . . No one could have categorically opposed such a development of events more than I." This statement was made during the very same days that American diplomacy, acting on the President's instruction, was secretly seeking any suitable pretext for just such an intervention. As was recorded in the report to the U.S. Congress on fulfillment of the so-called mutual security program, America's military deliveries to Indochina in 1953 exceeded the level of the preceding year by one-and-a-half times. Military aircraft, naval vessels, tanks, motor vehicles, ammunition and other arms and equipment were supplied in "significant quantities." It was later disclosed that the United States expended $1.4 billion in 1954 for the Vietnam war. For purposes of comparison, and so as to understand who actually financed the military operations in Indochina, it is worth noting that France expended $394 million for the same purposes during that year.

These facts make the position which Dulles advocated in Berlin understandable. While attempting to sabotage the conference on

Indochina, the United States was additionally trying to gain time for active intervention in the military operations. After the decision had already been made in Berlin to call the Geneva Conference on Indochina, the American ruling circles made a desperate attempt to wreck the projected conference by outright military intervention on a broad scale before the conference had begun. Such intervention required the consent of the U.S. Congress, and President Eisenhower directed Secretary of State Dulles to exert pressure upon the congressional leaders to that end.

Together with Deputy Secretary of Defense Kyes and the Chairman of the Joint Chiefs of Staff, Admiral Radford, Dulles met with eight leaders of both Houses of Congress. Those involved reached the conclusion that Congress would support the President's proposal for open U.S. military intervention in the Indochina war upon three conditions: First, the United States must not enter the war alone, but rather in a coalition with the countries of Southeast Asia, the British Commonwealth nations and the Philippines. Second, France must firmly announce the granting of independence to its colonies in Indochina, in order that U.S. intervention would not appear as support for French colonialism. Third, if U.S. armed forces were committed to action, France was not to withdraw its troops from Indochina.

As we see, the U.S. congressional leaders were less troubled by the fact of armed American intervention than by the difficulty of giving such intervention the appearance of "joint actions by the free countries." Eisenhower subsequently wrote: "While we recognized that the burden of the operations would fall on the United States, the token forces supplied by these other nations, as in Korea, would lend real moral standing to a venture that otherwise could be made to appear as a brutal example of imperialism." More definitive and more authoritative testimony would indeed be difficult to find!

Upon receipt of such encouraging news concerning congressional sentiments, Eisenhower decided to put together the necessary alliance of nations for intervention in the Indochina war even before the Geneva Conference began, thereby dooming the conference in advance to complete failure. In addition, steps were taken to prepare American public opinion for such a turn of events. Thus, Vice President Nixon, speaking on April 16, 1954, before members of the American Society of Newspaper Editors, stated that ". . . if to avoid further Communist expansion in Asia and Indochina, we must take the risk now by putting our boys in, I think the Executive has to take the politically unpopular decision and do it." However, as is generally known, these adventurist goals of the American reactionaries were not fated to succeed. The policy of the peace-loving countries, with the Soviet Union in the forefront, once again foiled the predatory plans of American imperialism.

Seriously perturbed by the growth in international influence of the U.S.S.R. and other countries of the socialist camp, including the People's Republic of China, Washington initiated an active anti-Communist campaign. Leading American figures were continuously making speeches on radio and television, at various dinners and luncheons, and before the most diverse audiences. Pathological hatred for the Communist movement and the socialist countries was the common thread running through all these speeches. The average American, who was made the target for every conceivable scare tactic, found it difficult to orient himself in the torrent of anti-Communist falsehoods which descended upon him. Secretary of State Dulles; his deputy, W. B. Smith; Assistant Secretary of State for Far Eastern Affairs Walter S. Robertson (the same man whom Dulles had agreed to appoint to this position as a concession to the influential "China lobbyists"); responsible figures in the Department of State, such as W. P. McConaughy, Alfred Jenkins and others—all took an active part in this campaign. One of the component elements of the campaign was an obvious effort to hinder the growth of the international prestige of the People's Republic of China and minimize the significance of the Soviet Union's victory at the Berlin meeting, which was manifested in the invitation of the People's Republic of China as a full and equal participant in the discussion of both main issues on the agenda—Korea and Indochina.

Washington attempted to prove to the whole world the rectitude of its policy of non-recognition of the People's Republic of China, and also made desperate efforts to demonstrate that such a policy allegedly had the broad support of American public opinion. In New York on February 18, 1954, W. S. Robertson said: "Far Eastern policy has been a subject of particular partisan conflict in the United States. However, I believe it is so no longer. I believe our country is now pretty generally of one mind in its appraisal of the situation in the Far East and its significance for us." Another leading figure in the Department of State, E. Martin, speaking in New York on March 24, 1954, emphasized that America's consent to sit at the negotiating table in Geneva with representatives of the People's Republic of China "does not signify any deviation from our policy toward China."

Moreover, the White House did not limit itself to speeches. On the very eve of the Geneva Conference, the United States increased its deliveries of armaments to the Chiang Kai-shek regime. Thus, wide publicity was given to the ceremony wherein two American destroyers were transferred "on loan" to the Chiang Kai-shek regime on February 26, 1954. At that ceremony, W. S. Robertson made extremely eloquent admissions: "Philosophy and the artistic masterpieces of a great culture have been among the many treasures brought back from China by traders to enrich our lives, in exchange for American machinery and manufactured goods and Western ideas. . . . You have given us landing fields, buildings, roads and hospitality. We have given you guns, planes, and vessels of war." As the saying goes, no explanation is needed!

After conclusion of military pacts with South Korea and Japan, the United States foisted upon a number of countries the sadly notorious SEATO pact and concluded a military agreement with the Chiang Kai-shek regime. In truth, as far back as December 1953 Chiang Kai-shek had proposed a mutual defense treaty with the Eisenhower government. Robertson arrived in Taiwan in October 1954 to discuss this matter, and on December 2, 1954, a new pact was signed in Washington. Article 7 of that pact stipulated that the United States had the right to station its army, air and naval forces in Taiwan and the Penghu islands. The conclusion of the agreement with the Chiang Kai-shekists constituted a direct American interference in the internal affairs of China, since, according to Dulles, the new pact was to show the People's Republic of China that "the United States views any armed attack directed against Taiwan and the Pescadores Islands as a threat to its own peace and security, and will undertake actions to repel this threat."

It is commonly known that the Soviet Union exposed the aggressive nature of this pact to the entire world. The U.S.S.R. Ministry of Foreign Affairs, in a statement of December 15, 1954, pointed out that "The aggressive treaty concluded on December 2, 1954, between the United States of America and the Chiang Kai-shek clique aims at finding a pretext for the illegal stationing of U.S. armed forces in Taiwan and the Penghu Islands, and for maintaining United States occupation of these territories. The conclusion of the treaty between the United States and the Chiang Kai-shek clique in Taiwan represents a gross violation of the sovereignty and territorial integrity of the People's Republic of China and, as such, is a violation of the Charter of the United Nations." The Soviet government stated additionally that "the responsibility for the consequences of the aggressive 'mutual defense treaty' concluded between the United States of America and the Chiang Kai-shek clique rests entirely with the government of the United States of America."

American-Chinese relations in late 1954 and early 1955 were marked by a whole series of events which, as President Eisenhower admitted, threatened "a break between the United States and almost all its allies," which could have "brought the country to the brink of war." Events unfolded around the small islands of Kinmen (Quemoy), Matsu and Tachen, located in the immediate vicinity of mainland China, which were then occupied by Chiang Kai-shek troops. According to American data, the Chiang Kai-shekists kept approximately 50,000 enlisted men and officers on Quemoy island, 15,000 on Tachen island and 9,000 on the Matsu islands. Moreover, it was observed that Chiang Kai-shek had strengthened his garrisons on these islands at the direct insistence of a group of American military advisers.

Joseph Alsop subsequently reported that the Eisenhower government, upon assumption of power, immediately began to exert the "strongest pressure" upon the Taiwanese authorities to reinforce the Chaing Kai-shek garrisons on the off-shore islands. This was not without success: Under pressure from the Eisenhower Administration and on direct instructions from the American military advisers, the Chiang Kai-shekists increased their garrisons on the off-shore islands by 1954, and from these islands made piratical attacks on peaceful Chinese villagers and obstructed navigation in that region. The Taiwanese pirates viewed the islands of Quemoy, Matsu and Tachen as springboards for their "future invasion of mainland China."

In early September 1954, units of the People's Liberation Army of the People's Republic of China subjected Quemoy, Matsu and Tachen to artillery fire. The actions of the People's Republic of China, taken within its own territory, created a furor in Washington. The point is that when these events occurred, Washington was under the impression that the Seventh Fleet was protecting only Taiwan itself and the Penghu Islands. According to well-informed observers, the American ruling circles thought that the question of ownership of the off-shore islands should be decided by military encounters between the People's Republic of China and the Chiang Kai-shekists. The United States thereby saw itself as the Chiang Kai-shekists' arsenal, but, in the opinion of those same observers, did not intend to intervene in a possible conflict.

President Eisenhower was now forced to decide America's future policy on this issue. The U.S. Joint Chiefs of Staff adhered to the opinion that even though the off-shore islands, from a military viewpoint, played no role in the defense of Taiwan, the loss of the islands by the Chiang Kai-shekists could nevertheless very seriously affect the morale of the Chiang Kai-shek army as a whole. It was therefore proposed to place the islands under the protection of American armed forces. Furthermore, a majority of the Joint Chiefs of Staff—Admirals

A.W. Radford and R.B. Carney, and General N.F. Twining—proposed the simultaneous bombing of mainland China, with atomic weapons "if necessary." Such American actions would have meant open warfare against the People's Republic of China, which, in Dulles' opinion, the United States would be forced to conduct alone, without its allies. Washington realized that hardly anyone could be found who wanted to participate in this new American adventure. The Generals' proposal was therefore "shelved."

The United States then decided to expedite the conclusion of a "mutual defense" pact with the Chiang Kai-shekists. Appended to, and made an integral part of this pact was an exchange of letters, which took place prior to the signing of the pact, between Dulles and Chiang Kai-shek's "Minister of Foreign Affairs." These letters stipulated that "either contracting party will undertake offensive military operations from the territory of the Chinese Republic* by mutual agreement only." There was actually nothing new in this stipulation, since without American assistance the Chiang Kai-shekists were not only unable to engage in military operations, but incapable of taking even a single step. Thus, the exchange of letters only legally confirmed on paper that situation which had in reality prevailed for several years—the complete dependence of the Chiang Kai-shekists upon American dictates. Some American scholars could later be found who interpreted this exchange of letters as a manifestation of the alleged "peace-loving" intentions of the United States, and even as a defense (!) of the interests of the People's Republic of China. There is nothing more hypocritical than these statements.

The Chiang Kai-shekists were at that time by no means ready for offensive operations. According to the authoritative opinion of the American Joint Chiefs of Staff, the Kuomintang troops were in no condition to defend the off-shore islands without significant U.S. military aid. And the reservation concerning "mutual agreement" for offensive military operations was demanded by the United States government primarily to reassure those among its allies who did not approve of Chiang Kai-shek's adventurist plans. The reservation was additionally designed to show the neutral countries that the United States was exerting a purportedly restraining influence upon Chiang Kai-shek.

It was clear that Chiang Kai-shek could not succeed in holding all the islands. After a series of meetings in Washington, it was decided, upon Dulles's suggestion, to evacuate the garrison from Tachen island and to

---

*i.e., from the territory held by the Chiang Kai-shekists (*Author's note*)

announce that the United States would assume the protection of the Quemoy and Matsu islands. Such action required the formal consent of the U.S. Congress, which the President requested on January 24, 1955, in a special message. Eisenhower, emphasizing in his message that Taiwan and the Penghu Islands under all circumstances "must remain in friendly hands,"* asked the Congress for emergency powers to deploy American armed forces in the Taiwan region, the Penghu Islands and "related territories and positions."

Promptly the next day, the House of Representatives approved the proposed resolution by a vote of 410-to-3 and submitted it for consideration by the Senate, where furious debates were held for three days. Senator Estes Kefauver proposed to entrust the United Nations with the protection of Taiwan. Senator Hubert Humphrey moved to restrict the right to deploy American armed forces to the territories of Taiwan and the Penghu Islands proper. Senator Wayne Morse stated that U.S. involvement in the civil war in China for the sake of the Quemoy and Matsu islands would set a "poor historical precedent," and that the proposed resolution would, in fact, give the President the right to start a war.

Senator Herbert Lehman introduced a formal motion to limit the scope of the resolution to the territories of Taiwan and the Penghu Islands. The Senate's defeat of the Lehman resolution, by a 74-13 vote, was the key to its approval of the resolution requested by the White House. It is extremely interesting to note that the 13 Senators who voted for Lehman's proposal included Fulbright, McNamara, Humphrey and Mansfield. By coincidence, two senators—John Kennedy and Lyndon Johnson—were ill on the day of the vote, but both publicly stated their points of view: Kennedy supported the minority position, and Johnson opposed Lehman's motion.

On January 28, 1955, the Senate approved the proposed "Formosa Defense" resolution, which granted the President of the United States the right "to employ the armed forces of the United States, as he deems necessary, for the specific purpose of securing and protecting Formosa and the Pescadores against armed attack, this authority to include the securing and protection of such related positions and territories of that area now in friendly hands, and the taking of such other measures as he judges to be required or appropriate in assuring the defense of Formosa and the Pescadores."

J. William Fulbright, the Chairman of the Senate Committee on Foreign Relations, stated a few years later that the adoption of such a

---

*friendly to the United States, of course (*Author's note*)

resolution was a fundamental congressional error, for the Congress had thereby surrendered to the President its basic right, granted in the U.S. Constitution, to declare a state of war. Fulbright also pointed out that the congressional practice of adoption of such resolutions was first exploited by Dulles, with the aim of substituting the personal authority of the President for the power of Congress by way of actions "which in outward appearance were acts of Congress, but in reality were not so at all."

President Eisenhower, making immediate use of the authority he had been granted, ordered the participation of American naval forces in the evacuation of the Chiang Kai-shek garrison from Tachen island. Furthermore, he granted to the Commander of the U.S. Pacific Fleet the authority to bomb airfields on mainland China territory "in case of necessity." Explaining his actions at that time with regard to the off-shore islands, Eisenhower wrote to British Prime Minister Winston Churchill: "To defend Formosa, the United States has been engaged in a long and costly program of arming and sustaining the Nationalist troops on that island. Those troops, however, and Chiang himself, are not content now to accept, irrevocably and permanently, the status of 'prisoners' on the island. They are held together by a conviction that some day they will go back to the mainland. As a consequence, their attitude toward Quemoy and the Matsus, which they deem the stepping stones between the two hostile regions, is that surrender of those islands would destroy the reason for the existence of the Nationalist forces on Formosa. . . .

"The Formosa Resolution, as passed by Congress, is our publicly stated position; the problem now is how to make it work. The morale of the Chinese Nationalists is important to us, so for the moment, and under the existing conditions, we feel they must have certain assurances with respect to the off-shore islands. We must remain ready, until some better solution can be found, to move promptly against any Communist force that is manifestly preparing to attack Formosa."

According to testimony of knowledgeable observers, the President's position was merely a reiteration of Chiang Kai-shek's current stance. *The Christian Science Monitor* wrote: "Chiang Kai-shek has more than once reported from Formosa that if evacuation of his troops from the off-shore islands would be demanded of him, morale of the Nationalist regime would fall to such a degree that his own control over Formosa would be threatened."

In compliance with the President's decision, Dulles, who had completed a routine trip to Taiwan in March 1955, concluded that the United States would have to use atomic weapons for the defense of the

off-shore islands. At the same time, he expressed doubt, in a conversation with Eisenhower, about the loyalty of the Kuomintang troops. A
member of the President's staff, Colonel Andrew J. Goodpaster, flew to
the General Headquarters of the U.S. Pacific Fleet at Pearl Harbor, in
order to clarify the views of its Commander.

On March 15, Goodpaster submitted a report to Eisenhower, who
announced at a press conference the following day that the United
States was prepared to use tactical atomic weapons in Asia against
"specific military objectives."

The American military preparations displeased many Western
countries. Anthony Eden, for instance, spoke out very clearly in the
British House of Commons on March 8, 1955, in favor of the withdrawal of Chiang Kai-shek's troops from the Quemoy and Matsu
islands. The Canadian Minister of Foreign Affairs, Lester B. Pearson,
announced that Canada had no intention to fight for the off-shore
islands. Summarizing the reaction of the Western Powers to this
problem, one American commentator wrote on March 25 that "all our
allies, with the exception of Generalissimo Chiang Kai-shek, regard this
as a wrong war, at a wrong time and in a wrong place."

Meanwhile, high-ranking U.S. military officers openly talked of the
"inevitability of war." These bellicose statements drew sharp objections
from many notable American figures. Senator Lyndon Johnson, for
example, acknowledged that he feared all these American actions would
end in an "irresponsible adventure." Adlai Stevenson, a leader of the
Democratic party, pointed out that he had "gravest misgivings about
risking a Third World War in defense of these little islands." Stevenson
asked whether these off-shore islands were really essential for United
States security, and called upon America and its allies to denounce the
use of force in the Taiwan Strait. He demanded an answer to the
question of how the prestige and honor of such a great power as the
United States had become staked on some little islands within the
shadow of the China coast.

Stevenson never received an intelligible answer. The Eisenhower
Administration was preoccupied at that time with something entirely
different: It was making every conceivable effort, as the President
noted in a secret memorandum to Dulles on April 5, 1955, to accelerate
the "concentrating, equipping and training of troops on Formosa," in
order that the Chiang Kai-shek troops would be "ready to take advantage of any political, military or economic circumstance on the mainland that would give to an invasion a reasonable chance of success."
Secretary of State Dulles threatened the People's Republic of China
with "complete destruction of military objectives." Assistant Secretary

of State for Far Eastern Affairs Robertson, speaking at a session of the Subcommittee on Appropriations of the U.S. House of Representatives, confirmed that the foundation of the Eisenhower Administration's Far East policy was the "maintenance of a constant threat of military action *vis-à-vis* Red China, with the hope that war might someday break out there."

The Soviet government sharply condemned America's aggressive actions against the People's Republic of China. In a letter to the Chairman of the United Nations Security Council, dated January 30, 1955, the Deputy Permanent U.S.S.R. Representative in the Security Council emphasized that "American interference in the internal affairs of China, and the recent escalation of aggressive American actions against the People's Republic of China in the Taiwan region, increases the tension in the Far East and magnifies the threat of a new war." The Soviet Union demanded the condemnation of these aggressive actions against the People's Republic of China and proposed that the U.S. government take immediate steps to cease its aggression, as well as its interference in the internal affairs of China.

The Soviet Union's actions, position and indisputable might once again had a sobering effect upon those enamored of military adventures, and thus served as the most important stabilizing force in the development of American-Chinese relations.

2. *GENEVA NEGOTIATIONS*

The actions and plans of the Eisenhower government with regard to the People's Republic of China demonstrate that the Republicans, during their first years in power, not only adopted the Democrats' "limited hostility" policy toward the People's Republic of China, but went even further, providing the traditional energetic support for Chiang Kai-shek's revanchist plans. Admiral Arthur W. Radford, appointed by Eisenhower in August 1953 as Chairman of the Joint Chiefs of Staff, unflaggingly reiterated in private conversations that the government of the People's Republic of China had to be overthrown, even if the United States would have to fight for 50 years to achieve that goal. U.S. Secretary of State Dulles stated in one of his speeches that the government of the People's Republic of China was "a passing and not a perpetual phase. . . . We owe it to . . . our allies . . . to do all that we can to contribute to that passing."

This policy was supported in every way possible by an influential group in the Congress led by Senator William Knowland, who was closely linked with the "China lobbyists"–the same Knowland who was often called, behind his back, the "Senator from Formosa." The well-informed American newspaper *The Washington Post* wrote that, despite the opposition of the U.S. Joint Chiefs of Staff to the large concentration of Chiang Kai-shek forces on the off-shore islands, Admiral Radford had repeatedly reassured Chiang Kai-shek during his trips to Taiwan that the United States fully supported an increase of garrisons on the islands. Admiral Stump, the Commander of the U.S. Pacific Fleet, also adhered to this position.

The situation in the Taiwan Strait remained tense, and, under these circumstances, a conference of Asian and African countries assembled in Bandung, Indonesia, in April 1955. The delegation of the People's Republic of China issued a statement during that conference pointing out that "the Chinese people are friendly toward the American people. The Chinese people do not want to fight with the United States of America. The Chinese government is prepared to sit down at the negotiating table with the U.S. government in order to discuss the question of reducing the tension in the Far East and, in particular, in the area of Taiwan." Incidentally, the idea of direct negotiations between the People's Republic of China and the United States was supported by eight major Asian countries.

The U.S. Department of State reacted to this statement with startling speed. The United States, it declared, would be ready to enter into negotiations, on the following conditions: First, the Chiang Kai-shekists should participate in the discussions on the situation in the Taiwan region as "equal participants in the negotiations." Second, the People's Republic of China should, prior to the beginning of the negotiations, free American prisoners of war captured in Korea. Third, the People's Republic of China should agree to take part in a United Nations Security Council discussion of the Taiwan situation.

Although *The London Times* characterized the State Department's reply as "unceremonious," it became clear that the United States was not rejecting the idea of direct contacts with the People's Republic of China. Under these circumstances, a number of U.S. allies exerted serious pressure upon Washington to obtain its agreement to the proposed negotiations, which many influential congressmen also favored. The Department of State had no choice but to "refine" its conditions, and on July 25, 1955, it was announced that direct negotiations would begin in Geneva between the American Ambassador to Czechoslovakia, U. Alexis Johnson, and the People's Republic of China Ambassador to Poland, Wang Ping-nan. Secretary of State Dulles announced the following day that he was not excluding the possibility of personal negotiations with Premier Chou En-lai. President Eisenhower also spoke of this plan on July 27, 1955, pointing out that negotiations between the United States and the People's Republic of China might "in due course" reach the ministerial level.

An agreement was reached at the first meeting between the Ambassadors of the People's Republic of China and the United States, on August 1, 1955, as to the following agenda for negotiations: (1) the return of civilians of both sides to their respective countries, and (2) other practical problems which were the subject of controversies between both sides. Fourteen closed meetings between the Ambassadors of the United States and the People's Republic of China were held during the following six weeks. On September 10, 1955, an agreement was reached on the first point of the agenda. In a joint communiqué, the United States recognized that any Chinese residing in America who desired to return to the People's Republic of China had the full right to do so. The People's Republic of China, in turn, recognized the right of Americans in the People's Republic of China to return to the United States. Both sides agreed to take the necessary measures to implement the agreement. To this end, it was proposed that India represent the interests of the Chinese in the United States, and England the interests of the Americans in the People's Republic of China.

On September 14, 1955, the Chinese representative at the Geneva negotiations proposed to move to the second point on the agenda, and to examine, first, the problem of removal of trade barriers, and second, the means of conducting the necessary preparatory work for continuation of the negotiations at a higher level. The American representative replied that strict compliance with the conditions of the agreement just reached would constitute a basis for negotiation on other practical problems. Although this statement by Ambassador Johnson did not, on first hearing, sound very reassuring, Johnson nevertheless presented for consideration at the meeting on October 8 a proposal for the renunciation of the use of force. This proposal did not envisage the "renunciation of the achievement of any political goals" which either side viewed as legitimate, but only required the "renunciation of the use of force in the implementation of a policy" to achieve those goals.

The United States proposed that the People's Republic of China announce that it "would not resort to force in the Taiwan region, except for purposes of defense." The United States, on the other hand, promised to issue a similar statement. On October 27, the Ambassador of the People's Republic of China introduced a counter-proposal that both parties declare their respective intention to refrain from the use of force, in accord with the United Nations Charter; and that in the interest of implementing this reciprocal restraint, a conference of the foreign ministers from both countries would be called to discuss the problem of the reduction and eventual complete elimination of the tension in the Taiwan area.

These proposals were actively discussed at the 18 meetings which occurred between September 11, 1955, and January 20, 1956. The representatives of both countries agreed, in principle, to repudiate the use of force, but the representatives of the People's Republic of China held in this regard that such repudiation on their part in no way represented a renunciation of China's sovereign right to liberate its legitimate territory—Taiwan.

On May 12, 1956, the representatives of the People's Republic of China proposed that a meeting of foreign ministers from both countries be held within two months. On June 12, the Department of State rejected this proposal on the pretext that the meeting was being called "on too short notice." Actually, the Geneva negotiations between the representatives of the United States and the People's Republic of China had by then reached a deadlock. Meetings of the Ambassadors continued, however, as did the discussion on the problem of returning both countries' civilians, on holding the conference of foreign ministers, and on the renunciation of the use of force. Such were the basic positions of both parties by mid-1956 at the Geneva negotiations, which continued at various intervals until December 1957, when Ambassador Johnson was recalled to Washington in connection with a new appointment.

Direct U.S. negotiations with representatives of the People's Republic of China seriously disturbed Chiang Kai-shek, who feared that the United States might reach an agreement with the People's Republic of China behind his back and at his expense. In order to reassure the Chiang Kai-shek regime, Vice President Richard Nixon visited Taiwan in July 1956 and delivered to Chiang Kai-shek a personal message from the President, in which Eisenhower reiterated America's "steadfastness" on the subject of "continuing support" for Chiang Kai-shek.

The establishment of direct American-Chinese contacts, the conclusion of an armistice in Panmunjom, the achievement of an agreement on the repatriation of American and Chinese civilians—all these factors intensified the interest of the American news media in the subject of American-Chinese relations. The question of a possible U.S. recognition of the People's Republic of China was again raised. *The New York Times*, *The New York Herald Tribune*, *The Christian Science Monitor*, *The Washington Post* and many others published scores of articles both favoring and opposing a policy of recognition. American officials spoke endlessly on this question, explaining the government's point of view before the most diverse audiences. Noting these facts, C. L. Sulzberger wrote in *The New York Times*: "Undoubtedly, now that the gamble of unseating China's Communist regime has long since failed, there is much interest in reports that at least some American opinion is openly discussing a grant of recognition to Peking as a means of easing tension."

U.S. Supreme Court Justice William O. Douglas and Senator Wayne Morse suggested at that time that Taiwan be placed under a United Nations trusteeship and that the People's Republic of China be admitted to the United Nations. From the floor of the Congress, Senators William Langer and Hubert Humphrey cast doubt on the wisdom of America's China policy. At the so-called "American Assembly," held at Columbia University in 1956, serious opposition to the policy of non-recognition became apparent.

An analysis of the numerous materials which are now available to researchers makes it possible to summarize the positions of both sides on this question.

Arguments against the recognition of the People's Republic of China: Opponents of recognition were spurred by obvious anti-Communist tendencies; these individuals reflected the points of view held by the most reactionary circles in the United States, as well as the most backward sectors of the population, which accepted at face value the official propaganda thesis of an imminent Communist threat to the country. Furthermore, the opponents of recognition tried in every way possible to conceal their anti-Communism by falling back upon a variety of arguments.

First, it was said that such recognition would be a violation of traditional U.S. policy on the question of recognition of new governments, since, the opponents contended, the government of the People's Republic of China did not exercise authority over the entire territory of China (Taiwan was still under Chiang Kai-shek's control), its authority was allegedly not recognized by all the Chinese people, and it was said to be unable and unwilling to fulfill its international obligations. Second, United States recognition would have signified approval by American public opinion of a Communist government of China. Third, since the government of the People's Republic of China was conducting a policy hostile toward the United States, recognition of that government was not at all in America's interests. Fourth, in the event of recognition of the People's Republic of China, the United States would have to support admission of that government to the United Nations and would thereby promote the growth of the international prestige of the People's Republic of China, in particular, and of international

Communism, in general, thereby striking a serious blow to American interests, especially in Southeast Asia. Fifth, such a step on the part of the United States, it was said, would signify an abandonment of support for the Chiang Kai-shekists, old allies and friends of America, and, in the final analysis, would facilitate the take-over of Taiwan by the Communists. Sixth, a policy of non-recognition of the People's Republic of China would allegedly boost the support of Chiang Kai-shek by millions of Chinese living outside the People's Republic of China and Taiwan. Seventh, this policy of psychological, diplomatic and economic pressure upon the People's Republic of China would promote the deterioration of relations between the People's Republic of China and the U.S.S.R., thus weakening the People's Republic of China. Eighth, the prevailing policy of the U.S. government already involved the tactic of economic blockade, thereby weakening not only the People's Republic of China, but also the U.S.S.R., which would be compelled to extend enormous economic aid to China.

These were the basic arguments advanced by those who were unwilling to consider the changes occurring in the world, who tried in every way possible to hold the United States to an adventurist policy course in the Far East, and who shared the opinion of the Washington ruling circles that the People's Republic of China was only a "passing phase" in this world. For such reasons, they urged the United States to make every conceivable effort to destroy the People's Republic of China.

Arguments in favor of recognition of the People's Republic of China: Advocates of recognition offered the following arguments in favor of such a step: First, they believed that the entire previous United States policy on the recognition of new governments, dating back to George Washington's time, had been based on recognition of governments exercising sovereignty over the territory of a specific country. The government of the People's Republic of China was the *de facto* government of China, and already recognized as such by 29 countries (as of 1956). There was no indication whatsoever that the population of China did not recognize that government which actually exercised control over the country's entire territory, with the exception of Taiwan. Second, the revolutionary origin of the People's Republic of China government was insufficient reason for non-recognition; the Chinese people had an absolute right to establish a new government by revolution, and the United States had often recognized such governments in the past—for example, the government of the French Republic. Third, United States recognition would promote the breaking-away of the People's Republic of China from the U.S.S.R., since it would, on the one hand, lead to the growth of nationalist sentiments, and, on the other, to the strengthening of still-existing goodwill feelings toward America on the part of "certain circles of the Chinese leadership." Fourth, even if United States recognition of the People's Republic of China would not lead to a complete break between China and the U.S.S.R., it could still foster a "more independent" Chinese foreign policy. Fifth, recognition of the People's Republic of China could eliminate the Chinese government's fear for its own security, since it was thought that the People's Republic of China viewed the United States as its primary threat. And this, in turn, could facilitate the solution of many problems in the Far East. Sixth, recognition would open the door for China's admission to the United Nations, which would undoubtedly strengthen that organization. Seventh, if the United States were truly interested in a People's Republic of China which would be friendly toward America and economically strong, then the United States would have to recognize and provide economic assistance to the Chinese People's Republic, which otherwise would still become an economically strong country, but one hostile toward the United States.

As is evident, the advocates of recognition of the new China proceeded, above all else, with America's interests in mind, predicating their arguments on the fact that recognition would provide for America more benefits than the policy pursued by the Eisenhower Administration. Thus, the debate between the opponents and the advocates of recognition did not go beyond the boundaries of a "family argument" and merely reflected differing views of what would be more advantageous to American imperialism. Both sides in this debate endeavored primarily to find ways to drive a wedge between the People's Republic of China and the U.S.S.R., and to undermine the unity of the countries in the socialist alliance. And both these factions were clearly impressed by the old policy of British imperialism, which found its true expression in the "divide and conquer" principle. The issue was not so much one of strategic policy goals as of finding appropriate tactics which would lead to achievement of those goals. For all their outward differences, the American advocates and opponents of the policy of recognition of the People's Republic of China basically agreed on the major point that, whatever the case, the policy must, above all else, serve the interests of American imperialism.

The Republican Administration expressed its attitude toward the discussion on recognition of the People's Republic of China in Secretary of State Dulles's well-known speech titled "Our Policy toward Communism in China," which was delivered on June 28, 1957, in San Francisco. Dulles therein analyzed almost all aspects of American policy toward the People's Republic of China, dwelling on the possible consequences of recognition, the questions of trade and cultural relations between the two countries, and the problem of China's representation in the United Nations. He countered the arguments of those who asserted that because the government of the People's Republic of China was the *de facto* government of the country, it must inevitably be recognized.

Dulles noted five possible consequences of recognition of the People's Republic of China, which, in his opinion, were telling arguments against such a policy. First, recognition, according to the Secretary of State, would most adversely affect those in China itself who were attempting to change the existing government. Second, in the event of recognition, millions of Chinese living abroad would be forced to accept the "guidelines" issued by the government of the People's Republic of China. Third, recognition of the People's Republic of China would constitute a betrayal of Chiang Kai-shek, to whom the United States was linked by a mutual defense treaty. Fourth, such a step by the United States would even further complicate the already difficult situation in Southeast Asia, where many governments allegedly pinned their hopes on America's steadfastness. And fifth, U.S. recognition would open the way to the United Nations for the People's Republic of China. Dulles also considered it necessary to emphasize that, in his opinion, recognition by the United States would strongly increase the "prestige and influence" of the recognized state both "at home and abroad."

Thus, the Republican Administration not only firmly adhered to the policy of non-recognition, but also openly supported the overthrow of the government of the People's Republic of China, and exerted strenuous pressure on other countries in an effort to keep them from establishing diplomatic relations with that government. True, this pressure was not very effective since, as is commonly known, the People's Republic of China was by the end of 1949 and early 1950 recognized by 26 countries. From 1953-60, *i.e.*, the period during which the Republicans were in the White House , 13 countries recognized the People's Republic of China, and most of them exchanged ambassadors. Dulles' arguments, therefore, did not have a very convincing effect upon the governments of other countries, and opposition to the American government's China policy grew stronger, even in the United States itself.

It is extremely important to emphasize that in shaping their policy toward the government of the People's Republic of China, the Republicans were guided primarily by the imperialist interests of the United

States, and not at all by the real interests of the Chinese people. "It was not necessary that they should have a good government," said Walter Judd, an influential Republican and member of the U.S. House of Representatives. "That was desirable, but wholly secondary. It did not necessarily need to be a democratic government, an honest government, or an efficient government. The key thing was that the manpower and the resources and the bases of China be under Chinese friendly to the United States." It is precisely this extremely blunt admission which holds the key to the entire policy of Eisenhower's Republican Administration toward the People's Republic of China.

3. REASSESSMENT OF VALUES

Dwight D. Eisenhower was elected President of the United States for a second term in November 1956, and in the opinion of a number of American political analysts, it was during just this period, beginning in 1957, that "dissension over China policy came to be heard frequently enough to have an impact on public opinion." By 1957, in fact, a number of distinguished American figures began to urge a reappraisal of the country's China policy. Theodore F. Green, the Democratic Chairman of the Senate Committee on Foreign Relations, spoke on February 18 in favor of a reassessment of that policy. Sooner or later, he plainly said, the United States "must recognize Red China." And, he added, "We don't like their form of government, but the country is a great country, and organized, and I do not myself see why we should recognize these other Communist countries and withhold recognition of China."

Senator Fulbright and Congressman Stewart Udall also criticized the government's China policy. U.S. Secretary of Commerce Sinclair Weeks stated that he favored a policy of reduction of trade restrictions with the People's Republic of China. The Senate Democratic leader, Lyndon Johnson, spoke out in favor of a reassessment of the trade policy toward the People's Republic of China, and the Democratic Senator Allen Ellender called for a complete lifting of the trade embargo against the People's Republic of China. Warren Magnuson, the Chairman of the Senate Committee on Domestic and Foreign Trade, announced the possibility of beginning passenger and air mail communications with the People's Republic of China. "It is time for us to become realists," Magnuson pointed out. "We cannot hold 400 million people behind an economic bamboo curtain only because we do not like their government." Senator Humphrey stated that "the time has come" to re-examine the entire U.S. policy toward Communist China. Members of the World Trade Advisory Committee of the U.S. Department of Commerce characterized American trade policy toward the People's Republic of China as "unrealistic."

A number of Western countries sharply curtailed their restrictions on trade with the People's Republic of China in 1957. On May 30, the British government announced that trade with the People's Republic of China would be conducted on the same basis as with other socialist countries. In June 1957, France, Italy, and Holland announced a significant lessening of trade restrictions with regard to the People's Republic of China. These decisions are all the more remarkable because they were made after the Department of State had, on April 20, 1957, specifically warned 14 nations friendly toward the United States that the White House intended to "continue the unilateral embargo on all trade with Communist China." Thus, the policy of economic blockade imposed by the United States was crumbling.

A broad-based discussion began in the United States during 1957 on the possibility that American journalists might visit the People's Republic of China. The discussion had begun in August 1956, when the government of the Chinese People's Republic agreed to issue visas for 15 American newsmen to enter the country. At that time, the Department of State reacted to China's decision with a statement that its ban on any travel to the People's Republic of China would remain in force. This problem surfaced once again at the beginning of 1957, when Secretary of State Dulles announced at a press conference in February that the Department of State had banned visits by journalists to the People's Republic of China. At his next press conference, however, only a month later, Dulles said that visits by American journalists to China would be "completely permissible." Emanuel Celler, the Democratic Chairman of the U.S. House of Representatives Judiciary Committee, introduced on March 18 for discussion in the House a resolution to give journalists freedom to travel anywhere in the world, including the People's Republic of China.

As a result, Dulles announced in April that the Department of State was prepared to allow a group of American correspondents to visit the People's Republic of China. After lengthy negotiations it was announced in August that the White House had granted permission for 24 newspapers, magazines, wire services and television networks to send their correspondents to the People's Republic of China for a seven-month trial period. The Department of State announcement emphasized that this decision was made because "new factors have come into the picture, making it desirable that additional information be made available to the American people respecting current conditions in China." The State Department representative pointed out, however, that it was out of the question to suggest that journalists from the People's Republic of China would be granted entry visas "on a reciprocal basis" to the United States. Sometime later, the Department of State also made this position "more specific." Assistant Secretary of State Christian Herter said that if China desired an exchange of journalists "on a reciprocal basis," its correspondents must apply for U.S. entry visas, and that the United States had thus far received no such applications.

It is, incidentally, extremely significant that the Department of State reconsidered its position toward the end of the summer of 1957, *i.e.*, after the Maoist group had conducted a recurrent campaign against dissenters in China. That campaign, which was bombastically named the "struggle against bourgeois rightist elements," occurred in the summer of 1957 and was specifically directed against those economists who opposed Mao Tse-tung's adventurist policy of unfounded rapid development of the country's economy, at the price of placing an extreme strain upon the entire work force and causing an artificial acceleration of numerous reforms. Were these not the "new facts" implied in the announcement of the Department of State—the facts of persecution of internationalist-minded members of the Chinese Communist Party?

The year 1958 was nevertheless marked by the recurrent U.S. effort to exert serious pressure upon the People's Republic of China. The Ambassadors' negotiations, which had continued since 1955 in Geneva, were terminated in December 1957. The United States officially explained that the negotiations were broken off because of Ambassador Johnson's recall from Europe. In an obvious attempt to lower considerably the level of negotiations, the United States proposed to replace Johnson with a minor diplomatic official from the U.S. Embassy in Great Britain. Speaking at the National Press Club in January 1958, Dulles said that he did not envisage at that time any necessity for high-level meetings with representatives of the People's Republic of China.

The U.S. Department of State deemed it necessary to issue one more statement concerning relations with China. "It is true," the statement conceded, "that there is no reason to believe that the Chinese Communist regime is on the verge of collapse; but there is equally no reason to accept its present rule in mainland China as permanent. . . . The United States holds the view that Communism's rule in China is not permanent and that it one day will pass. By withholding diplomatic recognition from Peiping, it seeks to hasten that passing."

Similar remarks by the Department of State, which were repeated with enviable constancy, had three primary purposes: First, they were meant to exert pressure on the many countries which had not only re-established and expanded trade and economic relations with the People's Republic of China during that period, but also had in many instances established official diplomatic relations. Second, the remarks were intended to strengthen Chiang Kai-shek's badly shaken prestige in the world arena. And third, they were directed against those progressive circles within the United States itself, which had raised their voices in defense of the People's Republic of China and demanded a fundamental re-examination of the U.S. policy in the Far East. Washington was obviously perturbed that not only U.S. allies, but also American corporations opposed a trade embargo upon China. It became apparent, for instance, at the end of March 1958 that one American and three Canadian companies had signed an agreement with the People's Republic of China for deliveries of Canadian grain to China.

It must be noted in this regard that beginning in 1958 the foreign policy of the People's Republic of China increasingly differed from the policy of the other socialist countries, and conflicted with that of the U.S.S.R. and the entire socialist camp, whose foreign policy was designed to resolve the "cold war" and other manifestations of international tension. A series of actions which the Maoists undertook in 1958 in the region of the Taiwan Strait exemplifies this type of conduct. The most significant military clashes between units of the People's Liberation Army and the Chiang Kai-shek forces occurred at the end of the summer in the vicinity of the off-shore Penghu and Matsu islands.

Events in that area developed as follows: On August 6, 1958, Chiang Kai-shek proclaimed a state of emergency in the Penghu and Matsu islands. It is necessary to realize that in initiating their operations, the Chiang Kai-shekists were counting on the support of the American military clique which had invested at least half-a-billion dollars in arming the garrisons on these islands.

By the summer of 1958, one-third of Chiang Kai-shek's combat-ready force was concentrated on the off-shore islands. Furthermore, 90,000 enlisted men and officers were deployed on Quemoy island, located only 7 kilometers from the mainland. From this island, the Chiang Kai-shek forces constantly undertook provocative actions against mainland China. Such actions suited in the best way possible the plans of those militant American circles which were endeavoring by every conceivable method to frustrate the course adopted by the Soviet Union and the other socialist countries, which was designed to lessen international tension. The Chiang Kai-shekists' actions of August 1958 were obviously meant to draw the People's Republic of China into a military confrontation.

These conditions required of the Peking leaders restraint, self-control and strict observance of the direct obligations imposed upon them by the Sino-Soviet treaty, which stated the necessity for consultations with the Soviet Union in such circumstances. The Chinese leaders, however, failed to inform the head of the Soviet government, who was in Peking at the beginning of August 1958, of their intentions when they decided to shell the Quemoy and Matsu islands as "punitive measures in reply to the Chiang Kai-shekists' provocations."

The shelling of the off-shore islands by troops of the People's Liberation Army caused a fit of military hysteria in the United States. Dulles, in a statement approved by the President of the United States, emphasized hurriedly that "Formosa's defense requires the use of U.S. armed forces. . . . The President will not hesitate to make such a decision, if he should find that conditions have been created that result in such a necessity." At a special briefing session for press representatives, Dulles explained that bombardment of the Chinese mainland by American armed forces was practically a foregone conclusion.

Walter Lippman wrote in this connection, on September 18, 1958, in *The New York Herald Tribune*: "Thus, we have been maneuvered into a position where the question is not whether we will defend Quemoy against invasion, but whether we will make war against the Chinese mainland. Was this maneuver forseen, it is fair to ask, when Mr. Dulles persuaded the President to stake American prestige on the defense of Quemoy? There is reason to doubt it. There is reason to doubt whether the President and Mr. Dulles and their military advisers had fully realized that Quemoy could be blockaded by artillery fire from the mainland. There is strong evidence that the commitment to defend Quemoy was made before there was a plan to defend Quemoy."

In mid-September, the U.S. Department of Defense announced that during the preceding three weeks alone, the United States had sent Chiang Kai-shek arms and ammunition valued at $90 million. The United States deployed on Quemoy island 8-inch howitzers, capable of shelling the Chinese coast with artillery carrying atomic warheads. A Pentagon representative simultaneously confirmed that American pilots had been granted permission to "pursue" aircraft of the People's Republic of China into China's own territory. The situation had clearly become inflammatory. Dulles, at one of his press conferences, went so far as to state that not only Quemoy and Matsu were at stake, but the "whole position of the United States and its allies in the western part of the Pacific Ocean, from Japan, Korea, Okinawa, Formosa, the Philippines and further into Southeast Asia."

Under these circumstances, the Soviet government, despite the Chinese leaders' clearly unfriendly posture, warned the United States that any attack upon the People's Republic of China would be viewed as an attack upon the Soviet Union. By this warning, the U.S.S.R. foiled the attempts of the aggressive imperialist circles to take advantage of the actions of the Chinese leaders and to expand the conflict over the off-shore islands into an armed confrontation in the Far East.

It should be noted that the "brink of war" policy pursued in the Far East by the Eisenhower Administration was subjected to serious criticism, both within the country and abroad. Former U.S. Secretary of State Dean Acheson noted that "the United States is sliding into a war with China . . . because of problems . . . which are not worth the life of even one American." Republican Senator John S. Cooper pointed out that he did "not believe that to start a war because of Quemoy and Matsu would be in the national interests" of the United States. Senator John F. Kennedy emphasized that "the weight of military, diplomatic, political and historical judgment would dictate a contrary policy concerning Formosa." Theodore Green, the Chairman of the Senate Committee on Foreign Relations, sent a personal message to the President on September 29 in which he expressed his "deep concern that the course of events in the Far East may result in involvement at the wrong time, in the wrong place, and on issues not of vital concern to our own security, and all this without allies either in fact or in heart." Four out of every five letters received at that time by the Department of State opposed the policy pursued by John Foster Dulles in the Far East. Nor did America's allies support the adventurist policy of the Eisenhower Administration.

The firm and unequivocal position of the Soviet Union and the other socialist countries, lack of support from the allies, and sharp domestic criticism forced the Eisenhower Administration to back down. On September 30, 1958, Dulles announced at a press conference that the United States had "no commitment of any kind" to Chiang Kai-shek, and that the United States favored the reduction of Chiang Kai-shek garrisons on the off-shore islands. Furthermore, Dulles noted, the concentration of such large forces on small islands was a "rather foolish" move. The next day, President Eisenhower noted that "as a soldier," he considered the concentration of all these forces "not a good thing to do." Assistant Secretary of State Herter characterized the attachment of the Chiang Kai-shekists to the off-shore islands as "almost pathological."

An example of the criticism heard in this regard within the United States was the measure adopted by a group of American congressmen. Ten Democratic congressmen, in a telegram to the President on October 4, demanded that he call a special session of Congress to discuss the Far East situation. The congressmen wrote that "the great majority of our constituents are deeply disturbed with the Administration's Quemoy policy" and "believe we should disentangle ourselves from Chiang Kai-shek's aspirations on Quemoy and should endeavor to bring the mantle of the UN over Formosa." Senator Humphrey, speaking before members of the International Chemical Workers Union, proposed a similar plan, expressing the opinion that the question of jurisdiction over the off-shore islands "should be given to the World Court to decide" and that Taiwan must be turned into "an independent nation under the umbrella of United Nations guarantees and protection."

A large number of American newspapers and magazines of widely varying political orientations described the American policy in the Taiwan Strait in extremely harsh terms. *The Nation* called it a policy of "deafness, dumbness, and blindness," the Protestant magazine *Christian Century* characterized it as "very poor," and *The New Republic* called it "disastrous." *The New York Times* spoke of the U.S. operations in the Taiwan region as being carried out "in the worst place, for the worst cause and together with the worst of our allies," and also as an "aimless, hopeless and senseless undertaking." Even such an ardent Republican supporter as Roscoe Drummond was compelled to concede in *The New York Herald Tribune* that the Republican Administration had led the United States into "unbearably unfavorable circumstances," forcing the country "to defend in complete isolation a very unpopular policy" and deal with the "hostility of the entire world of non-aligned countries."

Although all these statements were designed to influence the policy of the United States government toward restraint, they nevertheless failed to give the slightest consideration to the rights and interests of the Chinese people, whose legitimate right to Taiwan was at one time recognized unconditionally, even by the U.S. government. The discussions then about the "transfer of Taiwan to the United Nations' trusteeship" meant nothing more than a new attempt by American imperialism to seize the island. These proposals had nothing in common with serious attempts to resolve the Far East situation. Since all this could not fail to perturb Chiang Kai-shek, U.S. Secretary of Defense Neil McElroy was urgently dispatched to Taiwan. Several days later, U.S. Secretary of State Dulles also flew there.

After three days of discussions with Chiang Kai-shek, a joint communiqué was issued, which emphasized that "the sacred mission of the

Chiang Kai-shekists remains the return to mainland China." It was clear, however, from the text of the communiqué that, under the existing circumstances, the United States had no intention to aid Chiang Kai-shek in an immediate invasion of the mainland. And although Dulles stated that the most important result of his discussion was a "fresh formulation of the missions" of the Chiang Kai-shekists, it was clear to observers that a shift in the alignment of forces in favor of socialism had exerted a restraining influence on America's political course.

Thus, Dulles' policy to keep the world poised "on the brink of war" had once again suffered a crushing defeat—primarily as a result of the decisive and active policy of the Soviet state and of the firm unity of the countries in the socialist camp, which were supported by peace-loving forces throughout the entire world. And additionally, as Roger Hilsman, the former Director of the U.S. State Department's Bureau of Intelligence and Research, noted, an influential factor was that "it was certainly not in the United States' interest to become involved in a Chinese Nationalist attempt to retake the mainland, much less to permit Chiang to maneuver us into a war to restore him to power."

It is interesting to note that during all that time, discussions between the Ambassadors of the United States and the People's Republic of China continued regularly in Warsaw, and that on November 10, 1958, U.S. Ambassador Jacob Beam was recalled to Washington to give a detailed report on the course of the negotiations. The Department of State, however, did not wish to convey the impression that, by recalling Beam, negotiations were being indefinitely suspended, and it was therefore announced that the next meeting of the Ambassadors was scheduled for November 25, 1958.

The U.S. ruling circles, however, did not miss a single opportunity to reaffirm their policy of non-recognition of the People's Republic of China, as they continually tried to convince America's allies and world public opinion that the People's Republic of China was doomed. Speaking in San Francisco in December 1958, Dulles said: "It is certain that diplomatic recognition of the Chinese Communist regime would gravely jeopardize the political, economic and security interests of the United States." He further emphasized that the United States had an obligation to do all that it could to hasten the "passing of the Chinese People's Republic" from the scene of world history.

Neither Dulles's illness, retirement, and his death shortly thereafter, nor his replacement by Christian Herter as U.S. Secretary of State, on April 21, 1959, brought any changes in the Republican Administration's policy toward the People's Republic of China. The Eisenhower

Administration adhered to the same old Dulles "brink of war" policy for its entire period in power.

Politically, the Eisenhower-Dulles "brink of war" policy, aimed at the destruction of the People's Republic of China, found expression in the repeated threats to use atomic weapons against the People's Republic of China and to "unleash" Chiang Kai-shek; in the serious attempts to convince America's allies, primarily England, of the need to follow U.S. policy in this matter; in the open call for war against the People's Republic of China; and in the pushing of a resolution through the U.S. Congress which, in fact, granted authority to the President to start a war against the People's Republic of China without prior congressional consent.

Militarily, this policy placed the off-shore islands of mainland China under the protection of American armed forces and caused the Kuomintang to fortify military garrisons on these islands. It manifested itself in the further increase of military assistance to the Chiang Kai-shekists; in the direct order to the Commander of the U.S. Pacific Fleet to bomb Chinese airfields "if necessary"; and in the creation of a hotbed of war in the immediate proximity of the Chinese coast.

Economically, this policy was manifested not only in the complete trade embargo against the Chinese People's Republic, but also in the ever-increasing economic aid to the Chiang Kai-shekists, the lion's share of which went for military needs.

It is necessary to emphasize that all aspects of the policy of "limited hostility," which had been enunciated by Harry Truman, also remained in effect and, in the new circumstances, served the still more aggressive Republican policy, which was directed against the fundamental interests of the Chinese people.

During Eisenhower's last years in power, however, wide-spread efforts to call into question the propriety of the Administration's policy toward the People's Republic of China began to emerge in the United States. The yearbook *The United States in World Affairs, 1957*, published under the auspices of the Council on Foreign Relations, noted that "many of this country's allies and quite a few Americans, mainly in the opposition party, were visibly growing tired of Washington's inflexible stand and inclined to wish for a more normal relationship with the Peking regime. For the first time in several years, Americans were openly questioning the government's official China policy, hitherto regarded in most quarters as too 'controversial' (or too sacrosanct) for public discussion."

The discussion of the government's China policy became particularly far-ranging during 1957-59, when, as already pointed out, sharp domestic criticism of the Eisenhower-Dulles policy was one of the reasons for the American government's backing down on the question of support for an invasion of the mainland by Chiang Kai-shek. The discord reached such a level that even senators became aroused. The tension created in the Quemoy region provoked such stinging criticism from the most diverse circles of American public opinion that talk could be heard at that time in the congressional cloakrooms about the possibility of shifting from a "completely negative" policy toward the People's Republic of China, to one of so-called "limited contacts."

It should be noted that American big business circles also followed the development of events in the Far East with anxiety. And if the congressmen were more interested in the political side of events, the businessmen turned their attention primarily to the economic aspects. They well remembered that in 1947 the United States exported to China goods with a total value of $353.6 million. The trade embargo placed upon the People's Republic of China had reduced this trade to practically nothing. But certain American specialists calculated that if the embargo were lifted, trade between the United States and the People's Republic of China would, even in the first years after the change, easily reach $200-300 million annually.

As noted earlier, the strong and constant United States pressure notwithstanding, a number of countries considerably softened their restrictions on trade with the People's Republic of China in 1957, and, as a result, the year 1958 was marked by a sizable increase in trade between the People's Republic of China and these countries. Thus, England's exports to the People's Republic of China in 1958 amounted to $76 million, in comparison with $34 million in the preceding year, *i.e.*, a more than two-fold increase within one year. During the same year the Federal Republic of Germany almost quadrupled its exports to the People's Republic of China, and Italian and French exports more than doubled.

All these figures were reported in the pages of the American press and, of course, could not go unnoticed by the Congress. Measures were clearly needed which, on the one hand, could assuage public opinion and certain financial circles, but, on the other, would not require any immediate and important moves either by Congress or the U.S. government. Under these circumstances, the Senate Committee on Foreign Relations decided to undertake a series of studies on the problems of United States foreign policy. After a number of consultations between members of the Foreign Relations Committee and other interested persons, including Dean Rusk, then the president of the Rockefeller Foundation, and that eminent representative of the "China lobby,"

Henry Luce, the publisher of *Time* and *Life* magazines, fifteen basic subjects were outlined and assigned to various organizations for research. The San Francisco firm of "Conlon Associates" was commissioned to prepare a report on the subject of "U.S. Foreign Policy in the Far East and Southeast Asia."

It is interesting to note that Richard Conlon, the head of the firm, served for a time after World War II in the U.S. Department of State, and subsequently at the Central Intelligence Agency, where his duties included liaison with the State Department's Far East Office. He later headed the so-called Asia Foundation which, according to the American press, was heavily subsidized by the CIA. The firm headed by Conlon was at one time officially registered with the U.S. Department of Justice as an agent of the South Vietnamese government.

The study prepared by "Conlon Associates" contains a special section titled "Communist China and Taiwan." The authors of the report recognized that "Communist China presents the most complicated and serious problem faced by the United States in Asia. It is also a problem more likely to grow than to diminish, and one for which there are no easy answers." After an analysis of the internal situation of the People's Republic of China, the authors of the study reached the conclusion that "Communist China is very likely to emerge as one of the major world powers of the late Twentieth Century." Furthermore, the authors felt compelled to emphasize that the Soviet Union's assistance played no small role in the development of the People's Republic of China. The study detailed the areas in which Soviet aid to the Chinese people was particularly important, and noted that the friendly relations of the People's Republic of China with the Soviet Union had "increased her world prestige within as well as without the Communist orbit."

In addition, the authors of the report believed even then that "the coordination of policy toward the non-Communist world, particularly the United States, must also pose a problem to the Sino-Soviet alliance, a problem that will not become lighter as Chinese power grows." The report thus clearly pointed to the possibility that nationalist circles within the leadership of the People's Republic of China could pursue their own individual policy toward the United States, one separate and distinct from that of the Soviet Union and the other socialist countries.

Characterizing the Taiwan situation, the report noted that Chiang Kai-shek stationed on the island a disproportionately large army, the maintenance of which placed a heavy drain on the island's economy. Additionally, significant sums were being expended on an enormous bureaucratic apparatus. The political situation on the island, in the opinion of the authors of the report, was notable for its instability, which could lead to a "serious crisis."

The report concluded with a review of the problems of United States policy toward China. The authors were of the opinion that the decisions shaping this policy would enormously influence the future American position not only in Asia, but throughout the world. Thus, the report advocated a more realistic U.S. policy, one sufficiently flexible to lend itself to change, depending on the situation, yet simultaneously clear and firm. In accordance with these general conclusions, the report proposed three possible alternatives of U.S. policy toward the People's Republic of China.

1. *"Containment by isolation"* was the first alternative which, in the opinion of the authors of the report, the United States could (and, in fact, eventually did) adopt. The policy of "containment by isolation" was only a somewhat modernized version of the already well-known policy of "limited hostility." The authors of the report realized, however, that this policy would inevitably create numerous problems because, in their opinion, the United States had "long ago discovered that it could not impose its standards and criteria upon the entire world."

The main question, the authors of the report believed, was "how long the fiction can be maintained that the National government* is the government of China. Perhaps this situation can continue for some time, particularly if the United States exerts its full influence and if Communist China misbehaves." But, the report pointed out, the last few years had proved that such a policy was clearly destined to fail. A government which effectively controlled only 10 million of its population could not indefinitely pose as a "major power" in the name of 660 million Chinese. The report noted, in this connection, that a whole series of countries in Asia, including such large Asian powers as India, Japan and Indonesia, showed great restraint toward the existing U.S. policy on that question. Therefore, the authors of the report doubted the allegation of several American figures that any change in U.S. policy toward the People's Republic of China would be viewed as an American "surrender."

2. The authors of the report saw a second possible policy alternative with regard to the People's Republic of China—a so-called *"normalization of relations."* This, in their opinion, would consist of recognition of the People's Republic of China by the United States,

---

i.e., Chiang Kai-shek's government (*Author's note*)

U.S. support for a proposal to seat the People's Republic of China in the United Nations, and the pursuit of a policy toward the Chinese People's Republic generally "equal to that which the United States accords to the Soviet Union." The principal argument made by the authors of the report in favor of the policy of "normalization of relations" toward the People's Republic of China was the fact that the policy of non-recognition had, in fact, completely failed, and had led to the well-known isolation of the United States through a one-sided policy that was defensive and negative in nature. Besides, successful "normalization of relations" would, in the opinion of the report's authors, broaden the possibility for Washington to influence the Chinese people and allow the United States to exert "definite influence" upon the nationalist elements in the leadership of the People's Republic of China.

3. While not rejecting the first two alternatives, the authors of the report favored a third alternative for American policy toward China, which they themselves characterized as a policy of *"exploration and negotiations."* That policy, in the opinion of the authors of the report, was to be multi-faceted, and aimed at three basic goals. The first goal was to test the readiness of the leaders of the People's Republic of China to coexist with the United States. The second was to formulate a broader policy toward the People's Republic of China, which would retain the well-known firmness but would simultaneously be more dynamic, flexible and positive. The third goal was to achieve as much major agreement as possible among the principal Western Powers on the China question, and create a firmer basis for future joint actions by the Western countries in case such a necessity should arise.

The authors of the report recommended implementation of the "exploration and negotiations" policy in two stages. During the first, it would be necessary to clarify the attitude of the leadership of the People's Republic of China toward the idea of improving relations with the United States and, at the same time, to test the reaction of both the U.S. allies and certain neutral countries to such a change in American policy. In other words, that meant that the United States wanted to assure itself in advance that its allies and the neutral countries would blindly follow the so-called "new" U.S. policy toward the People's Republic of China. Finding itself in serious international isolation as a result of the "limited hostility" policy, the United States was trying not to repeat the same mistake in the future.

The report envisaged the enactment of the following practical measures during the initial stage. First, the United States would propose to the People's Republic of China a mutual exchange of journalists, to be followed by exchanges of scholars and trade representatives. Second, one or several groups of well-known American figures would be sent to the People's Republic of China from outside the government to "conduct such informal discussions ... as are possible." Third, the United States would begin a series of "informal, private" exchanges of views on questions of policy toward the People's Republic of China with its European allies, and with Japan, India, Burma, and Indonesia.

As is evident, it was contemplated that during the initial stage special emphasis would be placed on exploration of the domestic situation within the People's Republic of China. This was to be accomplished by sending there journalists, scientists and trade specialists, for clarification—by way of "unofficial" discussions—of the position taken by the Chinese leadership on questions of interest to the United States. Emphasis was also to be placed on efforts to win over America's European allies and the large Asian nations, without any substantive changes being made in the "limited hostility" policy.

Thus, the first stage of the so-called "exploration and negotiations" policy was to extricate the United States from its state of diplomatic isolation on the question of the People's Republic of China and, at the same time, to win over the European countries, above all England, although it was not even mentioned in the report, as well as a number of the Asian countries. It is also perfectly clear that these recommendations were prompted primarily by the interests of the United States itself and the desire to improve its position in the international arena, and least of all by the true interests of the Chinese people.

If the results of the first stage proved to some extent "encouraging" (for the United States, of course!), the plan was to proceed to the next stage, which was to consist of at least five basic measures. First, it was proposed to "allow trade" with the People's Republic of China on the same basis as United States trade with the U.S.S.R. Considering that in 1959 (the year the "Conlon Associates" report was published) the United States exported goods to the U.S.S.R. valued altogether at only $7 million, which constituted an insignificant share (0.04 percent) of the entire year's United States exports, it is clear that in this regard the United States was not offering anything of substance to the People's Republic of China, but was only making a concession to the interests of the U.S. West Coast monopolies, which had traditionally enjoyed trade relations with China and suffered considerable losses as a result of the U.S. trade embargo. It was no coincidence that in 1958 more than 730 San Francisco businessmen demanded the lifting of the trade embargo against the People's Republic of China.

Second, another series of "unofficial discussions" with the American allies and neutral nations was envisioned. Four problems were to be dealt with at these "unofficial discussions": (1) the "admission" of the People's Republic of China to the UN; (2) the creation and recognition of the so-called "Republic of Taiwan"; (3) measures required to ensure Taiwan's admission to UN membership; and (4) enlargement of the UN Security Council to include India and Japan as permanent members.

Third, Washington was simultaneously to reassure all its "lesser allies" that the United States intended to continue the fulfillment of its obligations toward these countries in accordance with existing treaties.

Fourth, the United States was to conduct parallel "special discussions" with Chiang Kai-shek in order to obtain his agreement to the following: (a) The United States would honor its "existing obligations" with regard to Taiwan and the Penghu islands, guaranteeing the defense of the "Republic of Taiwan" and providing it with increased economic and technical assistance; (b) Chiang Kai-shek's armed forces would withdraw from the off-shore islands, together with those from the civilian population "desiring to leave"; (c) the United States would "endeavor to help in the resettlement" of all emigrants from mainland China who now wished to leave Taiwan.

Fifth, "if feasible, the United States would negotiate a treaty of commerce with Communist China and, if successful, this would be followed by *de facto* recognition."

Certain circles in the United States have recently been attempting to depict the "Conlon Associates" report and its recommendations as being dictated by the interests of the Chinese people and aimed at normalization of the Far East situation. It is difficult, however, to agree with such assertions. First of all, if the recommendations contained in the report had been implemented, the People's Republic of China would have, for all practical purposes, lost forever a substantial part of its territory—Taiwan and the Penghu islands. Furthermore, notwithstanding the return of its legitimate seat in the United Nations Security Council and General Assembly, the international position of the People's Republic of China, rather than being strengthened, could actually have been weakened, since the United States unequivocally posited all these steps on the condition that numerous countries which had previously recognized and established normal diplomatic relations with the People's Republic of China would henceforth blindly follow America's lead in matters of China policy. These countries would have the obligation to share with America, at its discretion, some sort of "definite mutual responsibility."

Finally, the United States itself was not even obligated to recognize the People's Republic of China, and only intended to enter into negotiations on the conclusion of a trade agreement "if the opportunity arose." Thus, the question of actual recognition was bogged down by such conditions that it was, for all purposes, postponed indefinitely. The United States was to be the real beneficiary, for it would have subjected Taiwan and the Penghu islands to its still further control, after having torn them away from mainland China. The American monopolist circles would have received access to the vast Chinese market for peddling their shopworn merchandise, which was no longer saleable, even in the European and Latin American countries. All in all, as its authors admitted, the "Conlon Associates" report was an obvious attempt—as the saying goes—to kill two birds with one stone.

It is noteworthy that the association's report was attacked by those American circles for whom the very recognition of Communist China's existence constituted a mortal sin. Among these was the previously mentioned Admiral Arthur W. Radford, who had fought for the policy of a "Fifty Years War" against China, and other influential "China lobbyists." All this, however, offers no reason to doubt that the authors of the report had, first and foremost, the interests of the United States itself at heart, in accordance with the changing international situation.

The United States policy toward the People's Republic of China during that period was debated not only in the Congress and its cloakrooms. It gradually ceased to be a forbidden topic and, naturally, was discussed in newspapers, magazines and the small brochures published by various organizations. It is significant that talk of a possible alienation of the People's Republic of China from the world socialist system appeared in American mass publications in May 1958. This provides evidence that public opinion within the country was already being prepared for just such a turn of events. And there is also a striking coincidence of the period when these discussions commenced in American publications and when the People's Republic of China began to pursue the adventurist policy called "Three Red Banners." It is worth mentioning that among the English language books and journal articles on China recommended in 1958 and 1959 by the publications of the "Foreign Policy Association," half were published in 1957 or later.

Nor did the leading monopoly circles remain aloof from the China discussions. A clear example is the report prepared by the Rockefeller Foundation, titled "The Mid-Century Challenge to U.S. Foreign Policy," which appeared in 1959 and contained a special section on U.S. policy toward the People's Republic of China. It is interesting that the report was prepared by a special group headed by Dean Rusk, the president of the Foundation and a former U.S. Assistant Secretary of

State, who subsequently became Secretary of State in the Administrations of John F. Kennedy and Lyndon B. Johnson. In addition to
Rusk, the group consisted of such widely known financial magnates and
wheeler-dealers as the Carnegie Foundation's J. Johnson, RCA president David Sarnoff, John D. Rockefeller III, S. R. Davis of *The
Christian Science Monitor*, and others.

It is natural that a report prepared by people who frequently exerted
a decisive influence on the solution of American foreign policy problems should differ in tone, and even in entire orientation, from other
publications on the same topic. For example, while the majority of
publications seriously discussed the problems of U.S. recognition of the
People's Republic of China and its admission to the United Nations, the
Rockefeller Foundation report regarded these issues as merely "technical problems." The main American aim, according to the authors of the
report, ought to be the "candid recognition of what Communist China
is and where it is going. . . . The need for complete knowledge of what
is going on in China is so paramount that lesser interests or concerns
should give way to insure full reporting by Americans on the spot."
These lines, better than anything else, explain why all proposals for a
change in U.S. policy toward the People's Republic of China involved,
as one of the first steps, the exchange of journalists and the travel of
American scholars and businessmen to the People's Republic. It is not
just idle talk when they say that he who pays the piper calls the tune.
American monopolies wanted, above all, to ascertain from trusted
people what was really happening in the People's Republic of China.
And they insisted on obtaining such knowledge before even considering
the solution of such (in their opinion) "technical questions" as, for
example, diplomatic recognition.

The Rockefeller Foundation report contained only a single recommendation for the U.S. government with regard to a change in its policy
toward the People's Republic of China: "For the present, we must
avoid, wherever possible, courses of action which seem to drive China
closer to the Soviets; and be prepared for new situations as relations
between these two massive Powers undergo change." The American
monopolist circles pointed out frankly to their government the possibility of "new situations" developing between the People's Republic of
China and the world socialist system. These recommendations demonstrate not only that the U.S. ruling circles were then, and still are,
closely following the shifting events in the People's Republic of China
and the actions of the nationalist circles within the leadership of the
Communist Party of China, but also that the U.S. monopolist circles
intended to base their own concrete measures with regard to China
upon the path followed by the Chinese Communist Party leadership.

Thus, during the last years of the Republican Administration, U.S. policy on the China problem as a whole, and specifically toward the People's Republic of China, was subject to widespread debate within the most varied circles of American society; big business representatives and congressmen discussed the topic, and it was debated in American books, newspapers and magazines. This heretofore forbidden subject became, for a period, almost the center of the American public's attention.

The 1960 presidential elections were approaching, however, and these elections pushed all other problems into the background. The Republican party had no intention of relinquishing without a struggle the Presidency, which it had won with so much difficulty in 1952. And the Democrats, in turn, were firmly resolved to put a Democratic President in the White House.

Under these circumstances, President Eisenhower's Administration continued to conduct itself, literally on the eve of the presidential elections, as if all the criticism of its China policy, one of the mainstays of the Republican foreign policy, was of no concern at all. The President went to Taiwan in June 1960 and again reassured Chiang Kai-shek that the United States considered him the only legitimate representative of all China and had no intention to recognize the right of the People's Republic of China to "speak for all the Chinese people."

On January 2, 1960, the 43-year old Democratic Senator from the state of Massachusetts, John F. Kennedy, announced that he was a presidential candidate of the Democratic party. On July 13, the Democratic National Convention approved his candidacy, and on the next day, that of Senator Lyndon B. Johnson for Vice President. On July 27, the Republicans nominated Richard M. Nixon as their presidential candidate, and on the next day, Henry Cabot Lodge, the U.S. Permanent Representative to the United Nations, as Vice President.

It is significant that both parties considered it necessary to define in their pre-election platforms their attitudes on U.S. policy toward the People's Republic of China. The Republicans bluntly and laconically stated: "Recognition of Communist China and its admission to the United Nations have been firmly opposed by the Republican Administration. We will continue in this opposition." The Democrats expressed themselves in a more florid style in their election platform, continually attempting to place the entire blame for the prevailing state of American-Chinese relations on the People's Republic of China. The Democratic platform stated: "We deeply regret that the policies and actions of the government of Communist China have interrupted the generations of friendship between the Chinese and American peoples. We reaffirm our pledge of determined opposition to the present

admission of Communist China [to the United Nations] . . . . Although
normal diplomatic relations between our governments are impossible
under present conditions, we shall welcome any evidence that the
Chinese Communist government is genuinely prepared to create a new
relationship based on respect for international obligations."

Thus, the election platform of the Democratic party paid tribute, on
the one hand, to the traditional U.S. policy of non-recognition of the
People's Republic of China and refusal to admit it to the United
Nations, but, on the other hand, clearly took into consideration
American public opinion, *i.e.*, (and this was important prior to the
elections) the sentiments of those voters who favored a fundamental
re-examination of U.S. policy toward China.

The Democrats understood perfectly well that they assumed no
obligation whatsoever by any pre-election statements. However, they
considered it necessary to point out in their pre-election platform that
they were not rejecting out of hand the very idea of improving relations
with the People's Republic of China, and they thereby publicly recognized that the question concerning relations with the People's Republic
of China, which occupied the minds of Americans, was far from solved.
This acknowledgement alone, made by the Democratic National Convention on the eve of the presidential elections and less than a month
after President Eisenhower had rejected the right of the People's
Republic of China even "to speak in the name of the Chinese people,"
demonstrated not so much that the problem of relations with the
People's Republic of China had by this time grown from a "cloakroom"
issue into a national one, but rather that certain forces had risen to
prominence in the ranks of the Democratic leadership at that time,
which were capable of evaluating realistically the existing international
situation and which did not desire to relinquish even the smallest
opportunity to win over to their side the votes of thinking Americans.

The following fact partially substantiates such a conclusion: The
April 1960 issue of the extremely well-informed and influential magazine *Foreign Affairs* published an article by the not unknown Chester
Bowles, a member of the U.S. House of Representatives and a foreign
policy adviser to presidential candidate Kennedy. In Bowles' opinion,
the reaction of large numbers of Americans to the current state of
relations between the United States and the People's Republic of China
could be described in two words: "division and confusion." "The myth
that Chiang Kai-shek . . . remains the ruler of 650 million Chinese,"
Bowles said, ". . . rejected by most Asians, by our NATO allies, by our
closest friends the Canadians, and by a large number of Americans, is
supported only by three or four Asian governments under heavy

pressure from Washington, by our Department of State and by some members of Congress. . . . It seems to me that today we should be striving by all reasonable means to establish people-to-people contacts with mainland China. It may be useful as a first step to offer a fresh approach to the exchange of correspondents. . . . We are badly in need of the facts and perspective that able American reporters can give us. . . . But the freer flow of news is only the beginning. Educators, politicians, businessmen—all the many Americans who could profit by a firsthand understanding of the Chinese revolution and who could transmit their understanding to the rest of us—should be allowed access to the mainland by our authorities, with reciprocal privileges for the Chinese." Bowles further noted quite frankly in his article that the Chiang Kai-shek regime would "not be happy" about his statements.

Bowles' article was a "trial balloon" lofted by Kennedy's Democratic supporters, who were obviously attempting to determine the attitude of American public opinion toward the China problem prior to their party's national convention, in order to decide what priority should be placed upon this problem in the party's election platform, and how best to present the party's basic positions on the issue. As we have already seen, the Democrats were acting on the principle of "something for everybody." In their election platform they took into consideration the opinion of the most fervent opponents of a change in policy toward the People's Republic of China, while simultaneously leaving the door open for the advocates of a re-examination of this policy. This position gave the Democrats the option, if they won the elections, to act in accordance with whatever situation developed.

The question of U.S. policy toward China was raised several times during the election campaign. It is generally known that both presidential candidates appeared in four debates on American television, and twice during these debates—on October 7 and 13, 1960—the question was raised concerning the American attitude toward the defense of the off-shore islands of Quemoy and Matsu. It immediately became clear that the opinions of the presidential candidates differed sharply on this issue. Senator Kennedy, for example, answering a question on October 7 concerning the off-shore islands, said: "These islands are only a few miles—five or six—off the coast of Red China . . . and more than 100 miles from Formosa. We have never stated definitely that we would defend Quemoy and Matsu in case they were subject to attack. . . . I think it would be unwise to take the chance of being dragged into a war which may lead to a world war over two islands which are not strategically defensible and which . . . are not essential to the defense of Taiwan." Vice President Nixon disagreed with Kennedy. In his opinion there was at stake not merely these "two plots of land"—but the entire principle of support for the Chiang Kai-shek regime. In his next television appearance, on October 13, Nixon went even further and announced that the defense of the off-shore islands was inseparably linked to the question of the "containment of Communism."

In that later debate, the Democratic candidate again expressed an opinion contrary to that of Nixon. Kennedy emphasized that Nixon's position could only drag the United States into a war over what even Nixon himself had characterized as "two plots of land." At the same time, however, Kennedy said that he believed the United States would have to take military action for the defense of Taiwan proper and the Penghu islands, thus agreeing to U.S. military intervention in the internal affairs of China.

As is commonly known, the Democratic candidate Kennedy was elected as the 35th President of the United States of America in the election of November 8, 1960. And only two days after the election, his foreign policy adviser, Chester Bowles, speaking on a British television program, expressed support for the so-called "two Chinas" idea, based on the simultaneous existence of an "independent Formosa and an independent Communist China." Bowles' statement drew sharp criticism from influential senators, and only a day after his first appearance, Bowles stated that "recognition of Red China appears impossible."

The 1960 presidential campaign thus ended, bringing victory to the Democratic candidate John F. Kennedy, the man who was fated only to sketch the outlines of "new frontiers" for the largest country of the capitalist world.

CHAPTER V

"ISOLATION AND CONTAINMENT"

1. *PRESIDENT KENNEDY'S LEGACY*

As regards American-Chinese relations, the new President and his associates inherited from Eisenhower's Republican Administration the policy of "limited hostility" toward the People's Republic of China, as well as the policy of unconditional support of the Chiang Kai-shek regime, not only for its claim to be the sole legitimate representative of the Chinese people, but also for its efforts to return to mainland China.

Even prior to his official assumption of presidential duties, John Kennedy announced that he had chosen the president of the Rockefeller Foundation, Dean Rusk, as his Administration's Secretary of State; the president of the Ford Motor Company, Robert McNamara, as Secretary of Defense; and Chester Bowles as Assistant Secretary of State. Speaking at confirmation hearings held by the Senate Committee on Foreign Relations, Rusk flatly stated that he saw "no prospects at the present for the establishment of normal relations" with the People's Republic of China. Bowles, in turn, having forgotten all his pre-election statements, said that, in his opinion, U.S. recognition of the People's Republic of China was at present "out of the question" and that the United States was "ready to defend Formosa, regardless of the risk, at any cost."

Two events should be noted in this connection. First, the widely read American magazine *Look* published in its January 31, 1961, issue an interview by the American writer Edgar Snow with the Premier of the People's Republic of China, Chou En-lai. Chou En-lai, according to Snow, during the interview confirmed the existence of the well-known differences between the leadership of the People's Republic of China and that of the Soviet Union, and stated that an adjustment of relations between the People's Republic of China and the United States was possible, on condition that the United States recognize the problem of Taiwan as China's internal affair. American troops would have to leave the island, although the Chinese Premier did not specify any particular deadline for their withdrawal. Thus, literally during the very first days of the new Administration, Washington was informed of the readiness of the People's Republic of China to adjust its relations with the United States.

Second, the leaders of the American government received at approximately the same time a memorandum on the Chinese question prepared by General Li Tsung-jen, a former provisional President of China, who was at that time a United States resident. One might think there would be nothing in common between the thoughts expressed by the Premier of the People's Republic of China and the writings of a fugitive Chinese general who was one of the most ardent anti-Communists. Nevertheless, both these documents advocated, in fact, one and the same idea, creating the impression at times that they were written by the very same hand. Incidentally, Li Tsung-jen's departure several years later from the United States for the People's Republic of China and his triumphant reception by local leaders remove the last doubts on this score. It therefore makes sense to analyze Li Tsung-jen's memorandum to the American government.

As noted earlier, the leadership of the People's Republic of China pursued at the end of the Fifties a "special" foreign and domestic policy course which marked a departure from Marxism-Leninism and was profoundly in conflict with the principles of proletarian internationalism and the basic structural laws of a socialist society. In 1960, the Peking leaders openly opposed the general line of the international Communist movement, proposing in its place their own platform. This fact sheds new light on the interview with the Premier of the People's Republic of China, and on Li Tsung-jen's memorandum,

To begin with, we quote the following: "The Chinese on the mainland ... are exasperated beyond measure by America's constant interference with ... China's domestic affairs and by its imperialist or aggressive attitude toward matters which are specifically Chinese. ... There was a time when anything affecting China could be decided upon by London, Paris, Washington, and the other capitals of the Western world. That was in the second half of the Nineteenth Century, when China was at the mercy of the Western Powers. But that China is gone—forever."

The above quotation stems from Li Tsung-jen's pen. In his verbose memorandum, which fills some 27 pages, Li Tsung-jen is, as the saying goes, "more Catholic than the Pope." He scrupulously discussed all alternatives for a normalization of relations between the United States and the People's Republic of China and demonstrated the reasons why most of these were unacceptable for the leadership of the People's China. "The animosity between the United States and Communist China," wrote Li Tsung-jen, "has been intense, and will remain intense as long as the United States pursues its present policy." What alternative, then, did Li Tsung-jen propose? The very same as did Chou En-lai—settlement of the Taiwan problem. Furthermore, Li Tsung-jen directly quoted the words of the Premier of the People's Republic of China, which had appeared in *Look* magazine, and asserted that "United States acceptance of this solution would be in its own best interests."

This striking coincidence of views of people who at that time were, as many thought, at completely opposite poles of the world social systems, is not all that was interesting. Li Tsung-jen went even further and "dotted all the i's," proposing a deal between the United States and the leadership of the People's Republic of China. But let Li Tsung-jen speak for himself: "All that is required," he wrote, " is a simple statement by the United States, reaffirming in a few words that Taiwan is a sovereign part of China, and the results will be electrifying!" Li Tsung-jen further asserted that he had reason to "firmly believe" that the leadership of the People's Republic of China would agree to any solution of the question of Taiwan's actual control. The former provisional President suggested several options—a UN trusteeship, neutralization and demilitarization of the island, or its integration within the People's Republic of China. It was envisaged that, in the latter event, "the present Taiwanese government personnel would continue to carry out their functions." What a touching concern!

"The only thing needed is a nod from the United States," Li Tsung-jen plainly stated, noting that, as things then stood, the United States could achieve a great deal. The ongoing events in the region from "South Korea to Turkey provide a serious lesson," said Li Tsung-jen, and "one other lesson ... should be clear to those who have eyes to see: The search for a mutual understanding with Soviet Russia, without having reached a prior understanding and agreement with Communist China, would not greatly advance the solution of any international problem. A reverse order of events would ... yield better results."

Thus, Li Tsung-jen, and those who guided his hand in writing this memorandum, were pursuing a perfectly clear goal—an agreement between the leaderships of the People's Republic of China and the new United States Administration, at the expense of the interests of the

Chinese people and the unity of the socialist camp countries. Everything was disregarded, just to satisfy the wishes of certain leaders of the People's Republic of China.

Careful analysis of Li Tsung-jen's memorandum on the Chinese question and the entire subsequent course of events leaves no doubt that in this matter Li Tsung-jen merely played the role of a representative of those nationalist circles within the leadership of the People's Republic of China whose policy was to sever relations with the Soviet Union and the other socialist countries. Under these circumstances, the nationalist circles wished to strengthen their position by means of an agreement with the new government of the United States, at the expense of the fundamental interests of the Chinese people. In this regard, the statement made by Chiang Hsin-hai, a U.S. resident and former Kuomintang diplomat, in his book *America and China,* that "China would be prepared to dilute its Marxist pretensions in order to accommodate American sensibilities," inevitably arouses interest. Considering that Li Tsung-jen's memorandum was first published in this same book, this assertion not only acquires special meaning, but also gives cause for serious reflection.

True, for reasons beyond the two men's control, neither Chou En-lai's statements published in *Look* magazine nor Li Tsung-jen's memorandum led to any material changes in U.S. policy toward China. The Kennedy Administration, however, during its first days did make several cautious statements intended, at the very least, to create the impression that the Democratic government was not as hostile toward the People's Republic of China as the predecessor Republican government.

These extremely cautious steps of the American ruling circles can, of course, be explained as primarily an attempt to exploit for their own interests the Mao Tse-tung group's divisive activity and the Great Power policy course charted by Mao. To achieve these purposes, the United States ruling circles were prepared to initiate once more a re-examination of certain aspects of their policy toward the People's Republic of China. The President's statement, at a press conference on January 25, 1961, that the United States would, if requested, consider sending food to the People's Republic of China, was dictated by just such considerations. The United States made simultaneous efforts to broaden political contacts with the leadership of the People's Republic of China.

The new United States government, however, was simultaneously preoccupied with the search for measures which might exert political pressure upon Peking. The possibility of diplomatic recognition of the

Mongolian People's Republic was discussed as one such measure. The originator of this idea was, according to the American press, Chester Bowles. Among the apparent political advantages to be derived by the United States, such recognition would demonstrate to the other Asian countries that American policy was sufficiently flexible. And the fact that the U.S. Embassy in Ulan Bator could become a "window" on that part of the world to which the United States had almost no access and, thus, a "source of much needed information," played no small role in this regard. As soon as this possibility became known, however, the "storm broke." This potential American initiative so perturbed Chiang Kai-shek that, assisted by all the "China lobbyists," he forced the Kennedy Administration to abandon its intention in this regard. A State Department representative declared that "in view of the existing world situation, it is in the best interests of the United States to suspend further exploration of that matter at this time."

Some American Sinologists asserted that "almost imperceptible changes in the views, proposals, tone and expectations" of Washington on the China question began to appear during that period. These same specialists, however, were forced to admit that the basic aims of U.S. policy with regard to China "remained unchanged" during the Kennedy Administration. As for the possible "imperceptible changes" in America's China policy, these, as already noted, were determined by the policy pursued by the Maoist group and were aimed at exploiting for American interests that group's divisive activity. It is very likely that the formal agreement of the Chinese Communist Party's leadership with the decisions of the Congress of Representatives of Communist and Workers' Parties, which met in Moscow in November 1960, had a somewhat chilling effect upon the Washington politicians and caused them to adopt a more temporizing attitude, which marked the Kennedy Administration's subsequent policies toward the People's Republic of China. It is possible that the entire episode in which the United States acted as if it were about to recognize the Mongolian People's Republic was only an attempt to exert pressure upon China and to reach an agreement with its leadership at the expense of the Mongolian people's interests.

According to the Chinese calendar, 1962 was the "Year of the Tiger"—a good omen, in Chiang Kai-shek's opinion, for his "triumphant return" to the mainland. But this endeavor was influenced, of course, not so much by the "Year of the Tiger" as by the internal situation during that period of the People's Republic of China, where a widespread wave of dissatisfaction and critical speeches was occurring in connection with the Maoist group's adventurist policy of the "Great

Leap Forward." From the beginning of the year onward, Chiang Kai-shek continuously discussed an impending invasion of the mainland and exerted "official and unofficial, private and public" pressure upon the United States government for its necessary support.

The Chiang Kai-shekists counted in this regard primarily upon the fact that the People's Republic of China would find itself isolated in the event of an attack and would receive no support from the U.S.S.R. and other socialist countries, because of the actions of the Peking leaders who openly opposed the general line of the international Communist movement. In Taipei, of course, they understood that even in this event the Chiang Kai-shek army could not, on its own, oppose the People's Liberation Army with any measure of success. They therefore advanced the theory that it would be sufficient to land one or two Chiang Kai-shek divisions on the mainland for purposes of instigating an immediate general uprising. Neither were the American advocates of a mainland invasion by Chiang Kai- shek's troops standing idly by; due to their efforts, certain American newspapers began to favor such action. Top CIA intelligence reports were prepared in such a way as to suggest to influential readers that support for Chiang Kai-shek's invasion of the mainland was necessary.

Many in Washington understood, of course, that all of Chiang Kai-shek's verbiage as to the possibility of an uprising on the mainland was only a cheap trick. The high-ranking Washington leaders remembered only too well the lesson which they had learned just recently in the Cuban Bay of Pigs; they by no means wanted a repetition on a still greater scale. Washington thus demanded from Chiang Kai-shek exact intelligence data on the true state of affairs in the People's Republic of China. The President of the United States, meanwhile, ordered the reinforcement "for any eventuality" of the American Seventh Fleet located in the Taiwan Strait.

Under these circumstances, the Soviet government, faithful in its obligations to the Chinese people, publicly stated that any attack on the People's Republic of China would be repulsed not only by the Chinese people, but also by the Soviet Union. This warning had a very sobering effect upon Washington and, as subsequently became known, the American government directed its Ambassador in Warsaw to meet with and inform the Ambassador of the People's Republic of China that the United States would provide no assistance to Chiang Kai-shek if Chiang attempted to land his troops on mainland China. President Kennedy simultaneously stated that the United States would "take any action necessary to assure the defense of Formosa and the Pescadores" in accordance with the congressional resolution adopted in 1953.

Chiang Kai-shek, in the meantime, made feverish efforts to gather intelligence data. This became particularly clear when, in the first half of September 1962, an American-made U-2 reconnaissance aircraft was shot down over the People's Republic of China. After numerous inquiries, a State Department representative announced on October 10, 1962, that two U-2 aircraft had allegedly been sold by the Lockheed Aviation Corporation to the Chiang Kai-shekist forces "pursuant to a private commercial contract . . . in the last days of the Eisenhower Administration," and that the United States government had issued the necessary licenses to export these aircraft to Taiwan. The statement failed to clarify which Administration—Eisenhower's or Kennedy's—had issued the export licenses. But in light of the United States decision, mentioned earlier, to request additional intelligence data from Chiang Kai-shek, the conclusion is unmistakable: The reconnaissance aircraft were furnished by the new Democratic government.

Thus, the American government conducted a duplicitous policy during that period—on the one hand, reassuring the People's Republic of China, through its Ambassador in Warsaw, that the United States did not intend to support Chiang Kai-shek in the event that he landed troops on the mainland, while on the other hand, furnishing to Chiang Kai-shek the aircraft to gather intelligence information for assessing the advisability of such a landing. It is not without interest to note that U.S. representatives were at that very time participating jointly with those of the People's Republic of China in the Fourteen Nation Geneva Conference on Laos, which, as is generally known, concluded on July 23, 1962, with the signing of a corresponding agreement. The U.S. Secretary of State, Dean Rusk, and the Minister of Foreign Affairs of the People's Republic of China, Chen Yi, were present at the concluding ceremony of the conference. The Democratic government here, too, remained faithful to John Foster Dulles' principle—to participate in negotiations with the People's Republic of China, when required for America's best interests.

The "Year of the Tiger" did not see the realization of Chiang Kai-shek's cherished dream—the landing on mainland China. Support for his ambitious plans by officials in the Pentagon and CIA did not produce those results on which the aged Generalissimo had so greatly counted. The world socialist system, the fundamental foundation and support of the world revolutionary process, had placed under its protection the achievements of the Chinese proletariat, and thereby foiled the aggressive plans of Chiang Kai-shek and those agitators who stood behind him.

Specialists on Far East questions were forced to concede that the "limited hostility" policy had at least two negative consequences for the United States. First, the United States found itself isolated from its allies on the issue of its relations with the People's Republic of China; and second, it lost the support of world public opinion on this issue. Furthermore, despite the "limited hostility" policy, "a slow and insidious shift of the allegiance of hundreds of millions of people to Russian and Chinese Communism" was noticeable, according to the admission of the American professor Hans J. Morgenthau. "To try to stem this tide by military means," said Morgenthau, "is likely not only to be useless, but also self-defeating." Another American specialist on Far Eastern affairs, K. Younger, spoke in the same vein, acknowledging that "The danger of existing American policy is that it is drifting increasingly far from the realities of world power, and the moment of truth is bound to come one day."

The same Hans Morgenthau, however, did not expect any fundamental change in the new U.S. government's policy toward the People's Republic of China. "The chances that the government of the United States will take the initiative in revising its China policy are virtually nil," he wrote in 1962. "A considerable number of high officials are aware of the facts of life in the Far East, yet quite a number, especially in the military establishment, are not. Furthermore, and most importantly, public opinion has been conditioned for more than a decade to support a negative policy towards China, unaware of the risks, expecting at worst an indefinite continuation of the status quo and at best some kind of miracle which will make the Chinese Communists go away."

It is commonly known that President Kennedy and his closest associates were extremely sensitive about this position adopted by the leading academic specialists. And this is not surprising. Among the assistants to the President and his highest appointed officials in the various departments, quite a large number were former professors from leading American universities, and many were prominent scholars. There can be no doubt that the Kennedy Administration was highly cognizant of the opinions of American specialists on China.

According to Roger Hilsman, the "isolation and containment" policy was to have been replaced by one of "firmness, flexibility, and dispassion." What was needed, above all, was a clear formulation of the principles of this new policy in order to secure the support of American "public opinion"—or rather of those who create and direct that "public opinion," the major press, television and radio magnates. It was suggested that the "new policy" be formulated in a speech by one of the leading State Department figures.

It must be emphasized at the outset that this alleged "new" policy was based primarily on the assumption, according to Hilsman, that it would "demonstrate to the world that it was not the United States that was 'isolating' Communist China, but Communist China that was isolating itself." At the same time, implementation of an "open door" policy was suggested, meaning, in this case, that the United States was prepared to adjust American-Chinese relations on the condition that the People's Republic of China would be willing to make compromises. The United States announced that it would always hold open the door for compromises which indicated, in its delicate phrase, a "possibility of change" in the People's Republic of China, in accordance with America's interests.

Thus, the policy of "firmness, flexibility, and dispassion" was essentially no different from the policy of "isolation and containment." "Isolation" of the People's Republic of China was also to be pursued through this "new" policy, but now the Washington ruling circles proposed to make China responsible for this "isolation." Nor could the readiness to negotiate with the People's Republic of China be in any way called a "fundamental change" in U.S. policy. As is generally well known, such negotiations had been conducted almost without interruption since 1954, first in Geneva, then Warsaw, and later in Paris.

However, the very replacement of the term "isolation and containment" with "firmness, flexibility, and dispassion," though only "political trickery," is nonetheless evidence that the old U.S. policy toward the People's Republic of China was finally outdated, and that Washington was prepared to initiate changes in the obsolescent policy, the faster the better. But the need for change was recognized only in words, whereas in reality the old "isolation and containment" policy was persistently continued.

Thus, even those figures in Washington who recognized the true state of affairs in the Far East went no further than engaging in semantics and were not yet prepared for a fundamental change in United States policy in this region. As Robert Blum pointed out: "If there was any serious intention of moving toward a change in policy, it was halted, or at least interrupted, by President Kennedy's death." Furthermore, any "moving toward a change in policy" was undoubtedly determined by hopes for change in the policy of the People's Republic of China itself. The American ruling circles were betting, as in the past, on the nationalist circles in the leadership of the Chinese People's Republic.

2. NEW "CHINA LOBBYISTS"

It would be naive to think that the departure from the political

arena of McCarthy, Knowland, Kohlberg and others who were closely
linked with the work of the "China lobbyists" during the late Fifties
and early Sixties, led to the elimination of the "China lobby" as such.
Nothing of the sort! "As the old China lobby faded away, other
influences, employing a more sophisticated assortment of techniques,
took over"—that was the conclusion reached in 1966 by the well-
known American journalist Archibald T. Steele.

A good idea of the manner in which the new "China lobbyists"
operated can be drawn from the activity of a New York corporation,
the "Hamilton Wright Organization," which specialized, according to its
prospectuses, in "publicity, public relations and advertising." The
activity of this organization was secretly investigated in 1963 by the
U.S. Senate Committee on Foreign Relations, under the chairmanship
of Senator J. William Fulbright. Part of the material from this
investigation was later published for official use, and thus became
available to American journalists.

The story began in the spring of 1957, with a letter sent by the
president of the corporation, Hamilton Wright, Sr., to the Chiang
Kai-shek representative at the United Nations, Tsiang Ting-fu. In this
letter to the Chiang Kai-shek authorities, Wright offered to launch a
worldwide pro-Chiang Kai-shek propaganda campaign, which would be
designed, Wright said, "to arouse public opinion in the United States,
Canada, South America, and Europe, and to create a sympathetic
understanding of Free China* that would have dramatic impact on
members of the United Nations and prevent the seating of Red China in
the United Nations.... Too, this campaign will bring vociferous moral
support from the American people when the day comes for a return to
the mainland."

Shortly thereafter, Wright arrived in Taipei to negotiate with the
official Chiang Kai-shek representatives, who willingly responded to the
tempting proposal. Sampson Shen, the director of Chiang Kai-shek's
Office of Information, acknowledged that the Chiang Kai-shek propaganda effort in the United States had heretofore encountered "certain
sales resistance" from the American public and urgently needed help.
The offer of the "Hamilton Wright" firm was thus accepted immediately. The Chiang Kai-shek representatives themselves determined the
immediate campaign goals—to discredit the so-called "two Chinas"
theory, oppose the admission of the People's Republic of China to the
United Nations, prevent a relaxation of the embargo on the export of

---

*of the Chiang Kai-shek regime on Taiwan (*Author's note*) strategic materials to China, and suppress all attempts to reassess the general American policy toward China. It was further proposed to emphasize that the Chiang Kai-shekists' main task was to return to mainland China. The Chiang Kai-shek representatives demanded in this regard that the company should also try to refute the growing opinion in the United States that "Chiang's army is aging," and that the "Taiwanese are not Chinese." The company's entire activity in this direction was to be conducted with the "advice and consent" of the Chiang Kai-shek Office of Information in New York.

The "Hamilton Wright" company thus went to work and began to produce documentary movies, newsreels, television programs, articles, photographs and other propaganda material whose main purpose was to praise Chiang Kai-shek and his Taiwan regime. All these materials were approved by the Chiang Kai-shek representatives and sent free of charge to the leading movie and television companies, magazines and newspapers. Photography exhibits were organized in many large cities. The operation was conducted on a grand scale. Specifically, a major campaign was conducted during 1960 in South and Central America, for, as Wright noted, these countries had 21 votes in the United Nations and thus could not be ignored.

No expense was spared. Company representatives traveled to many countries and met with editors of local newspapers and magazines, the presidents of radio and television companies, and the editors in public information departments. Films were supplied in various languages. The campaign was conducted consecutively in the European countries, the Middle East, and the Southeast Asian nations.

The main emphasis of the propaganda campaign, however, was centered in the United States itself. Here, the public relations men used not only the achievements of modern technology, but bribery and deception as well. Free pleasure trips abroad were arranged for "necessary people" from film distribution companies and newspaper-magazine syndicates; these individuals also received expensive gifts, and their relatives were offered jobs with the "Hamilton Wright" company. A certain Richard Kuhn, for example, was invited to make a Chiang Kai-shek propaganda film. Kuhn's father was at that time in charge of the film shorts division of the "Twentieth Century Fox" movie company, and was responsible for distribution of many films prepared by the "Hamilton Wright" organization upon the order of the Chiang Kai-shek authorities.

During the subsequent hearings on this matter in the Senate Committee on Foreign Relations, top secret materials from the company's files were produced. Wright strongly maintained that these disclosures could cause great difficulties, not only for the company, but also for the Chiang Kai-shek authorities. These materials, however, are extremely interesting and shed new light on the methods and activities of the new "China lobby." In top secret correspondence with the Chiang Kai-shek representatives, Wright boasted that, in the overwhelming majority of cases (more than 75 percent), not only the readers, but the newspaper and magazine editors themselves had not the slightest idea where the material came from, and were totally unaware that it was not only paid for by, but even prepared under direction of the Chiang Kai-shekists. The company's materials were represented as objective testimony by unbiased observers. The documentary films, prepared according to the instructions and scenarios of the Chiang Kai-shekists, were released as though produced by large American film companies, for, as Wright cynically remarked, what sort of fool would pay money to watch Chiang Kai-shek propaganda movies?

The following facts indicate the scale of the treatment to which American public opinion was subjected on behalf of Chiang Kai-shek. Materials prepared by the "Hamilton Wright" company were printed in 900 newspapers, including *The New York Times, New York Herald Tribune, Washington Star*, and *Chicago Tribune*; publicized by the three largest American television networks; distributed by eight wire services, including the world-renowned Associated Press and United Press; and given space in the pages of such influential magazines as *Time, Newsweek, Reader's Digest* and *Esquire.* Documentary films were released under the trademark of nine well-known American film companies. A large amount of pictorial material was printed in journals specializing in agriculture, railroads, finance, mining, etc. In addition, the Chiang Kai-shekists subsidized, through the "Hamilton Wright" company, certain publications, such as *The New Leader* magazine, which carried, to use Wright's description, "sensational anti-communist stories."

The owners of the company reacted immediately to any important American political statement which touched on China. After John Kennedy's above-mentioned television appearance during the pre-election campaign, for instance, Wright wrote to the director of the Chiang Kai-shek information service: "In view of the critical United Nations developments and statements by Senator Kennedy that he would abandon Quemoy if elected President—it is our considered opinion that the time has come for Taiwan to fight back with a full-scale counter-attack in the form of stepped-up, high-powered publicity." It was emphasized further that the propaganda campaign should be particularly strong "during the U.S. presidential election campaign and after the new U.S. President takes office."

Hamilton Wright and his colleagues tried by every possible means to bolster the prestige of the Chiang Kai-shekists and to present them in the most favorable light. In its operation, the company utilized purely political propaganda methods, but emphasized simultaneously the "value of positive non-political propaganda to create an effect essentially political." The main goal of the propaganda outflow, as J. W. Fulbright, the Chairman of the Senate Committee on Foreign Relations, commented, was to "influence policies and interests" of the United States of America. It is interesting to note that the company's material was also widely used by American government offices, primarily the U.S. Information Agency, which distributed these materials in many countries through its own channels. Company-produced propaganda films about Taiwan were also used by the U.S. Department of State.

One of the most important aspects of the company's operations was the preparation of articles favorable to the Chiang Kai-shek regime in Taiwan, which were published under the signatures of U.S. Senators and congressmen. Wright's correspondence with the Chiang Kai-shek representatives indicates that a number of such articles appeared in the largest American newspapers. The Senate Committee on Foreign Relations, however, did not try very hard to wash its dirty linen in public, and for that reason the Committee named publicly as an "author" of such articles only one senator, Paul Douglas, who was compelled to admit that an article, published under his name, in support of the policy of non-recognition of the People's Republic of China, was written for him by an employee of the "Hamilton Wright" corporation. The American public never did learn the names of other senators and congressmen involved in this episode.

Another important aspect of the "Hamilton Wright" corporation's activities was its energetic support of organizations pursuing a policy favorable to the Chiang Kai-shekists. Hamilton Wright, Sr., named the "Committee of One Million" as one such organization. Established in 1953 at the initiative of the well known "China lobbyist" and Congressman, Walter Judd, this committee had as its initial goal the collection of one million signatures for a petition, addressed to the President of the United States, demanding that the People's Republic of China be denied admission to the United Nations.

The necessary number of signatures was collected during the year, and in 1954 the committee was dissolved. The very next year, however, it renewed its activity under the name "Committee of One Million Against the Admission of Communist China to the United Nations," with a membership that included representatives of the old "China lobby," such as Senators Knowland and Bridges; former Congressman

Judd; Henry Luce, the publisher of *Time* and *Life* magazines; and
Generals A. C. Wedemeyer and J. A. Van Fleet. Frederick McKee, an
active Chiang Kai-shek lobbyist, was the committee treasurer. Senators
Barry Goldwater (well-known for his reactionary views), Everett
Dirksen and Mike Mansfield; the former Vice President of the United
States, Hubert Humphrey (who subsequently left the committee);
Admiral A. W. Radford and others, became members of the new com-
mittee. In 1958 the committee counted among its active members 23
senators, 23 congressmen, 4 state governors, and 15 admirals and
generals.

The committee defined its tasks in a published statement as follows:
first, to prevent the admission of the People's Republic of China to the
United Nations; second, to oppose in every way possible United States
diplomatic recognition of the People's Republic of China; third, to
prevent the normalization of trade relations between the two countries;
and fourth, to oppose, in general, "any political settlement" between
the United States and People's Republic of China. The committee also
attempted to counteract "any measures which could strengthen the
political, economic or military positions" of the People's Republic of
China. Pressure was exerted to this end on the members of both Houses
of the American Congress.

The committee reacted quickly to any more or less serious statements which it regarded as a threat to its point of view. Thus, when
Assistant Secretary of State Roger Hilsman stated in a 1963 speech
merely that United States policy should proceed from the simple fact
that the People's Republic of China does exist, the "Committee of One
Million" immediately circulated among all influential people an eight-
page message strongly objecting even to the recognition of the very
existence of the People's Republic of China. The committee's entire
work was infused with a spirit of dyed-in-the-wool anti-Communism,
and it was no coincidence that Barry Goldwater was from the very
beginning among its most active figures. The anti-Communist character
of the committee's work assumed such forms that, according to the
admission of the American press, a number of well-known liberals who
had participated in the work of the committee during its early years
"became increasingly uncomfortable with the organization's policies. A
number of them have withdrawn."

The "Committee of One Million," however, enjoyed for quite some
time the support of many congressmen. It is significant that the
committee's appeal to the delegates at the XXIst Session of the United
Nations General Assembly, published on October 31, 1966, which
urged them not to admit the People's Republic of China to the UN, was

signed by 50 senators and 231 congressmen. The significance of this committee's work should, of course, not be overestimated, but neither should it be forgotten that it exerted over an extended period enormous pressure upon American public opinion, in general, and, particularly, upon the United States Congress, to forestall any changes in U.S. policy toward China.

Numerous ultra-right organizations and associations have spoken, and continue to speak out as ardent Chiang Kai-shek "lobbyists." Although the problem of relations with China is undoubtedly of secondary importance in the work of the overwhelming majority of these organizations, all nonetheless firmly favor a policy of non-recognition of the People's Republic of China, and of unconditional support for Chiang Kai-shek. The most implacable of these ultra-right organizations, the well-known "John Birch Society," believes that the United States is "in a state of war" with the People's Republic of China.

Right-wing organizations are receiving enormous financial support from big business. Many retired generals and admirals, including General A. C. Wedemeyer, former commander of U.S. forces in China, Major General C. A. Willoughby, the former chief of MacArthur's intelligence staff, and others are playing an active role therein. The availability of significant funds allows the ultra-right to use television and radio broadcasts, newspapers and magazines for its own purposes. American observers have noted that the ultra-right inundates the average American with an "enormous quantity of propaganda materials." And by no means does it limit its activity only to legal methods. The American press has been compelled to acknowledge that the ultra-right fairly frequently resorts to outright intimidation of individuals.

American journalists explain that the fear of revenge by the ultra-right precludes a free and open discussion in many American cities of the entire complex set of questions relating to United States policy toward China. Not only ordinary American citizens, but also many congressmen and senators have been, and are still being subjected to threats by ultra-right organizations. For example, Thomas G. Kuchel, a senator from California, admitted in one of his Senate speeches that during a period of several months he had received approximately 6,000 threatening letters.

The Washington Post observed that even though many active "China lobby" representatives have either died or ceased active participation, the "China lobby" has by no means departed the political scene. The *Far Eastern Economic Review* wrote in February 1970 that the "ghost of the Taiwan lobby still stalks the halls of Congress and prevents members from being more forthright in their statements about China." The radical reassessment of America's China policy undertaken by the Nixon Administration was a powerful blow to the interests of the "China lobbyists," forcing them to regroup on a new platform. The creation of a new organization, the "Committee for a Free China," established to replace the "Committee of One Million," was announced at a press conference held in Washington in February 1972. In fulfilling its aims, the new committee is proceeding from the prevailing factual situation, and plans to devote itself to a broad study of the People's Republic of China. To this end, it has added a special department to its organization. Thus, the old "China lobby" is endeavoring to preserve the remnants of its influence and to adapt its operations to the changing realities of present-day political life.

CHAPTER VI

THE UNITED STATES, CHINA AND THE VIETNAM WAR

1. *"TACIT MUTUAL UNDERSTANDING"*

For a short period after the assassination of John F. Kennedy, United States foreign policy continued along the course charted by the late President. During this brief interlude, Roger Hilsman, Assistant Secretary of State for Far Eastern Affairs, spoke in San Francisco on the problem of America's China policy. In this December 1963 address, Hilsman did not spell out any policies which were fundamentally new. His remarks did, however, suggest a certain departure from the notorious Dulles doctrine on the "transient nature" of the existence of the People's Republic of China. "We have no reason to believe that there is a present likelihood that the Communist regime will be overthrown," Hilsman said. In this manner the United States government for the first time acknowledged, by verbal statement of its official representative, the irrevocable nature of the changes which had occurred in China. True, Hilsman's speech contained no indications whatsoever of a possible early change in America's policy toward the People's Republic of China. Moreover, the speech emphasized that the defense of Taiwan continued to remain a "fundamental principle" of U.S. policy toward China and that "fundamental changes" in American-Chinese relations remained impossible as long as the People's Republic of China failed to recognize this fact.

The next policy statement on China was made a month-and-a-half later, on January 27, 1964, by the Johnson Administration, in response to France's recognition of the People's Republic of China. Characterizing France's action as an "unfortunate step," the Department of State reaffirmed that the United States would "firmly observe its obligations" toward the Chiang Kai-shek regime in Taiwan. Secretary of State

Dean Rusk, then in Tokyo, spoke in the same vein. American observers explain that the haste with which both these statements were made, and also their rather harsh tone, resulted from Washington's desire to emphasize its displeasure at France's political step and its fear that America's silence might be interpreted as approval of the measures taken by France. Speaking before the Senate Committee on Foreign Relations on March 14, 1964, Secretary of State Rusk deemed it necessary to emphasize once again the immutability of United States policy toward the People's Republic of China, which, he pointed out, was "based primarily on political considerations."

Notwithstanding the assertion by the new U.S. President that his foreign policy course would be a direct continuation of Kennedy's policy, well-informed American observers noted that the change of Presidents and Lyndon Johnson's assumption of power brought new problems to the forefront. These primarily concerned U.S. actions in Vietnam, which directly influenced America's policy toward the People's Republic of China.

As is generally known, United States intervention in the war in Vietnam began in 1950, when Secretary of State Dean Acheson offered France economic and military aid to "re-establish stability" in Indochina. The extent of this intervention may be judged by the fact that in 1954 alone the war in Vietnam cost the American taxpayers roughly $1.4 billion. In fact, even then the United States was contributing 78 percent of the entire cost of the military operations in Vietnam. In addition, the United States was gradually increasing its military personnel in South Vietnam. While there were, according to official statistics of the American military command, 3,164 American servicemen there by the end of 1961, their number had increased to 9,865 by the end of 1962, and to 14,000 by October 1963.

The American press indicates that Kennedy was very disturbed during the last months of his life by the American commitments in Vietnam. At his direction, Secretary of Defense Robert McNamara and the Chairman of the Joint Chiefs of Staff, Maxwell Taylor, flew to South Vietnam at the end of September 1963 on an inspection tour. They reported the results of the tour to the President, and on October 2, 1963, the White House issued a statement acknowledging that "the political situation in South Vietnam remains deeply serious." It was officially announced simultaneously that 1,000 military advisers would be withdrawn from South Vietnam before the end of 1963 and that, "on the whole," all of the 14,000 American military personnel in Vietnam would be withdrawn by the end of 1965.

The American press now notes that Kennedy was scheduled to meet with Henry Cabot Lodge, the U.S. Ambassador to South Vietnam, after the President's trip to Dallas. It is generally well known, however, that Lodge had already discussed the situation in South Vietnam with the new President. Soon thereafter, Secretary of Defense McNamara left again for a two-day visit to Vietnam. After his return it was officially announced that the earlier plans for a reduction of American armed forces in Vietnam had been changed; there would, in fact, be no reduction, but rather an increase of American forces.

The decision to expand American intervention in Vietnam raised the specific question concerning the attitude of the leadership of the People's Republic of China toward the events in that region. Once more, the problems of American-Chinese relations emerged in all their complexity, now to be faced by Lyndon Johnson's Administration.

On January 27, 1964, Secretary of Defense McNamara, appearing before the Armed Services Committee of the U.S. House of Representatives, asserted that as a result of Mao Tse-tung's anti-Soviet policy, the People's Republic of China would not be in a position to undertake in the near future active military operations against the Americans in Vietnam. A few days later, President Johnson rejected General de Gaulle's plan for the neutralization of South Vietnam and stated bluntly that the United States intended to expand significantly its military operations in that region. Secretary of State Dean Rusk, in turn, speaking on February 25, 1964, in Washington, attempted to create the impression that the United States had reliable information regarding the intentions of the People's Republic of China in Vietnam, and that further U.S. actions in that region would take into consideration a possible reaction by the People's Republic of China. He stated openly that he wanted to "clear away one myth. We* do not ignore the Chinese Communist regime. . . . We talk with it regularly through our respective ambassadors to Warsaw. There have been 119 of these talks."

1964 was a presidential election year in the United States, and Lyndon Johnson, who found himself in the presidential chair "by accident," passionately desired to become the "legitimately elected President." Johnson's election campaign managers realized that he would not get very far with bellicose speeches. At the same time, everyone in Washington well knew that after the elections nothing could prevent Johnson from discarding his peace-loving statements like unnecessary husks and initiating a policy of escalation of the war. The pre-election campaign period could, in addition, be used to clarify the real intentions of Mao Tse-tung and his associates.

---

*the United States of America (*Author's note*)

Thus, 1964 was the year of preparation for a serious escalation of the war in Vietnam. During the first half of the year, Secretary of Defense McNamara and the Chairman of the Joint Chiefs of Staff, Maxwell Taylor, visited South Vietnam twice (in March and May). After each of these visits, the Johnson Administration issued official statements regarding its intention to increase military support for the South Vietnamese authorities. It is significant that the first of these statements was issued by the White House on March 17, 1961, after a special meeting of the National Security Council. In the opinion of American journalists, this constituted a radical departure from the established practice in which no statements are released about National Security Council sessions.

Notwithstanding the ever-increasing American aid, the political, economic and military situation of the constantly changing South Vietnamese regimes deteriorated steadily. Under these circumstances, after a routine inspection trip to Vietnam by McNamara and Taylor, Washington decided in May 1964 to send there an additional contingent of American servicemen and a large number of military aircraft.

One of the principal aims of the Johnson Administration's China policy was the clarification of the attitude of the leadership of the People's Republic of China toward the decision to expand American armed intervention in Vietnam and begin bombing that country. The Pentagon, according to the testimony of American Sinologists, was seriously concerned over the potential intervention of the People's Republic of China, and the President was also worried. Hence, weighing the "pros and cons" of the impending escalation of the war, Washington carefully examined the possible alternative Peking reactions. President Johnson wrote to the U.S. Ambassador in Saigon, Henry Cabot Lodge: "There is an additional international reason for avoiding immediate overt action,* in that we expect a showdown between the Chinese and Soviet Communist parties soon, and actions against the North will be more practicable after than before a showdown."

In a move which underscored the expansion of direct U.S. military intervention in Vietnam, the Johnson Administration decided to strengthen its military leadership on the scene, and in June 1964 General Maxwell D. Taylor, the Chairman of the Joint Chiefs of Staff, was appointed as the new U.S. Ambassador to South Vietnam. Several days before that appointment, Secretary of State Dean Rusk announced at a briefing of leading American journalists that the Democratic Republic of Vietnam and the People's Republic of China

---

*against the Democratic Republic of Vietnam (*Author's note*)

were "running the risk" of finding themselves in a state of war with the United States. President Johnson and other top officials in Washington relentlessly asserted in public statements during that period that the United States had no intention to "expand the war."

The true value of all these statements became clear early in August 1964, when the American Navy began a series of provocations in the Tonkin Gulf; within a few days, the size of U.S. naval forces along the coast of the Democratic Republic of Vietnam was doubled, upon personal orders of the President. This demonstration of sea power was accompanied by unusual U.S. diplomatic activity and an outburst of bellicose speeches in the Congress. The President stated that he had instructed the Secretary of State to explain the U.S. position "to friends, foes and, in general, to everybody"(!). The U.S. representative at the United Nations received instructions to prepare for an "urgent and immediate" session of the Security Council. The congressional leaders—both Democrats and Republicans—were asked to adopt immediately a resolution ratifying the President's actions in the Gulf of Tonkin. Former Ambassador to South Vietnam Lodge was simultaneously dispatched on a round-the-world journey to explain the policy of the United States to its allies.

On August 7, 1964, the U.S. Congress, in an atmosphere fraught with militarism, adopted the resolution authorizing the President to take "any measures, including the use of the armed forces," to aid any SEATO member nation. Even then, individual senators and congressmen opposed this resolution. For example, Eugene Siler, a member of the House of Representatives, characterized the proposed resolution as a futile effort to shift the blame for all subsequent actions of the Administration to the U.S. Congress and to silence congressional criticism. Senators Morse and Gruening voted against the resolution, but it was adopted by an overwhelming majority of votes and subsequently constituted the "legal basis" upon which the United States Administration began to escalate the war in Vietnam.

United States naval operations in the Tonkin Gulf shed light on the true position of the leadership of the People's Republic of China, and on its attitude toward the war of national liberation waged by the Vietnamese people. The fact is, as Secretary of Defense McNamara stated to reporters on August 5, 1964, that aircraft carriers of the U.S. Seventh Fleet, whose main task was patrolling the Taiwan Strait, participated in the Tonkin Gulf operations. American military figures, who well remembered the events of 1954 and 1958 in the region of the Quemoy and Matsu islands, undoubtedly had exact information on the intentions and capabilities of the Chinese Army in that area. And, in truth, nothing unforeseen by the Americans occurred in the Taiwan Strait. There are compelling reasons to believe that this circumstance did not go unnoticed in Washington. In any event, the election platform of the Democratic party, made public toward the end of August 1964, not only omitted the almost traditional demands to oppose recognition of the People's Republic of China and to support Chiang Kai-shek, but totally ignored the general issue of U.S. policy toward the People's Republic of China. Diplomats and journalists noticed that the usual slogans in opposition to the People's Republic of China were in this instance replaced by a promise "to support a growing understanding among peoples" of the Pacific basin.

In this sense, the Democratic election platform differed sharply from that of the Republicans, who, as in the past, opposed the recognition of the People's Republic of China and its admission to the United Nations, and favored continued support for Chiang Kai-shek. How strange that the American press, which is usually very sensitive to the finest nuances of an election campaign, this time overlooked—as if on command—these aspects of the election platform. The impression was created that certain extremely influential circles in Washington did not wish to focus attention upon this change in the Democratic party position on one of the most important problems of United States foreign policy. In any event, it would not be a great exaggeration to say that the authors of the Democratic party's election platform were obviously unwilling to burden the Administration with any kind of promises regarding future U.S. policy on China.

Thus, the Democratic party, still in power in the United States during the summer of 1964, excluded from its most important political document—the election platform—any mention of the policy of "isolation and containment" of the People's Republic of China. One might conclude that the United States ruling circles, encouraged by the inaction of Mao Tse-tung and his group during the Tonkin Gulf episode, and carefully pondering the general policy of the Maoist group in the international arena, had already begun by mid-1964 to search for ways to achieve a "tacit mutual understanding" with the People's Republic of China concerning the expansion of American intervention in Vietnam. These ruling circles were endeavoring to determine the possible consequences of such intervention and the exact intentions of China's leadership.

Washington was at that time already aware of the re-orientation of the Mao Tse-tung group on many issues. A special report published by the U.S. Information Agency on April 8, 1964, emphasized that in 1963 the Mao Tse-tung group, attempting to curtail economic ties with the socialist countries, had "made a prodigious effort to seek out technical assistance, capital goods and raw materials from the West." It cited, as an example, new trade agreements entered into by the People's Republic of China in 1963 with England, Holland, Italy, Finland, Canada, Australia, Argentina, Mexico, and other countries. President Johnson felt compelled to emphasize in one of his campaign speeches that he did not intend to involve the United States "in a war with 700 million Chinese." This statement was obviously intended more for certain people in Peking than for the American voters.

The first explosion of an atomic device in the People's Republic of China took place on October 16, 1964. President Johnson, speaking on television on October 18, stated that this explosion "was no unexpected surprise" for the United States, and he warned against possible "exaggeration of [its] military significance." Secretary of State Rusk also delivered a speech in the same vein. The extremely restrained tone of these statements differed sharply from all earlier remarks by official Washington representatives on the policy and actions of the People's Republic of China. Such restraint by the President and Secretary of State would, of course, have been most welcome, if they had not been concealing far-reaching plans for a possible agreement with Peking at the expense of the Vietnamese people's fundamental interests.

In the presidential elections of November 3, 1964, Lyndon Johnson was elected for a new four-year term as President of the United States, defeating General Barry Goldwater, who had advocated an undisguised program for expanding the war in Vietnam. Less than three weeks after the elections, *Life* magazine published an interview with Maxwell Taylor, the Ambassador in South Vietnam, in which Taylor mentioned the possibility that America would bomb so-called military objectives in the Democratic Republic of Vietnam and Laos. A State Department representative hastened to point out that Taylor's statement did not reflect "policy," but merely indicated a "possibility" which "would not necessarily occur." It became known several days later, however, early in December 1964, that Taylor had been in Washington and discussed with President Johnson various proposals for further major expansion of military operations, including American bombing of the Democratic Republic of Vietnam and Laos. But the time for such a step, which would have marked a fundamental change in the entire U.S. policy in Vietnam, had not yet arrived.

The United States needed precise information on the attitude of the leadership of the People's Republic of China, which it received from an extensive interview which Mao Tse-tung had granted to the American journalist Edgar Snow, on January 9, 1965, in Peking, and which was published in the American press on January 20, 1965. Several circumstances relating to its publication in the United States are noteworthy.

It is commonly known that Mao Tse-tung almost never grants interviews to foreign journalists, and for this reason it is extremely significant that the only interview granted in recent years was to an American journalist. It is also well known that the U.S. government did not at that time allow American journalists to visit the People's Republic of China, and yet Snow's passport was not lifted by the American authorities after his trip there, which in itself suggests that this trip was sanctioned by the Department of State. It is also extremely significant that an American magazine published in full the extensive interview, covering 25 typewritten pages.

But let us turn to the text of the interview itself, or rather to those of its aspects which concern relations between the People's Republic of China and the United States, and the events in Vietnam. To Snow's direct question whether the South Vietnamese partisans could then "win victory by their own efforts alone," Mao replied affirmatively. Furthermore, Mao emphasized that he considered the current situation of the South Vietnamese partisans significantly improved over that of the Chinese Communists during the 1927-37 period of the first civil war, for "at that time there was no direct foreign intervention." Mao pointed out further that the expansion of American intervention would only "hasten the arming of the people against them."

It turned out, in fact, that the more American troops there were in Vietnam, the better off was the cause of the Vietnamese people's national liberation war. And Mao made his remarks at a time when the heroic Vietnamese fighters demanded the immediate and unconditional withdrawal of American troops from Vietnam!

As regards the relations between the United States and the People's Republic of China, Mao Tse-tung stated that he did not believe that the prevailing state of these relations could lead to war. "Mao said . . . there would be no war. That could occur only if American troops came to China. . . . Probably the American leaders knew that, and consequently they would not invade China. Then there would be no war . . . ."

"What of the possibilities of war arising out of Vietnam?" Snow persisted in asking. "I have read many newspaper stories indicating that the United States has considered expanding the war into North Vietnam."

"No, Mao said, . . . Mr. Rusk had now made it clear that the U.S. would not do that. Mr. Rusk may have earlier said something like that, but now he had corrected himself and said that he had never made such a statement. Therefore, there need not be any war in North Vietnam."

"I do not believe that the makers and administrators of United States policy understand you," Snow said.

"Why not?" asked Mao, who stressed that "China's armies would not go beyond her borders to fight. That was clear enough. Only if the United States attacked China would the Chinese fight. Wasn't that clear? The Chinese were very busy with their internal affairs. Fighting beyond one's own borders was criminal. Why should the Chinese do that? The Vietnamese could cope with their situation." And Mao Tse-tung then categorically denied that any Chinese troops whatsoever were in Vietnam.

As we see, Mao Tse-tung left no doubt that the People's Republic of China had no intention to intervene under any circumstances in the events in Vietnam. The conclusion automatically suggests itself that as long as the United States did not intend to invade China, America had a free hand to do whatever it wanted in Vietnam. It is common knowledge that Washington understood Mao Tse-tung perfectly well and drew the appropriate conclusions from his statements.

Two more points expressed by Mao Tse-tung in this interview merit attention. First, Mao pointed out that the People's Republic of China would aid the national liberation movements by "publishing statements and calling demonstrations to support" these popular movements. In Mao Tse-tung's opinion, it was just such verbiage by Peking, along with the demonstrations on its streets, that "vexed the imperialists." Thus, while Mao Tse-tung and his group are ardent verbal supporters of the people's anti-imperialist struggles, in actuality they refuse real support for the national liberation struggles, limiting their so-called support to loud and empty statements. Second, Mao Tse-tung noted that the United States was reacting very sensitively to each "blank shell," as he put it, fired by the People's Liberation Army in the region of the Taiwan Strait. "It seemed," he boasted, "that China could order the American forces to march here, to march there.... Consider what could be accomplished by firing some blank shells within those Chinese territorial waters." The question inevitably arises as to why the forces of the People's Republic of China failed to fire "some blank shells" during the summer of 1964, in order to keep U.S. aircraft carriers in the Taiwan Strait and prevent their dispatch to the shores of the Democratic Republic of Vietnam. Only one explanation is possible: Mao Tse-tung and his group did not, and still do not want to complicate relations with the United States ruling circles. Mao was compelled to make this unnecessary retroactive boast just to reassure the Pentagon once more that he and his group had no intention of giving military aid to the Vietnamese people in their heroic struggle against American imperialism.

Thus, after starting off by mouthing ultra-left phrases, Peking concluded by directly betraying the interests of the socialist camp. In fact, Mao Tse-tung's group not only substituted a struggle against the Soviet Union, the other socialist countries and the Communist movement as a whole, for the struggle against imperialism, but also stabbed in the back the heroic Vietnamese who were fighting the American aggressors.

It is noteworthy that during that same period official Washington representatives began to stress in their statements the development of contacts with the People's Republic of China. A speech given by Marshall Green, Deputy Assistant Secretary of State for Far Eastern Affairs, at a Princeton University conference at the end of February 1965 (*i.e.,* a month after the Mao Tse-tung interview was published by the American press), is significant in this regard. Green characterized U.S. policy toward the People's Republic of China primarily as a combination of "strength and patience," and emphasized additionally the following: "A significant but oft-times overlooked aspect of our current policy is the fact that . . . we . . . would improve some of our contacts with Communist China. Under this general heading we have held more than 120 diplomatic level talks with Peiping representatives in Geneva and Warsaw; we have participated with Peiping in international gatherings such as the Geneva talks of 1954 and 1962; we have authorized virtually every newspaperman who has so desired travel to Communist China; we have authorized a number of other visits to Communist China by Americans for humanitarian or national interest reasons. . . . There is no prohibition on correspondence to and from China, or even on the export of films. We are holding out the possibility and prospect of expanding such contacts."

Green's statement, not intended for the public-at-large and published in a limited number of copies, demonstrated the new course adopted by the U.S. ruling circles in their relations with the People's Republic of China after the 1964 events in the Tonkin Gulf. Here, there was no hint of those threats which only recently comprised the basic subject of all official statements addressed to the People's Republic of China. Thus, a certain wing within the U.S. ruling circles began persistently to attempt to "build bridges" to Peking on an anti-Soviet foundation, and to search for points of contact with the People's Republic of China.

The fact that Washington's somewhat ameliorated position toward the People's Republic of China exactly coincided with the intensive escalation of U.S. military actions in Vietnam must not be regarded as coincidental. On President Johnson's orders, the American Air Force began bombing the territory of the Democratic Republic of Vietnam on February 7, 1965. The barbaric bombings took place regularly, and

February 7, 1965, became a turning point in the history of American military intervention in Vietnam. If the Americans had tried in the past somehow to conceal their intervention in the South Vietnam events with talk about their alleged advisory role, they now openly began armed incursions against a sovereign state—the Democratic Republic of Vietnam.

Almost simultaneously, the American Air Force initiated operations against the forces of the South Vietnamese National Liberation Front. The U.S. Democratic Senator Wayne Morse, in characterizing these operations, said: "The United States is carrying out the war escalation plans that both the Pentagon Building and the State Department have been manipulating for the past several months." Morse called America's policy in Vietnam "immoral and godless," and said that the United States was "drunk with its military might."

A sharp escalation of the Vietnam war, with a substantial increase in troop strength, began in February 1965. At the end of March, the Americans admitted they were using gas in Vietnam. On April 2, the U.S. National Security Council decided to increase the number and intensity of bombings close to the North. On April 26, Secretary of Defense McNamara significantly stated that there was "no military requirement for the use of nuclear weapons in the *current** situation." At the beginning of May, the United States Congress made a supplementary appropriation of $700 million to meet the needs of the war in Vietnam. Speaking on May 4 before a joint session of the Committees on Foreign Relations, Armed Services and Finance of the U.S. Senate and the House of Representatives, President Johnson explained the necessity for additional appropriations and noted that the number of American servicemen in Vietnam had increased from 3,164 soldiers in 1961, to more than 35,000 at the end of April 1965. U.S. military helicopters in Vietnam had flown 30,000 flight hours during the first quarter of 1963, and 90,000 flight hours during the same period of 1965. In February 1965, the U.S. Air Force conducted 160 sorties against the Democratic Republic of Vietnam, and in April of the same year, more than 1,500 sorties. The day after the President's speech, 8,000 more U.S. marines landed in Vietnam. The escalation of the war continued.

It is significant that during the very period when American imperialism began aggressive operations against the Democratic Republic of Vietnam, Premier Chou En-lai of the People's Republic of China made several statements regarding China's position to representatives of the

---

*emphasis supplied by the author

foreign press. Thus, on March 20, the *Manila Times* published an interview with Chou En-lai in which he emphasized that China was "showing restraint" toward the events in Vietnam. On June 3, the Egyptian magazine *Al Mussawar* reported that Chou En-lai, in an interview in Peking, had stated that the "war in Vietnam cannot lead to a world war."

Reading these statements leads to the conclusion that Peking was obviously trying to minimize the significance of the war escalation and the aggressive American actions against the Democratic Republic of Vietnam. And the remarks also bring to mind the "infallible confidence" with which Mao Tse-tung, less than two months before the American Air Force began to bomb the Democratic Republic of Vietnam, rejected the very possibility of such operations, citing Secretary of State Rusk as the "authority." It is now perfectly clear that the statements of both Mao Tse-tung and Chou En-lai were not and, indeed, could not have been coincidental. These were elements of a single policy aimed at the heightening of international tension.

Washington drew the appropriate conclusions from the position adopted by the leadership of the People's Republic of China. In June 1965, military operations were escalated at an unprecedented pace. On June 8, the Department of State announced that the U.S. military command in Vietnam would use American military units in combat operations against the partisans. On June 16, Secretary of Defense McNamara reported that the number of American troops in Vietnam, which by that time had reached 54,000 men, would be increased by 21,000 men in the near future. The next day, on June 17, hefty B-52 jet bombers were put into operation there for the first time. On June 22, American bombers raided areas of the Democratic Republic of Vietnam north of Hanoi. On June 28, American paratroopers began operations against the partisans in South Vietnam.

Thus, the American imperialists had by July 1965 completely discarded the peacemaker's mask and shown the whole world their true face—that of an aggressor. The socialist countries gave considerable aid to the people of Vietnam in their struggle against the American aggressors; however, because of the position adopted by China, the socialist countries were unable to develop a unified policy on assistance to the Vietnamese people. And Peking's position, of course, enjoyed the silent support of the Pentagon and the Department of State. By their actions, or, more accurately, by their inaction, Mao Tse-tung and his associates practically gave a *carte blanche* to the American aggressors.

On July 28, 1965, President Johnson stated that the number of American enlisted men and officers in Vietnam would be increased to 125,000. On August 4, the President asked Congress for an additional appropriation in the amount of $1.7 billion for the war in Vietnam. Secretary of Defense McNamara, appearing before the U.S. Senate Subcommittee on Military Appropriations, explained that the amounts requested would be adequate until January 1966.

The sharp escalation of military operations conducted by the American government in Vietnam resulted in a series of even more aggressive statements by certain extremely responsible American figures. Thus, on August 11, 1965, L. Mendel Rivers, the Democratic Chairman of the Committee on Armed Services of the U.S. House of Representatives, urged the U.S. government to prepare for the use of atomic weapons against the People's Republic of China. Rivers received the immediate support of another congressman—the Democrat F. Edward Hebert, who expressed the opinion that Rivers, by his statement, had made a "great contribution to the national defense of the U.S." Gerald Ford, the Republican leader in the House of Representatives, favored "immediate and more effective" bombing of the Democratic Republic of Vietnam. Reasonable voices, however, were also heard. Congressman Don Edwards, a Democrat from the state of California, called Rivers' speech "dangerous and inflammatory," stating that it "undercut the very basis of American foreign policy." Senator Stephen M. Young also criticized Rivers' speech.

Washington announced in July that Henry Cabot Lodge was being re-appointed as Ambassador to South Vietnam. In mid-July, Lodge and Secretary of Defense McNamara flew to Vietnam to appraise the situation. As a result of this sixth trip to Vietnam, McNamara was forced to admit that the sharp escalation of military operations had not only failed to improve the position of the Americans and their South Vietnamese puppets, but had even led to a worsening of the situation. "The overall situation continues to be serious," he said at a press conference in Saigon on July 21, 1965. "As a matter of fact . . . there has been a deterioration since I was here 15 months ago. The size of the Viet Cong forces has increased. Their rate of operations and the intensity of their attacks has been expanded."

But the increased resistance of the Vietnamese people failed to bring the high-handed militarists to their senses. They continued the escalation of the war, with the bombing of peaceful villages in Cambodia, the construction of an enormous military base in Thailand, and the continuing deployment of more new military units in Vietnam. According to official Pentagon statistics, 181,000 American enlisted men and officers were stationed in Vietnam by the end of December 1965—*i.e.*, the number had increased eight times within one year. It is interesting to note that during the same period, according to (obviously underestimated) official records of the South Vietnamese authorities, 96,000

South Vietnamese soldiers deserted from their units because they were unwilling to fight against their brother-partisans.

At the end of 1965, Washington was forced to admit that the sharp escalation of military operations in South Vietnam and the bombardment of the Democratic Republic of Vietnam, which had begun in February, constituted a desperate attempt to hold its ground in Vietnam at any cost. McGeorge Bundy, the Special Assistant to the President for national security problems, stated openly that the situation in South Vietnam, even in January 1965, had tottered "on the brink of a military failure, which undoubtedly overshadowed all aspects of the problem." Washington subsequently published an official document which noted that "by February 1965, it had become absolutely clear that . . . South Vietnam was almost lost" for the United States. In turn, a group of senators headed by Mike Mansfield, the Senate Democratic leader, noted in its report to the Senate Committee on Foreign Relations, which was prepared after a trip to the European and Asian countries, that "during the early months of 1965, a complete failure of the Saigon government seemed inevitable."

If the Americans succeeded in holding their ground in Vietnam, it was only due to the position of Mao Tse-tung and his group, which had substituted for the struggle against imperialism a struggle against the Soviet Union, the other socialist countries, and the entire Communist movement. Of course, the escalation of the war in Vietnam did not go unnoticed in Peking. They were clearly perturbed there that the Americans might become carried away and take steps which could place Peking in a difficult situation, by exposing the true face of the Peking leaders to the entire world.

Chou En-lai, under these circumstances, delivered a speech on December 20, 1965, in which he characterized America's "possible future" steps to expand military operations in Indochina. According to Chou En-lai's outline, "These actions include: extensively bombing Northern Vietnam, including Haiphong and Hanoi, in an attempt to sap the fighting will of the North Vietnamese people . . . and support and assist the South; harassing and blockading the Bac Bo Gulf in the hope of cutting the sea communications of the Democratic Republic of Vietnam; bombing the central and southern parts of Laos liberated by the Neo Lao Haksat, and preparing to dispatch U.S. and Thai troops, together with the troops of the Laotian rightists, to occupy this area, in an attempt to link it with Thailand and South Vietnam; bombing and attacking the Xieng Khouang area of Laos, in an attempt to block the main highways linking the Democratic Republic of Vietnam and Laos; and instigating the puppet cliques of Thailand and South Vietnam to intensify attacks and disruptive activities against Cambodia, in the hope of sealing off the borders between Cambodia and South Vietnam. Obviously, the aim of the United States is to enforce a water-tight blockade on South Vietnam and render the South Vietnamese people isolated." Chou En-lai further noted that, according to the logic of aggressive wars, it was possible that the United States would expand the war in the future "to the whole of Indochina and to China."

It is extremely significant that, having enumerated the steps in the escalation of the war, the Premier of the People's Republic of China did not deem it necessary to state Peking's attitude toward these actions, and never mentioned what steps China intended to take to prevent these operations. Without such a statement, Chou En-lai's entire tirade may be interpreted as an obvious attempt to delineate the possible limits of Washington's aggressive actions, and as a direct hint to the Pentagon on how far it could go in expanding the war without the risk of incurring China's wrath. That the Pentagon did not overlook Chou En-lai's statements was demonstrated by the bombing of strategic highways in Laos, and by the further expansion of the bombing of the Democratic Republic of Vietnam, including Hanoi and the seaport of Haiphong, and the subsequent mining of Vietnam's ports.

Mao Tse-tung and his group did not miss the opportunity once again to bring to the attention of the White House their reluctance to risk a serious conflict with the United States over the expanded American aggression in Vietnam. Significant in this regard is an article titled "When and How China Will Go to War," written in 1966 by the American journalist Anna Louise Strong, a permanent resident of Peking at that time. She wrote openly that "As is clearly visible from Peking, China has no intention of entering the war." Obviously replying to reports published in the American press on the alleged presence of numerous Chinese soldiers in the Democratic Republic of Vietnam, Anna Louise Strong gave her assurance that "China does not have one soldier beyond its borders. . . . It is, however, prepared to defend its country . . . in case of attack."

As an example of Peking's "good behavior," Anna Louise Strong cited its reaction to the bombing and strafing of Chinese fishing vessels in international waters by American aircraft: "In recent years China has issued more than 400 'serious warnings' in connection with violations of the Chinese air space and territorial waters by the U.S. Seventh Fleet. . . . China is patient. It is Mao's strategy to allow the aggressor to commit a multitude of aggressive acts, exposing himself thereby before the entire world, so that world public opinion will know whom to blame in case of war." The tenor of the entire article is: China will not wage war because of Vietnam unless China itself is attacked. In support of her conclusions, the author quoted statements of Mao Tse-tung, Lin Piao and others.

It is noteworthy that after each such signal from Peking, the United States implemented the next stage of escalation of the Vietnam war. Thus, less than a month after the publication of Edgar Snow's interview with Mao Tse-tung in the American press, U.S. aircraft began bombing the Democratic Republic of Vietnam. Literally the day following Chou En-lai's December 20, 1965, speech in Peking, a State Department representative announced that the American command in Vietnam had received authorization to bomb Cambodia and initiate the invasion of its territory by American military forces. In May 1966, soon after publication of the article "When and How China Will Go to War," American artillery began the massive shelling of Cambodian territory.

The leading American figures who were escalating military operations in Vietnam came forward during the same period—spring and summer of 1966—with a series of public statements explaining United States policy toward the People's Republic of China. While the American leaders had in the past untiringly alleged on every occasion (and even without any occasion at all) aggressive intentions on the part of the People's Republic of China, the pages of the American press were now replete with discussions concerning the caution of the Peking leaders, and their reluctance to become involved in a conflict with the United States. Mao Tse-tung and his associates, it was reported, no longer considered United States imperialists as their principal enemy. American public opinion was obviously being led to think that a major improvement of relations with the People's Republic of China might be in the offing.

It should not be forgotten that this genuflection toward Mao Tse-tung and his group was accompanied by the relentless expansion of American intervention in Vietnam. At the beginning of 1966, President Johnson requested supplementary appropriations in the amount of $12 billion for the Pentagon requirements in Vietnam. The number of American military personnel in Vietnam was increased every day, and by the end of 1966 exceeded 390,000 men—*i.e.*, more than doubled that year. And in the U.S. Senate, voices were already heard speaking of the necessity to increase the number of American soldiers in Vietnam to half-a-million men.

At the same time, certain Americans launched an appeal "to settle" the situation in Southeast Asia through direct negotiations with the leadership of the People's Republic of China. On June 16, 1966, Senator Mike Mansfield, speaking in New York, said that "an initiative for a direct contact between the Peking government and our own government on the problem of peace in Vietnam and Southeast Asia" was urgently needed. Senator Mansfield frankly suggested a meeting between the U.S. Secretary of State and the Minister of Foreign Affairs of the People's Republic of China. If one considers that Mansfield replaced President Lyndon Johnson as the Democratic party leader in the U.S. Senate and was always his own man in Washington's highest governmental echelon, then this proposal acquires a special meaning.

The advances made by the Washington politicians toward Mao Tse-tung and his group inevitably caused anxiety in Taiwan, where Chiang Kai-shek still persisted in his sole ambition: the return to mainland China. The improvement in relations between the People's Republic of China and the United States had no place at all in his plans, and he tried to exert pressure upon Washington through both his official representatives and the influential Chiang Kai-shek lobbyists. The Minister of Defense of the Chiang Kai-shek government visited Washington at the end of 1965, met with President Johnson, and held a full series of discussions with leading representatives of the United States Armed Forces and intelligence services. The Chiang Kai-shek representatives simultaneously offered the South Vietnamese authorities technical aid, as well as assistance in organizing so-called "psychological warfare" against both the National Liberation Front of South Vietnam and the Democratic Republic of Vietnam.

It was rumored in Washington that Chiang Kai-shek troops might be used in Vietnam. That talk reached the point where Senator Dirksen introduced an official proposal to increase military aid to the Chiang Kai-shek regime by $100 million, to modernize its army for use in Vietnam. Dirksen withdrew his proposal only when representatives of the Departments of State and Defense assured him that if the decision were made to deploy Chiang Kai-shekist forces in Vietnam, the forces would be armed and equipped with everything that they needed.

It is also interesting that during this period the traditional demands from Peking for the liberation of Taiwan were heard with significantly less frequency, and that units of the People's Liberation Army which were deployed in the region of the Taiwan Strait took no action whatsoever against the Chiang Kai-shekists. From all appearances, the "tacit mutual understanding" reached between the United States and the People's Republic of China on the Vietnam problem extended additionally to the Taiwan Strait.

At that very time, on July 10, 1966, the Peking newspaper *Jenmin Jihpao* published an article with the extremely eloquent title: "Depend on your own forces and you will be invincible." This advice, the article made clear, was addressed to the Vietnamese people and obviously pointed out that they could not count on any aid from Peking in the struggle against American aggression. The American press interpreted this article in just this way.

The change in Washington's policy toward the People's Republic of China received wide commentary in the American press. Earlier even important reports from the People's Republic of China would not be covered by newspapers and magazines; but now, the American press not only watched closely the important events, but even printed many photographs of Mao Tse-tung and his closest associates. The press began to note not just the content, but the slightest change in nuance of the statements issued from Peking. In many instances, reports on events in the People's Republic of China began to receive large headlines and front page press coverage. The American press was pursuing two goals: first, to discredit the successes achieved in the building of socialism in the People's Republic of China and, by the same token, to discredit the Communist movement as a whole; and second, to portray as clearly as possible the readiness of the Peking leaders to "reach an amicable agreement" with the United States.

An article by Max Frankel, published in *The New York Times* on November 16, 1966, is very significant in this connection. "A remarkable byproduct of the upheaval in China known as the 'cultural revolution' is the simultaneous moderation of Peking's threats of intervention in the war in Vietnam," Frankel wrote. "Although ideological dogmatists appear to have the upper hand in Peking, they have not been as strident or menacing toward the United States as they were a year ago." American Sinologists, Frankel observed, "have found a marked reduction in the belligerence of the Chinese commentaries on the war" in Vietnam. U.S. observers, he wrote, were aware of the fact that, ever since the "cultural revolution," the Chinese "have been even more circumspect than usual in defining this threshold" beyond which the People's Republic of China would take retaliatory measures, "and they have not for several months uttered the once familiar threat that they would not indefinitely stand idly by if Hanoi summoned their direct help."

In the opinion of American Sinologists, this position taken by the People's Republic of China was attributable to at least two factors. First, there was "the diminishing fear in Peking of a United States attack on China." The Peking leaders, Frankel emphasized, "are thought to have been reassured by strenuous signals from Washington that the United States is not seeking an opportunity to widen the war, to bomb Chinese nuclear installations, or otherwise attack the Chinese directly." And second, the Sinologists noted, there was a feeling of weakness produced by the political confusion which accompanied the "cultural revolution."

Thus, the rumors of a "tacit mutual understanding" between the United States and the People's Republic of China were widely discussed by the American press, without prompting any denials from either the Washington authorities or the Peking leaders. In light of this, a UPI wire service report on the growing trade between the United States and China came as no surprise to anyone. The American press noted simultaneously that trade between the People's Republic of China and the Soviet Union, which in 1955 comprised 21.4 percent of the total volume of Soviet trade, declined in 1966 to 1.9 percent, and the volume of trade between the People's Republic of China and the capitalist countries increased significantly. In 1966 alone, exports from China to six capitalist countries—Canada, Great Britain (including Hong Kong), Japan, France, the Federal Republic of Germany, and Italy—grew by 25 percent over the previous year, and imports from these countries by 37.5 percent.

The world press paid particular attention to the "tacit mutual understanding" between the United States and the People's Republic of China concerning Hong Kong and Singapore. Hong Kong was widely used by the American military clique for resupply and repairs of U.S. warships which directly participated in the Vietnam war. U.S. Navy servicemen vacationed and "recuperated" in Hong Kong before being sent to Vietnam. According to records of the Hsin Hua agency, American warships visited Hong Kong approximately 80 times during the first two-and-a-half months of 1967 alone. Among these were the flagship of the U.S. Seventh Fleet, the "Providence," the nuclear aircraft carrier "Enterprise," the aircraft carriers "Franklin D. Roosevelt" and "Bennington," the cruiser "Long Beach" and others.

It might seem at first glance that these visits by American warships to the British colony of Hong Kong had no relevance to American-Chinese relations. But the fact is that Hong Kong receives practically all its provisions and drinking water from the People's Republic of China, and thus the American warriors in Hong Kong were literally fed on "Chinese chow," while the potable water tanks of the American warships were overflowing with Chinese water. This fact may seem unimportant, but it is actually very noteworthy. In any case, both the American and Chinese press were of a rare unanimity in their mutual silence. Peking's taciturnity is fully explained by its mercenary considerations—the delivery of Chinese provisions and drinking water to Hong Kong brought Peking over $480 million in 1966 alone. And

Washington, certainly, had no reason to expose the true face of the Peking leaders.

Some additional light was shed on the behind-the-scenes trade arrangements between the People's Republic of China and the United States in December 1966. According to a report by the British journalist Dennis Bloodworth, the People's Republic of China sold several thousand tons of steel in 1966 to Singapore industrialists, who promptly redirected the steel to South Vietnam for construction of American military bases. As Dennis Bloodworth pointed out, steel was provided by the People's Republic of China at that moment "when only Peking could plug a crucial gap in American supplies by meeting the specifications, the quantities and the six-week delivery date that would satisfy . . . U.S. military purchasing officers." Several days later, these reports were confirmed by the Singapore correspondents of the UPI wire service and *The New York Times*. According to various records, the total amount of steel purchases ranged between $600,000 and $1 million, with payments made through Hong Kong banks. These figures were subsequently confirmed by the official trade statistics of Singapore.

2. *"CONTAINMENT WITH CONCILIATION"*

By mid-1966, according to *The New York Times*, "a review of American policy toward Peking was no longer in doubt, it was only a question of time." In the opinion of the Foreign Policy Association specialists, 1966 was the year in which the United States began its "new" China policy, which may best be described as "containment with conciliation." These same specialists simultaneously noted that the new policy was based on the old colonial principle of the "carrot and stick."

American political scientists give several reasons for the shift of the American ruling circles from the policy of "isolation and limited hostility" to one of "containment with conciliation." First, Mao Tse-tung's anti-Soviet course continued to exert a major influence upon the change in American policy. As the Foreign Policy Association experts wrote: "The Sino-Soviet rift was a development of singular importance, for it opened a sweeping new range of possibilities to U.S. policy-makers for exploitation." *The New York Times* stated in plain terms just what these possibilities were. "It is necessary to work out a strategy," the newspaper advised, "which would influence the discussions in Peking, and also between Peking and Moscow, in a direction favorable to us." Second, Washington finally understood that the policy of isolation had failed. Third, the atomic explosion in the People's Republic of China required the American government to review the situation in light of changed conditions. And fourth, the policy of sharp escalation of the Vietnam war called into question the advisability of the policy of "limited hostility" toward the People's Republic of China, and generated an effort to "thaw by any means the existing state of mutual hostility" between the United States and the People's Republic of China. The fact that a number of American specialists were of the opinion that the People's Republic of China was in no position to threaten the fundamental interests of the United States also played a major role. All these circumstances, taken in their full complexity, caused the United States government to re-examine its policy, in words if not by deed.

The fundamental aspects of the "new" U.S. policy toward China, a policy characterized by the American press as a political counter-strike, were formulated by Secretary of State Dean Rusk. The policy had the following main features: First, an increase in the so-called unofficial contacts between the United States and the People's Republic of China, by means of exchanges between scholars, businessmen, journalists, etc., was contemplated. Second, the United States proclaimed an "open door" principle, which in this case envisaged an expansion of diplomatic contacts and a readiness to discuss with the People's Republic of China such problems as disarmament and non-proliferation of nuclear weapons. At the same time, the United States calculated that the leaders of the People's Republic of China would announce that they were not hostile toward America. Furthermore, the United States intended to continue its objection to the exclusion of the Chiang Kai-shek regime from the United Nations, and to maintain programs of assistance to all Asian countries which were "fighting Communism."

An analysis of these characteristics of America's "new" China policy makes it impossible to quarrel with those who assert that it was based on the old principle of the "carrot and stick." One can add only that this policy reeked of the musty spirit of anti-Communism and was intended primarily to draw its support from the anti-Soviet tendencies in the leadership of the People's Republic of China.

On May 13, 1967, the *Chicago Daily News* began to publish a series of ten articles by Simon Malley, a "naturalized citizen of the United States." Malley wrote the articles after a visit to the People's Republic of China, where he claimed to have had lengthy interviews with Chou En-lai and other leading figures among Mao Tse-tung's associates. According to Malley, the Peking leaders assured him that the People's

Republic of China did not intend openly to come to the aid of the Democratic Republic of Vietnam, or to send its volunteers there. Chou En-lai pointed out to Malley, however, that the "position" of the People's Republic of China could be re-examined if American troops invaded the Democratic Republic of Vietnam and approached the Chinese border, or if a "sell-out peace" were concluded in Vietnam.

Many American newspapers reprinted these revelations under bold headlines on their front pages. At the same time, "unofficial comments" by a State Department representative appeared in a number of newspapers, primarily expressing the view that Malley's stories contained no new information for the Department of State, because its staff had read all ten articles prior to publication. An extremely significant confession! One cannot overlook the fact that an anonymous State Department representative deemed it necessary to comment on and clarify Chou En-lai's statement. The spokesman emphasized that the People's Republic of China might intervene in the Vietnam war only if U.S. troops, after invading the Democratic Republic of Vietnam, directly approached the Chinese borders. If U.S. forces invaded the southern part of the Democratic Republic of Vietnam, located far from the Chinese border, there was no danger of intervention by the People's Republic of China. One can only marvel at the striking familiarity of the American State Department officials with the intentions of the People's Republic of China.

Also notable in this regard is a statement which appeared in the newspaper *Paris Jour* at the beginning of 1967, following the 132nd regular meeting of American and Chinese ambassadors in Warsaw on January 25, 1967. "There exists a more or less tacit agreement between Washington and Peking on the limitation of the Vietnam conflict," wrote *Paris Jour.* "Authoritative representatives of the United States and People's China have continued uninterrupted the confidential negotiations on this subject. These have been held in Warsaw and elsewhere, both within and outside of the framework of the regular Chinese-American meetings on the ambassadorial level. More important yet, the sessions have taken place continuously, with the consent even of Mao himself and the adherents of the 'hard line.' Furthermore, it is well known that Chou En-lai is, in fact, personally responsible for these contacts. As for the substance of the agreement, its principal component is as follows: In exchange for the silent promise of the Americans not to carry their aggression into the territory of China itself, Peking must avoid any direct intervention in Vietnam."

Commenting on these reports, the world press came to the unanimous conclusion that a major improvement in relations between

Washington and Peking was really not such an impossibility. "President Johnson regularly returns to his plan to 'build a bridge' between the U.S. and China," wrote the newspaper *Combat*. "Now the news concerning the beginning of a constructive dialogue between the U.S. Ambassador in Warsaw, John Gronouski, and his Chinese colleague Wang Kuo-chan, has, after their 133rd meeting, been confirmed. Vietnam, of course is not the only obstacle to relations between Peking and Washington. There is still Taiwan, SEATO and everything else. But nonetheless, normalization of relations between Washington and Peking does not seem at all impossible."

Combat drew attention additionally to an extremely important circumstance in American-Chinese relations, namely, the existing contradictions between the United States and the People's Republic of China on a number of important problems, such as Vietnam, Taiwan, the U.S. position in the United Nations, and the aggressive U.S. blocs in Asia. There were, in fact, major areas of dispute, which sometimes seemed, at first glance, even irreconcilable. It undoubtedly would be impossible to disregard the influence which these problems had on the further development of American-Chinese relations. It should be emphasized, however, that the evolution of U.S. foreign policy toward the People's Republic of China was not determined primarily by these contradictions, but by the shift in the foreign policy of the People's Republic of China from a socialist to a nationalist position, and by the creation, on this basis, of conditions for new relations between the U.S. ruling circles and the chauvinist Mao Tse-tung group.

The U.S. ruling circles, as the verbal advocates of "peaceful normalization," extended to the leadership of the People's Republic of China the "carrot" of economic cooperation. But they did not at the same time relinquish the "stick," for they further escalated military operations in Vietnam and brought the flame of war ever closer to the borders of the People's Republic of China. During the summer and early fall of 1967, the President of the United States issued an order to begin the bombing of targets located within the immediate vicinity of the borders of the People's Republic of China, which produced a new wave of questions concerning Peking's possible reaction. White House Press Secretary George Christian stated in response, on behalf of the President, that the U.S. authorities were "confident Peking is aware that the United States does not seek involvement in Red China." *The New York Times* stressed that President Johnson had "expressed confidence that Peking will not react dangerously."

The official White House assurances, however, inevitably caused astonishment among many Americans who asked, very reasonably, in letters to newspaper editors: What basis has the United States government for the prediction of possible actions of the Peking leaders? Furthermore, many readers stressed their inability to understand how Peking could know the exact intentions of the United States if, to quote the writers of a collective letter to *The New York Times*, "responsible people throughout the world differ as to the Administration's true intent." These same readers asked: "How can the American government be confident of China's reaction, even if China is aware of the United States' intentions?"

Public officials furnished no straight answers to this question, although American newspapers and magazines continued to print reports from Hong Kong during 1967 that "the lack of desire to intervene in the Vietnam events was ever increasing" within the leadership of the People's Republic of China. Furthermore, the best informed journalists hinted that American-Chinese negotiations were being held not only in Warsaw, but in some "Hong Kong bar room."

The events of 1964-67, and especially the escalation of the Vietnam war by the United States ruling circles, constitute irrefutable evidence that a "tacit mutual understanding" existed even at that time between Washington and Peking, and it was, if not a written agreement, a factual one. There is also every reason to assert that a similar "mutual understanding" continues in effect regarding the region around the Taiwan Strait, which has been noticeably quiet since 1964. This "tacit mutual understanding" with the United States imperialist circles is part of the chauvinist, Great Power course of the Mao Tse-tung group, a course designed, as *Pravda* observed, to "undermine the unity of the world socialist alliance and the international Communist movement, and which contradicts the interests of the people's revolutionary struggle." It formed, at the same time, the basis of the new U.S. policy toward the People's Republic of China—"containment with conciliation."

CHAPTER VII

"ISOLATION WITHOUT CONTAINMENT"

1. *THE AMERICAN CONGRESS AND THE CHINA PROBLEM*

The final years of the Democratic party's occupancy of the White House were marked by the initiation of a widespread propaganda campaign designed to prepare the ordinary American for a possible fundamental change in policy toward the People's Republic of China. Newspapers and magazines began to publish regularly articles on China, and the production of books on this subject increased sharply. The three-volume *China Reader*, issued in 1967 by the large New York publisher Random House, the eight-volume series titled *The United States and China in World Affairs*, published between 1966 and 1968 by the McGraw-Hill book company, and a whole series of other publications may be cited as examples.

In the United States Congress, one hearing followed another during this period on various aspects of American policy toward the People's Republic of China and the problems of Sino-Soviet relations. Leading figures in the Department of State appeared before various public organizations to explain the "realistic approach" toward the People's Republic of China. The well-known American satirist Art Buchwald wrote in this connection that "one of the most astounding discoveries in history was made recently when a group of State Department people found a new country named Red China." The humorist's words convey rather accurately the atmosphere of that period. Earlier, even simple mention of the People's Republic of China was considered a sign of "bad taste," but now, many people—from the President of the United States and leading congressmen to reporters for local newspapers—began to discuss the desirability of improved relations with the People's Republic of China.

During these years the U.S. Congress played a considerable role in the reorientation of the country's public opinion with regard to the People's Republic of China. This was not just coincidence. As the American journalist Archibald T. Steele asserted: "It is natural for Americans to look to Congress to take the lead in debating and evaluating problems of transcendent national importance." Steele emphasized that "United States policy toward China is a product of the interplay between the Administration, the Congress, public opinion and various pressure groups." One such group, mentioned earlier, is the "China lobby."

The U.S. Senate and the House of Representatives repeatedly discussed U.S. policy toward China, both in open sessions of each House and behind closed doors—in various committees and subcommittees. High-ranking representatives of the American government, diplomats and generals, professors and intelligence officers, appeared before the congressmen to comment on the most varied aspects of American policy toward the People's Republic of China and, dwelling on the finest nuances, to discuss the numerous options and counter-alternatives for possible changes in this policy. It should be noted that the congressmen did not dare at first to discuss publicly the government's policy toward China. The U.S. Senate Committee on Foreign Relations intended to conduct open hearings in 1959 on this problem, with emphasis upon the Conlon Report. But the government unmistakably hinted at that time that such hearings would be both inopportune and undesirable, and the senators did not press the issue.

The congressmen's attention was once more directed to the problem of China only a few years later, in the spring of 1964, when the Democratic Senator from Arkansas, J. William Fulbright, the Chairman of the Senate Committee on Foreign Relations, delivered a speech titled "Old Myths and New Realities," in which he sharply criticized the government's entire foreign policy, and particularly its China policy. Fulbright observed that "We are committed, with respect to China . . . to inflexible policies of long standing, from which we hesitate to depart because of the attribution to these policies of an aura of mystical sanctity." The Senator drew further attention to the fact that there are not, in reality, "two Chinas," but instead only one "mainland China, and that is ruled by Communists and likely to remain so for the indefinite future." Gazing into the future, Fulbright asserted that "It is not impossible that in time our relations with China will change again, if not to friendship, then perhaps to 'competitive coexistence.' " He therefore advised the American government to retain "the capacity to be flexible in our relations with Communist China."

In the opinion of a number of American specialists, Fulbright's speech preceded a serious reawakening of congressional interest in the China problem. The fact that the Senator received more than 12,000 letters in response to his speech, with the overwhelming majority of writers approving of Fulbright's proposals, contributed to this renewed interest. The speech received wide coverage in the American press, not so much because of the Senator's own prominence, but because the thesis of his speech reflected the opinion of extremely influential circles within American society.

Reaction to the Senator's speech among government circles, big business and the influential news media, as well as ordinary Americans demonstrated that it was clearly time for the U.S. Congress to arouse itself from what A. T. Steele called its "frozen" state on the question of the government's China policy—the state in which it found itself as a result of "pressures of the right, on one side, and the failures of our China policy on the other."

The first hearings on the China problem were held in March 1965 by the Subcommittee on the Far East and Pacific of the U.S. House of Representatives Foreign Affairs Committee. The subject of these hearings, as it turned out, was the anti-Soviet policy of the Mao Tse-tung group and its possible consequences for the United States. This time, the American government not only refrained from objecting to the discussion of China policy in the U.S. Congress, but even actively cooperated with the subcommittee, which held ten sessions, including four behind closed doors. At its open sessions, the subcommittee heard 17 witnesses, including such well-known American figures as Professor George Kennan of Princeton University, the former U.S. Ambassador to the U.S.S.R. and Yugoslavia; Roger Hilsman, the former Assistant Secretary of State for Far Eastern Affairs; China specialists Lucian Pye, Robert A. Scalapino, George Taylor, Donald Zagoria, and Harold Hinton; and the leading American "specialists on problems of Communism," Zbigniew Brzezinski and William Griffith.

Appearing at the closed subcommittee sessions were Secretary of State Rusk; leading officials of the Department of State, including Marshall Green, Richard Davis, and James Leonard; and officials of the Central Intelligence Agency and military intelligence. Secretary of State Rusk noted in his statement that the congressmen were discussing a question which "is one of the most important matters that we have in front of us as a nation." Nonetheless, the American press, according to A. T. Steele, gave these hearings "only cursory attention, and congressional reactions were scanty."

Less than a year later, the same congressional subcommittee held new hearings, this time on the subject of "United States Policy in Asia." In fact, the government's China policy was discussed at these sessions once again, and Dean Rusk's remarks therein received wide publicity, both in the American press and in special publications of the Department of State. Rusk called attention to the fact that the words of the Peking leaders differed sharply from their actions. "It is true," he said, "that they* have been more cautious in action than in words . . . more cautious in what they do themselves than in what they have urged the Soviet Union to do. . . . They have shown, in many ways, that they have a healthy respect for the power of the United States." Rusk considered it essential at that point to state that the United States had, for its part, reassured the leaders of the People's Republic of China "both publicly and privately" that the United States did not want war with China.

Outlining future American policy toward China, the Secretary of State emphasized that Washington intended to "enlarge the possibilities for unofficial contacts." Rusk noted in this regard that certain steps had already been taken in this direction. The American authorities, for example, had "gradually expanded the categories of American citizens who may travel to Communist China. American libraries may freely purchase Chinese Communist publications. American citizens may send and receive mail from the mainland." Rusk also stated that Washington had "indicated . . . willingness" to permit journalists from the People's Republic of China to visit the United States, and would also allow American universities to invite Chinese scholars to the United States.

It is noteworthy that the proposal to admit Chinese journalists to the United States was first made confidentially during the Warsaw discussions. It is significant that the United States, having made this proposal, frankly stated that it did not envision reciprocal travel by American journalists to the People's Republic of China. Thus, a substantial exception was made for the People's Republic of China, because the exchange of journalists with the socialist countries had traditionally been conducted on a bilateral basis. In fact, the United States granted to the People's Republic of China the same terms which, until then, had been given only to capitalist countries.

Several days before Rusk made his remarks, the President lifted the ban on travel by American scholars to the People's Republic of China, and Rusk announced that Chinese scholars would be permitted to visit the United States. All these measures might have been welcomed, if only they had not been engendered by the peculiar position adopted by the Peking leadership, the anti-Sovietism of the Maoist group, the

---

*Mao Tse-tung and his group (*Author's note*)

efforts to split the international Communist movement, and the desire to prolong the Vietnam war. And it was no coincidence that Rusk, in announcing these steps by the American government, once again emphasized that "The Chinese Communists . . . acted with caution when they foresaw the possibility of a confrontation with the United States."

Secretary of Defense McNamara expressed himself in the same vein when he appeared before the Senate Armed Services Committee in February 1966. "The Chinese Communists," McNamara said, "have thus far displayed great caution in an effort to avoid direct confrontation with the United States military forces in Asia. . . . There is every reason to conclude that Peiping is determined to press the conflict in Vietnam at the expense of the Vietnamese people." During these very same days, the United States resumed the bombing of the Democratic Republic of Vietnam.

The following people, in addition to Rusk, appeared before the congressmen: William Bundy, Assistant Secretary of State for Far Eastern Affairs; Harald Jacobson, the director of a State Department office; John D. Rockefeller III, Bronson Clark, Willem Holst and other representatives of big business; retired generals Thomas A. Lane and Samuel B. Griffith; China specialists A. Doak Barnett, O. Edmund Clubb (the former U.S. Consul-General in Peking) and Alexander Eckstein; Professors Hans J. Morgenthau and Ralph Powell; Kenneth Young, president of the Asia Society; former officials of the Department of State, and journalists. Invited to appear from Canada were James Duncan, the Deputy Canadian Minister of Defense, who had visited the People's Republic of China in 1959 and 1964, and the journalist Charles Taylor, who was in Peking from May 1964 to October 1965 as a correspondent for *The Toronto Globe and Mail*. The subcommittee's conclusions were hardly notable for their novelty. The United States' European allies were urged to support American policy toward the People's Republic of China and to assume part of the expenditures for maintenance of the Western Powers' armed forces in Asia. The subcommittee simultaneously took cognizance of the new trends by recommending "that we enlarge our limited peaceful contacts with the mainland of China."

While the House subcommittee was still in session, another organ of the U.S. Congress—the Senate Foreign Relations Committee—had already begun its own hearings on the problem of "United States Policy toward Mainland China." J. William Fulbright, the Chairman of the committee, emphasized that "The immediate purpose of these hearings is educational. At this stage, perhaps the most effective contribution the committee can make is to provide a forum for recognized experts and scholars in the field of China. I hope that these hearings in this way will increase the knowledge of China, our knowledge in Congress and the public's knowledge."

The following prominent U.S. Sinologists appeared before the committee: Fairbank, Scalapino, Barnett, Eckstein, Lindbeck, Zagoria, Taylor and others, as well as the former Congressman Judd and General Griffith. During these hearings the "new" United States policy toward the People's Republic of China was characterized as "containment without isolation," a policy of promoting "maximum contacts" with the People's Republic of China, while maintaining its "minimum of involvement" in the affairs of the international community.

These sessions, unofficially called the "Fulbright hearings," attracted the widespread attention of the American public. One *New York Times* reader wrote in a letter to the editor that the hearings were "an exercise in political sanity," because Americans were in a "neurotic darkness" about China, which manifested itself particularly in the fact that Americans "pretend that China does not exist." *The New York Herald Tribune* said that the Fulbright hearings demonstrated, first and foremost, an "astonishing tolerance" by the fact that such hearings could even take place. In the newspaper's opinion, congressional hearings on this issue, if held just a few years earlier, would have aroused a storm of protest from supporters of the late Senator McCarthy. And the fact that this furor did not arise was indicative of the dramatic shift in public opinion with regard to China. Second, the hearings showed a "striking lack of knowledge" about Communist China among a large number of senators. *The New York Herald Tribune* contended, with good reason, that the Fulbright hearings had evoked "unexpected interest in China" among many people in Washington as well as throughout the entire country.

Others, while not denying the significance of the Fulbright hearings, cautioned against exaggerating their impact. Professor Charles B. McLane, for example, wrote that "American policy toward China is an immensely complex political question and must be determined by fully responsible political figures in the government. No one, of course, would question the relevance of the senators studying the problem, though it is the President who must make the ultimate determination, on advice from the State Department and other counsel." Retired General Barry Goldwater, the mouthpiece of American reactionaries, found the Fulbright hearings disgusting.

The United States government, however, reacted to the Senate committee proceedings very favorably. As the American press pointed out, President Johnson was "greatly pleased with these hearings" and totally concurred with Fulbright's opinion that the hearings "cast some light on this immense land whose politics we may not approve, but whose existence we cannot ignore." It was further noted that the fact that the China specialists who appeared before the Senate supported the war in Vietnam "with varying degrees of enthusiasm" played no minor role in determining the government's attitude toward the hearings. At the same time, those who appeared at the hearings completely agreed with the opinion of Washington's ruling circles that there was little chance of direct intervention by the People's Republic of China in the Vietnam war as long as the war did not directly threaten China itself. The Fulbright hearings, in the opinion of the Washington Administration, were simultaneously advantageous for minimizing the significance of the possible admission of the People's Republic of China to the United Nations.

The influential *New York Times*, in an editorial titled "The 'Open Door'," published on February 28, 1966, stated: "After long internal debate, the Administration is beginning to move cautiously to increase contact with Communist China. The new policy has begun with an easing of travel restrictions. . . . The struggle in Washington against political timidity, ideological rigidity and bureaucratic inertia that was required to bring about even these minor moves entitles those responsible to an accolade."

At the same time when specialists and scholars on the question of U.S. policy toward China were appearing before the Senate Foreign Relations Committee, high-ranking representatives of the Washington Administration also delivered a series of speeches on this problem. And while official Washington had only recently reacted with harsh criticism to the discussion of the Vietnam problem in that same committee, the government spokesmen—to the surprise of journalists—now showered effusive praise on those whose critical remarks were resounding through the chamber in which the Senate Foreign Relations Committee held its sessions. Vice President Hubert Humphrey's appeal to American journalists "to stimulate broader interest of Americans in the problems of Asia, including China," was extremely significant in this regard.

The United States had, of course, understood for a long time that the "policy of isolation" had completely failed, but still continued to keep it alive until the divisive actions of the Mao Tse-tung group compelled the White House to adopt new measures. And it was no coincidence that leading figures of the Department of State and the President himself began to speak loudly within the United States of a new policy, at the very time when the U.S. imperialist forces sharply expanded the war in Vietnam and instigated their bandit raids on the Democratic Republic of Vietnam. Washington saw the divisive actions of Peking as a distinct call for rapprochement; it understood that Peking was now seeking allies other than the socialist countries, and drew from this realization the appropriate conclusions.

Vice President Hubert H. Humphrey, appearing on the NBC television program "Meet the Press" on March 13, 1966, made a telling comment in this regard. Humphrey dwelt specifically on the problem of American-Chinese relations and spoke out frankly in support of the "containment without isolation" formula proposed by Professor A. Doak Barnett during the Fulbright hearings. The Vice President emphasized at the same time that the new policy would not, in his opinion, in any way reflect on the "Administration's determination to pursue the Vietnam war to a successful conclusion." The newspapers noted that the Vice President then took an extremely unusual position: He began to praise publicly the Senate Foreign Relations Committee hearings on the question of United States policy toward China. By way of explanation, the press pointed out the probability that Humphrey's remarks were an answer to Peking's efforts to reduce the tension between the People's Republic of China and the United States.

These conclusions were borne out by the further actions of American officials. The same Vice President Humphrey, speaking on June 8, 1966, to the graduates of the West Point Military Academy, pointed out that the United States was seeking, and would continue to seek opportunities to "build bridges" between the United States and the People's Republic of China, and that America was "holding open the doors" for negotiations with China. It is interesting to note that only two days after Humphrey's speech, the U.S. Secretaries of Defense and State announced at a joint press conference the dispatch of another contingent of American troops to Vietnam. Neither McNamara nor Rusk, of course, indicated whether any of the West Point graduates to whom Vice President Humphrey had stressed the need to "build bridges" between the United States and the People's Republic of China were included in this contingent.

Commenting on Vice President Humphrey's speech at West Point, the American press emphasized that the U.S. government was endeavoring in every way possible to change its attitude toward the People's Republic of China, "if not in fact, then in words." Interesting in this regard are the comments which appeared in *The New York Times* on June 9, 1966, in a special article concerning Humphrey's speech: "In recent weeks, after years of virtual silence on the subject, Secretary of State Dean Rusk, Secretary of Defense Robert S. McNamara and now

Mr. Humphrey have held out the metaphoric promise of change, if only the Chinese leaders would transform themselves into the more acceptable kind of Communists [!].... The Vice President even hinted a willingness to share the blame for Peking's past isolation.... But the widespread impression here is that at least some of the official speeches are meant to encourage ..." the critics of the American government's China policy.

As in times past, this recurrent thaw in the relations between the United States and People's Republic of China was accompanied by a renewal of the U.S. military clique's aggressive actions in Vietnam. In fact, the Senate hearings on China held during the first half of 1966 culminated in the Senate's direct support of the American Administration on the fundamental issue—waging war in Vietnam—while simultaneously paving the way for a more flexible U.S. policy toward the People's Republic of China, a policy which, at that particular stage, was more in line with the interests of American monopolies. And, of course, the Fulbright hearings focused the interests of the American press on the People's Republic of China and led to wide publicity of the China problem in a way that was advantageous to the U.S. ruling circles.

A year passed, and in April 1967 the Joint Economic Committee of the U.S. Congress held a four-day hearing on the problem of "Mainland China in the World Economy." The hearing was preceded by twenty reports on varied aspects of economic life in the People's Republic of China, prepared by "recognized specialists on China." Additional assistance in the preparation of reports was provided by the Department of State, the Central Intelligence Agency, the Department of the Interior, the Department of Agriculture, and other U.S. government agencies. The reports covered a broad and diverse array of topics, including the economic problems of China's defense system; the availability of mineral resources; main trends of economic policy; the tempo of economic development; agriculture; problems of planning and management; population growth and its employment; the monetary and banking system; scientific research activity and education; foreign trade of the Chinese People's Republic; its aid to developing countries, and a whole list of other important problems related to the country's economic development.

The participants in the discussion of problems raised in the committee sessions were the former U.S. Ambassador to Japan, Edwin O. Reischauer, Professors Gurley, Hoffman, Eckstein, Richman and others. As a result of the hearings, the Joint Economic Committee of the U.S. Congress reached the conclusion that the American embargo on trade in non-strategic goods with the People's Republic of China actually accomplished nothing, and was even possibly harmful to the United States from the standpoint of its long-range interests. The committee stated plainly that, from an economic vantage point, the trade embargo against the Chinese People's Republic was in no way justified, and could only be sanctioned as a part of America's international political activity. The Joint Economic Committee thereby unequivocally recognized that the United States economic blockade was utilized as a means of placing political pressure upon the People's Republic of China.

The discussion of U.S. policy toward China in the various congressional committees culminated in a proposal advanced by a number of senators that the President of the United States should appoint a special commission which, according to Senator Edward Kennedy, would conduct a "major reassessment" of America's entire China policy. Senator George McGovern, speaking in favor of Kennedy's proposal in the Congress, observed that the United States, in making "anti-Communism the guiding principle of our policy in Asia," very often had "become identified with corrupt, stupid and ineffective dictators" in a number of Asian countries.

Senator Kennedy's proposal was supported by many congressmen. A State Department spokesman, however, "showed little enthusiasm for the proposal," according to American journalists. It is nevertheless significant that a short time thereafter, the Secretary of State appointed two advisory commissions composed of scholars, businessmen and journalists. One was to concern itself with problems of East Asia and the Pacific Basin, and the other with China problems. The China problem was additionally reflected in the hearings conducted by the Senate Foreign Relations Committee in February and March of 1968 on the subject "Essence of Revolution." Professors R. Solomon of the University of Michigan and J. Thomson of Harvard University discussed during these hearings the characteristics of the Chinese revolution, and emphasized the need to understand these in order to determine the general political course of the United States in Asia.

2. *AMERICA'S PRESS VIEWS CHINA*

The China hearings held on Capitol Hill received extensive coverage in the American press. Detailed transcripts were made available to academic circles in the United States, and several publishing houses reprinted lengthy excerpts from these transcripts for the broad masses of readers. The hearings stimulated a series of conferences on the problems of China, held at various universities around the country, which quite often attracted a very large attendance. Professors who were China specialists, State Department officials and journalists often lectured at these conferences, and the local press devoted a great deal of attention to the materials presented therein.

A number of large American newspapers published special articles on China during the last years of the Johnson Administration. *The New York Times*, for example, carried a series of articles by its own leading correspondent, Harrison Salisbury, as well as a series of reports by the Peking correspondent of the Canadian newspaper *The Globe and Mail*. The Boston *Christian Science Monitor* published ten articles by Professor Lucian Pye. During these years influential American magazines devoted entire issues to China and published lengthy extracts from books about the country. Television and radio networks sharply increased the number of programs on China. Several State Department officials, including Assistant Secretaries of State Nicholas Katzenbach and Eugene Rostow, delivered speeches on China problems.

Many well known Sinologists began to give public lectures on China during that period. At the beginning of 1968, for example, Alexander Eckstein, a professor of economics at the University of Michigan, addressed the Americans for Democratic Action on the topic "Events in China and Their Significance for U.S. Policy." Eckstein, author of the book *Communist China's Economic Growth and Foreign Trade: Implications for U.S. Policy*, was a member of the U.S. State Department advisory group on China. In his report Eckstein stated that the United States must adhere to a conciliatory position toward the People's Republic of China. He deemed it necessary to emphasize the "striking caution" of the People's Republic of China in its actions. "Despite the cultural revolution," Eckstein observed, "China is taking a very cautious position with regard to Vietnam and the presence of the American Navy in Asia." Eckstein pointed out that, according to President Johnson's "State of the Union" message, the United States was prepared to relax the embargo on trade and enter into economic and commercial relations with the People's Republic of China; he stressed that such a step on Washington's part "would have political significance. It would demonstrate the willingness and desire of the United States to end the isolation and begin a policy of dialogue with China."

It is characteristic that the American press noted in a headline during this period that "Some Specialists Say U.S. Aides Exaggerate Peking's Threat" to America. At the same time, certain American political commentators began to hint cautiously at the possibility of a "military conflict" between the People's Republic of China and the U.S.S.R. Extremely significant in this regard is the speech by *The New York Times* commentator Harrison Salisbury, before the members of the Detroit Economic Club on November 11, 1968, in which he flatly "predicted war between the People's Republic of China and the U.S.S.R." The portrayal of a "Peking regime hostile to the United States" gradually disappeared from the pages of American newspapers, magazines and books, and its place was taken by the portrayal of the Peking leadership as an eminently respectable, though somewhat eccentric, circle of people who were leading the most populous nation in the world.

The thrust of the research on China simultaneously underwent major changes. While earlier studies of the People's Republic of China were devoted exclusively to its military-strategic, political and economic situation, the China researchers in the late Sixties began to study as well such problems as the methods employed by the People's Republic of China in conducting foreign policy and foreign economic negotiations. Thus, one of the "Rand Corporation" reports of February 1968 was devoted to problems relating to the "style" of the political life and foreign policy of the People's Republic of China. The former American Ambassador to Thailand, Kenneth T. Young, authored a major study titled *Negotiating with the Chinese Communists: The United States Experience, 1953-1967*, which dealt with the course of American-Chinese negotiations on the ambassadorial level in Warsaw. Other works on similar subjects were also published. It is significant that a number of writers were attempting to predict what direction the relations between the United States and the People's Republic of China would take. In this sense, Young's book is characteristic. Young, well acquainted with the plans of the Department of State, thought that the "new approach" of the United States to the People's Republic of China could best be expressed by the formula "understanding before contact." Young believed that America's "new strategy" in its relations with China must include six basic features: First, the United States must, above all, strengthen and improve "the sub-diplomatic system of the ambassadorial talks." In time, these negotiations would, Young believed, include meetings between the foreign ministers of both countries. Young considered the discussions between the United States and Chinese ambassadors to have been more beneficial to the United States than normal diplomatic relations with the People's Republic of China had been to other countries. For this reason, Young believed that "the sub-diplomatic system of the ambassadorial talks" must remain for some time as the only diplomatic channel between the United States and the People's Republic of China.

Young believed that it was preferable for the United States not to hasten formal recognition of the People's Republic of China and the establishment of diplomatic relations. But he felt that the subject matter of the discussions between the ambassadors of both countries should at the same time be expanded to include such problems as the conclusion of a bilateral agreement on the non-proliferation of nuclear weapons. The negotiations might also include discussions of the problems of resolving the situation of, and guarantees for, Southeast Asia, determining a mutually acceptable evolution (!) of the situation in the Taiwan Strait, and settling the problems of American-Chinese trade, with even a possibility of U.S. economic aid.

It is most interesting that Young was proposing a discussion at the Ambassadors' talks of the problems of mutual relations between Peking, Washington and Moscow "in terms of the bilateral interests of the Chinese People's Republic and the United States, to safeguard and maintain the integrity, viability, and utility of their joint dealings." In other words, it was proposed to make a deal between the ruling circles of the United States and the People's Republic of China, at the expense of the interests of the Soviet Union and other peace-loving countries. Thus, if Kenneth Young is to be believed (and there is no reason not to believe him), the American ruling circles were even then quite seriously examining the possibility of a behind-the-scenes deal with Mao Tse-tung and his group. Young's report acquires special significance in light of the fact that it was approved by the Department of State even before his book was published.

The second component of America's "new strategy" was to consist, in Young's opinion, of broad "preparatory studies" of China by private and non-governmental American organizations in order to establish a basis for the renewal of contacts with mainland China, with the aim of building "a strong bridge based on objective understanding." We see the reflection herein of President Johnson's so-called "theory of building bridges," a theory which was already in practice at that time, because of the ever-increasing research on China in the United States. As shown previously, this trend toward rapprochement occurred primarily as a result of the anti-Soviet policy of Mao Tse-tung and his group.

Third, the "new strategy" of the United States toward China was to place particular emphasis on the trade and technical exchange of non-strategic goods and materials, in contrast to the exchange of journalists, scholars and businessmen which was proposed in 1966-67. The exchange of books and other materials was to be the first step on the road to restoration of American-Chinese contacts. The implementation of the proposed exchange could be entrusted to a "joint

Chinese-American secretariat," located in Hong Kong or Shanghai. Subsequently, a small number of representatives from the wire services and commercial firms of each country would receive the right to reside in each other's country.

Fourth, the United States should, according to Young, "encourage" the participation of the People's Republic of China in various international conferences, and also "induce" Peking to take part in various bilateral or multilateral arrangements, both within and outside of the United Nations system. American representatives at such conferences and other activities would have the opportunity to enter into unofficial contacts with representatives of the People's Republic of China.

Fifth, Young believed that the "Chinese-American association" should develop only in accordance with the national interests of the United States, which should pursue in regard to the People's Republic of China a "policy of contact and conciliation, with modified containment." It was further understood that such a policy would be pursued regardless of other major international events and would not be subject to pressure from third countries.

And sixth, the issues of American-Chinese relations would be examined in their entire complexity, including mainland China and the problem of Taiwan, as well as that of the Chinese population in other countries.

Young concluded that such a "strategy" would help to "regularize relations between the United States and Peking, and lead to genuine coexistence between the United States and the People's Republic of China."

Kenneth Young's views and recommendations are interesting primarily as evidence that toward the end of the Johnson Administration, the U.S. Department of State was seriously considering possibilities of improving relations with the Peking leaders, and was preparing various positive programs for the development of such relations with the People's Republic of China. The publication of one such program, drafted by Young, was a "trial balloon" of sorts, to test public reaction to this kind of program. The strategic aims of these programs— "contacts and conciliation"—were simultaneously indicated quite plainly.

Regular meetings between the Ambassadors of both Powers were reconvened in Warsaw in mid-1967, in accordance with these aims. It is significant that at the 134th meeting, on January 8, 1968, the Chinese side was not represented by an Ambassador, but by a Chargé d'Affaires. The official U.S. representative explained that Washington agreed to such representation because it considered the Warsaw talks as the only direct contact, and an extremely important one, between the two governments. This meeting continued for more than two hours. In the words of the American Ambassador to the Polish People's Republic, John Gronouski, there was a "frank and serious exchange of views on a large number of problems facing the United States and the Chinese People's Republic."

3. *AMERICA STUDIES CHINA*

The United States has always followed events in Peking with rapt attention. Within the government, the Department of State is officially concerned with problems of relations with China; among its other duties, the Department informs the President and the Congress about all important changes relating to China, and recommends appropriate measures to be taken. Specialists on China problems are concentrated mainly in three divisions of the Department of State: the Offices of Intelligence and Research, Political Affairs, and Planning and Coordination. One Sinologist, A. Doak Barnett, was a Deputy Assistant Secretary of State. There are approximately 70 officials, including a number of leading specialists, in the Department of State who are concerned with China problems.

A special advisory committee on China problems was established in late 1966 at the Department of State. Among its members were Professors A. Doak Barnett, Alexander Eckstein, John K. Fairbank, Robert A. Scalapino, George C. Taylor, Ralph L. Powell, Lucian Pye, and Paul A. Varg; and the retired diplomats Julius C. Holmes, the former U.S. Consul-General in Hong Kong, and Philip Sprouse, the former U.S. Ambassador to Cambodia, who had spent 11 years in China and often met with Chou En-lai. The inclusion in this committee of professors who had criticized official American policy was regarded as a "reflection of Washington's desire to take advantage of new thinking and to display greater flexibility in its China policy." However, it was emphasized that the committee's conclusions were only to be advisory in nature.

American diplomatic representatives in Hong Kong, Japan, Thailand, Taiwan, Singapore, Pakistan, India and certain other countries are the principal sources for the State Department's information on China. But the central collection point for such data is undoubtedly Hong Kong. A. T. Steele, an American journalist who has often traveled to Hong Kong, describes the significance of this British colony: "Hong Kong is by all odds the best listening post for information from Communist China—in some ways better than being stationed in mainland China itself. Here ... observers are in a position to keep a close check on Peking broadcasts, scrutinize translations from mainland newspapers, consult China experts ... of many nationalities, interview travelers and refugees from China, [and] maintain contact with diplomats and intelligence agents. ... Hong Kong attracts a vastly greater volume of reliable information and has better facilities for separating fact from fiction."

American ruling circles devote a great deal of attention to Hong Kong. The U.S. Consulate General located there is the largest American diplomatic representation abroad. According to various figures, 500 to-1,000 diplomats work there. Since the end of 1967, this enormous apparatus has been headed by E. Martin, whom the American press describes as one of the "leading U.S. diplomatic experts on China." American observers in Hong Kong, according to A. T. Steele, are preoccupied with "digging out meaningful bits of information, weighing them, checking them, comparing for hidden meanings, fitting them together into a pattern. ..."

American observers face the task of clarifying, as much as possible, what steps the Peking government intends to take, both in the domestic and international arena. All available political, economic and military information is analyzed, mainly by the officials of the American intelligence community. The magazine *Eastern World* estimates that approximately 85 percent of the American diplomatic, consular and press corps in Hong Kong are CIA employees.

The main source of information for American observers, as mentioned earlier, is the central and local periodical press of the People's Republic of China, as well as its radio broadcasts. The United States government maintains in Hong Kong a whole army of qualified translators, who, according to Steele, translate no less than 33,000 words a day into English. The demand for Chinese newspapers is so great that a contraband trade in these papers flourishes in Hong Kong. Furthermore, "fantastic prices" are often paid for individual issues of newspapers from remote provinces. Reference books, textbooks, scientific works and other printed materials published in the People's Republic of China are also in great demand in Hong Kong. Interested organizations literally snatch them from each other's hands.

Emigrants from the various provinces of the People's Republic of China, whose number increased once the "cultural revolution" began, serve as another important source of information. All emigrants are subject to prejudiced interrogation, first by the representatives of the official authorities and then by journalists. All reports are painstakingly studied, compared and verified. A significant number of foreigners—businessmen and tourists traveling to the People's Republic of China—pass through Hong Kong, and their impressions and testimony serve as one more source of information on events in mainland China. The American consulate in Hong Kong regularly publishes at least three periodicals—*Survey of China Mainland Press, Current Background* and *Selections from China Mainland Magazines.* These publications print translations of almost all basic materials from the Chinese press, quote from the recordings of broadcasts by a number of Chinese radio stations, and provide various reference materials. All this information is immediately sent to Washington. According to the American press, the United States government publishes more than 100 pages of such material each day. A significant number of translations is received by cable from the American consulate in Hong Kong. American services such as the U.S. Information Agency, the "Voice of America" and others also maintain large staffs there. The leading American wire services, newspapers and magazines are widely represented in Hong Kong, as are many American universities and private companies. It is no coincidence that the world press has drawn attention to Hong Kong's gradual emergence as the center of the entire U.S. anti-Communist activity in Southeast Asia. It is from Hong Kong that "world public opinion" is supplied with "news" concocted in the "kitchens" of the American consulate and other United States organizations which finance various pro-American publications; from there, the "Voice of America" broadcasts are transmitted in various languages.

American agencies, according to the magazine *Eastern World*, are financing no less than 26 newspapers and 38 magazines in Hong Kong—not counting the numerous press reviews, special news releases, and other printed matter financed or published by the U.S. Information Agency. The radio interception and translation service of the U.S. Information Agency in Hong Kong issues an enormous quantity of specially selected material for journalists, scholars and other specialists. The American press has very cautiously hinted that Hong Kong is also being used by the U.S. authorities for secret unofficial contacts with representatives of the People's Republic of China.

Hong Kong has also served for many years as an intermediate point through which foreign currency enters the People's Republic of China. However, since the beginning of 1966, well-informed observers have begun to note a reverse movement of currency. *Eastern World* reports that: "It has been known for many years that Chinese private bankers and other leading businessmen in Hong Kong have channeled huge investment funds originated from overseas Chinese sources (and their

American and other associates) into China. Early this year a reverse traffic opened. Hong Kong now serves as a channel for mainland funds placed in Taiwan for investment there. . . . 'Communist' investment in Taiwan is still small, but glaringly symptomatic."

At first glance, these facts might seem implausible. However, they are links in that invisible chain which in recent years has connected the Peking authorities to Washington figures. In this regard, the report that the United States has "shifted the center of regional political and propagandist activities, as well as the center of its defense communications, from Taiwan to Hong Kong," cannot fail to arouse interest.

Information received from Hong Kong is collected in the Department of State and there compared with information received from other points, after which a general picture of events in the People's Republic of China is pieced together. A leading Sinologist in the Department of State, who wished to remain anonymous, drew for an American correspondent the following picture of the kind of information on China which is available to the U.S. ruling circles: "We have pretty good information on the general picture. . . . For example, we have been able to make very accurate estimates of grain production, calculated on a basis of what refugees tell us about weather conditions, food supplies, and so forth. We have an accurate picture of the situation in the coastal areas—Kwantung, Fukien, Chekiang, Shantung, Hopei. . . . We know what life is like in those areas. Also, by analyzing the Communist press, we can tell what the regime is thinking and what it is likely to do. We have a fairly good picture of political conditions and economic conditions—enough on which to base policy." The same State Department staff member admitted additionally that there is a whole series of regions and problems about which Washington "is in the dark." This is primarily the case with regard to the situation in Tientsin, Inner Mongolia and Tibet, the general situation of the national minorities within the People's Republic of China, the mood of the broad masses of workers, as well as certain other problems.

In addition to the Department of State, a number of other U.S. government agencies, primarily the CIA and the Pentagon, are studying, in one way or another, China and problems related to it. The CIA activity surfaces at times and becomes public knowledge. At the beginning of 1967, for example, the Joint Economic Committee of the U.S. Congress published a two-volume *Economic Profile of Mainland China*, which contained information prepared by CIA officials on China's balance of payments for the years 1950-65. According to information in the American press, no less than two other research reports for the "economic profile" were produced by CIA staff members: Robert M. Field's work on "Chinese Communist Industrial Production," and J. G. Godaire's study of "Communist China's Defense Establishment: Some Economic Implications." Earlier yet, in 1960, the CIA prepared information on the foreign and domestic deficit in China's balance of payments.

The American Department of Defense also devotes much serious attention to China. The nature and scale of this research may be judged by two publications of the U.S. Army Headquarters. The first, which appeared in January 1962, was called *Communist China—Ruthless Enemy or Paper Tiger?* The second, *Communist China: A Strategic Survey*, was published in February 1966. As noted in the introduction to the latter, this collection was intended "to probe into the economic, sociological, military and political fabric" of the People's Republic of China, and it was designed for use by those persons who "are charged with the responsibility of planning and making policy."

Most of the research on China is being done by the Pentagon within the framework of the so-called National Defense Education Act, adopted in 1958. Harvard University, in particular, prepared a study on "China and the Atom Bomb," with funds provided by the U.S. Department of Defense. Within the Department of Defense itself, the Far Eastern Division is concerned with China problems. All this demonstrates that at the Headquarters of the U.S. Armed Forces, serious research on the People's Republic of China is being performed. This research is a component part of the entire activity of the government apparatus, and is geared to the study of China as a whole, as well as the specific prospects for American-Chinese relations.

The American press has reported that other U.S. government agencies, including the Departments of Labor, and Health, Education and Welfare, are also involved in the study of various aspects of China. A special joint publication research service exists within the Department of Commerce, which translates into English materials from the People's Republic of China on problems of industry, agriculture, food and materials supply, trade, finance, science, transportation, communication, and so forth.

All the China information which is collected and processed by various government departments is channeled into the residence of the President of the United States—the White House. Here, on the staff of the Special Assistant to the President for National Security Problems, China specialists are also at work. As James Reston has pointed out: "The amount of information on China available to all these men is voluminous. It is sifted, summarized and analyzed, and shipped every day to the officials concerned."

This is the general picture of research on China carried out by the U.S. government apparatus. It is evident that the American government has a large army of specialists concerned only with China problems, which demonstrates the considerable importance which the U.S. ruling circles attribute to the study of American-Chinese relations and prospects for their further development.

It was not without reason that *The New York Times* published in the summer of 1966 an article which asserted that the United States leads the world in the study of China. In support, the newspaper cited statements by the well-known Sinologists William T. de Bary, John K. Fairbank, and Charles O. Hucker. In the opinion of these specialists, America's "leading position" in the study of China was explained, first, by the significant financial support which the American government provides to the Sinologists; second, the generous subsidies of big business; third, the organization within government agencies of a large service for Chinese translations; and fourth, the establishment of a special committee on problems of contemporary China, which encourages scientific research activity relating to China.

Academic research on China is extensively prepared at such universities as Harvard, Columbia, Yale, Michigan, Chicago, California, Washington (Seattle), Stanford, Indiana, Illinois, Wisconsin, Minnesota, Pennsylvania, Princeton, Pittsburgh, Kansas, Colorado, San Francisco and several others. It should be noted, in addition, that many universities have enormous specialized libraries at their disposal. Harvard University, for example, where more than 100 graduate students are engaged in the study of China, has 300,000 volumes on China. Columbia University, where in 1966 the problems of China were studied by 90 graduate students and 225 undergraduates, has at its disposal a library of books on China totalling more than 150,000 volumes. Incidentally, the American press has pointed out that many American universities have been receiving for years, without any difficulty, all necessary literature from the People's Republic of China.

A number of universities have organized centers for the study of the Chinese language, with funds specially appropriated by the government. It is also significant that in recent years the study of the Chinese language has been introduced as well in many American secondary schools. The Ford, Rockefeller and Carnegie Foundations grant to universities enormous sums for the study of various problems, including those of China. Columbia University, for example, received at one time approximately half-a-million dollars for purposes of "research on the political evolution of modern China." Harvard University was allocated a quarter-of-a-million dollars for research on the contemporary Chinese economy. The Social Science Research Council received for similar studies almost a million dollars. Columbia University received $250,000 from the Carnegie Foundation for training 12 newspaper correspondents who were to elucidate in the press the problems of China and Japan. It is possible to cite many such instances.

The availability of sizable funds allows a number of universities to organize academic conferences on China problems. One can note, for example, the four-day conference held at the University of Chicago in February 1967, which discussed foreign policy problems of the People's Republic of China, and also the "worldwide implications of the domestic power struggle" in that country for international relations. The conference reports were not published; it did become known, however, that the participants were unanimous in their opinion that a victory of the Mao Tse-tung group was more advantageous to the West than a victory of Mao's opponents. Those who presented papers believed that "a victory by Mao excludes even a partial reconciliation [of China] with the Soviet Union. If he wins, China will not solve its economic problems." The conferees were in agreement that the Mao Tse-tung group considered the Soviet Union "Enemy Number One," and thus, since China was unwilling to wage a war on two fronts, it would be anxious to avoid "a confrontation with the United States."

The American ruling circles were in complete agreement with this conclusion. "Officials in Washington consider that Mao is serving American interests," wrote *The Washington Post*, "and for that reason they are even thinking of cultivating Maoism as a means to pressure Moscow." The well-informed American weekly *United States News and World Report* did not conceal, in this regard, that the "United States is counting on Mao," because "American officials are inclined to prefer the victory of Mao Tse-tung in his struggle to liquidate the more moderate elements, since they believe that this would mean a continuation of trouble for Soviet Russia."

A great deal of the research on China is being done by numerous societies and councils which exist on contributions from big business. The most active among these is the extremely influential Council on Foreign Relations, which is well known in the United States. Several years ago the Ford Foundation gave the Council $900,000 for research on the subject "The United States and China in International Relations." The entire work was conducted under the direction of a special committee, headed by the not unknown former CIA Director, Allen Dulles, who, incidentally, has been since 1927 a permanent director of the Council. It was proposed to publish the results of this research, which was begun in 1962, in eleven volumes, each to discuss a specific subject. Only eight books were actually published: *The United States and China in World Affairs, The American People and China, Policies toward China: Views from Six Continents, Communist China's Economic Growth and Foreign Trade: Implications for U.S. Policy, The Chinese People's Liberation Army, Future of the Overseas Chinese in Southeast Asia, U.S. Policy and the Security of Asia,* and *Negotiating with the Chinese Communists: The United States Experience, 1953-1967.*

It should be noted at this point that the number of books devoted to China problems published in the United States has sharply increased in recent years. According to the most conservative estimates, approximately 200 major works on China were published in the United States between 1963 and 1972. Furthermore, the fact that the majority of these are devoted to current problems of China—foreign policy, economics, foreign trade, the army, etc.—merits attention. The studies which were published include: *China and the Bomb, Communist China's Strategy in the Nuclear Age, China and the Peace of Asia, Communist China in World Politics, The Economy of Communist China, China and the World in Asia, China and Russia: The "Great Game," Law and Policy in China's Foreign Relations, A New U.S. Policy toward China, Remaking China Policy: U.S.-China Relations and Governmental Decision-Making, Communist China's Leading Figures, Communist China and Asia,* and *Prospects for Trade with China and U.S. Policy.* A whole series of works examines problems relating to the anti-Soviet policy of the Mao Tse-tung group.

Even a simple listing of titles irrefutably shows that the United States has in recent years done significant research on the vital problems of contemporary China. This research has focused upon China's economic and military potential and the possible consequences of its acquisition of nuclear weapons. This shift in emphasis is revealing, for in the not too distant past, American Sinologists preferred to devote their time to the study of China's ancient history, archaeology, ancient literature and art. The United States now regards research on China as highly significant, as demonstrated by one extremely telling piece of information: A national committee on American-Chinese relations, composed of 99 China specialists representing the largest research organizations, was established in July 1966 with the support of the American authorities.

It is interesting to note that at the end of the Sixties the American government permitted free entry into the United States of printed matter from the People's Republic of China. One can now easily purchase in most American bookstores Mao Tse-tung's collected sayings, translated into English. The point has even been reached that a number of American newspapers have published in full three essays of Mao Tse-tung which were part of the compulsory study program for the *hungweipings*.

Thus, American scholars, political figures, journalists, and intelligence agents carefully study and continually analyze everything which occurs in China. Even during President Johnson's Administration, the firm hope was expressed in Washington that "certain extremely important events which are taking place right now in China will facilitate ... better mutual understanding between the People's Republic of China and the United States." In anticipation of such a "better mutual understanding," a broad propaganda campaign, skillfully orchestrated by Washington, was initiated in the United States. As a result of this campaign, serious shifts occurred toward the end of the Johnson Administration in the attitudes of large circles of the American public, which eventually came to favor a re-examination of official government policy toward the People's Republic of China.

CHAPTER VIII

"CONTACTS AND CONCILIATION": A NEW APPROACH

1. OLD SLOGANS REVIEWED

Richard M. Nixon's ascent to power marked the beginning of a new stage in American-Chinese relations, although the first public steps of the new Administration in no way indicated an abrupt and fundamental change in policy with regard to the People's Republic of China. Ordinary Americans did not even expect such changes because, for many of them, Richard Nixon "personified," in the words of American scholars, "the tired and time-worn old American leadership." Prospects for further relaxation of tension between the United States and the People's Republic of China seemed to a number of American specialists "more remote than ever."

And the new President's first official statements only served to confirm this view. During a press conference on January 27, 1969, which was broadcast on radio and television, Richard Nixon emphasized that the United States would continue to oppose the admission of the People's Republic of China to the United Nations. The President also expressed the hope that during the forthcoming Warsaw meeting between representatives of the United States and the People's Republic of China in February 1969, it could be ascertained whether China had in any way changed its attitude on basic issues. "Until some changes occur on their side," the President concluded, "I see no immediate prospect of any change in our policy." *The New York Times,* in an editorial, characterized the President's remarks as "most disappointing."

It later became known, however, that the President's public statements in no sense reflected his true intentions. According to informed sources, as early as "ten days after assuming office," Nixon asked trusted White House officials to investigate the possibility of establishing direct contacts with the People's Republic of China. Knowledgeable American journalists noted that the Peking leaders were using their contacts among the Japanese to communicate to Washington that they, in turn, were interested "in doing business with the new occupant of the White House." As early as November 1968, Peking communicated to Washington its readiness to hold the 135th regular meeting in Warsaw on February 20, 1969, and to discuss there the possibilities of concluding "agreements on five principles of peaceful coexistence." *The Washington Post* wrote that "In proposing 'peaceful coexistence' with the United States, they* rejected the idea of a like agreement with Moscow, thereby implying that the American 'imperialists' are preferable to the Soviet Union."

On the very eve of the meeting, Americans began to speculate on the cause of Peking's desire for this session. The Associated Press columnist John M. Hightower, quoting the remarks of certain State Department officials, noted that Peking "possibly is not against changing its policy" with the aim of "exploring the ground for the establishment of new relations with the United States." The journalist Harry Schwartz expressed himself in the same vein in *The New York Times,* and called attention, moreover, to the fact that "Peking's outpourings of venom against Moscow are far more bitter and more frequent than the attacks against this country." The influential American foreign policy journal *Foreign Affairs* wrote in its January 1969 issue that many Americans were "struck . . . by the contrast between Peking's wild words and its relatively sober deeds." Among such "sober deeds," the journal singled out the "cultural revolution," for it was "accompanied by the final rejection" by China of the socialist countries' call for unity of action against the imperialist forces.

Zbigniew Brzezinski, a Columbia University professor who is well known for his anti-Sovietism, said at that time that "The United States must react favorably to any signs of a manifestation of China's interest in broadening contacts." Brzezinski and others like him called for rapprochement with the People's Republic of China, on the basis of the Chinese leaders' hostile policy toward the Soviet Union and their divisive course in the revolutionary and liberation movements. At the same time, progressive American circles and some liberals who had spoken out long ago against the "cold war" policy continued to demand improvement of relations with the U.S.S.R. and other socialist

---

*the Peking leaders (*Author's note*)

countries, including the People's Republic of China, and an end to all manifestations of the "cold war" in American policy.

Several influential senators also spoke out during that period in favor of a "new China policy" for the government. J. W. Fulbright, the Chairman of the Senate Foreign Relations Committee, urged the use of "the scheduled meeting with the Chinese Communists in Warsaw . . . to signal the start of a new China policy." Fulbright suggested that this meeting be held at the ministerial level, in order to "show sincerity in wishing to remove long-standing barriers." Senator Edward M. Kennedy stated that the time had long since come "to reassess American policy toward mainland China. We must begin to take creative initiatives in an effort to break down the great wall of estrangement existing between the two countries." Kennedy emphasized that the shift of power in Washington to "new national leadership" and the "changing conditions within China" created an "appropriate moment to refocus attention on developing mutual understanding and respect." Senators John Sherman Cooper, Mark Hatfield and others expressed similar sentiments.

The American press drew attention at this time to the fact that, in the opinion of certain China specialists, the Mao Tse-tung leadership had somewhat "softened" its position on the question of Taiwan and was even prepared to make "certain concessions." Specifically, a commentary published simultaneously in the Peking newspaper *Jenmin Jihpao* and the magazine *Hung-ch'i* attracted the attention of American journalists. This commentary contained a long list of places around the world from which, in Peking's opinion, the United States should withdraw its troops. It was striking that Taiwan was not listed, although the Chinese leadership had until then invariably made such demands to the United States. In regard to this commentary, the journal *Foreign Affairs* very significantly implied that the question of Taiwan's future status would easily lend itself to a "compromise settlement by means of the expanding dialogue." *The New York Times* explained Peking's position as follows: "China, having probably become reconciled to the prospect of a peaceful settlement in Vietnam, is attempting to secure for itself some role in this settlement by means of bilateral negotiations with the United States."

In Washington, instructions for the representatives at the Warsaw talks had already been formulated. According to a statement by Secretary of State William Rogers, the United States was prepared to accept a Peking proposal to discuss the possibility of concluding an agreement between the two countries on the basis of principles of peaceful coexistence. The U.S. Ambassador was instructed to propose the settlement of problems of postal and telegraph communications between the United States and the People's Republic of China. As a "trial balloon," it was also proposed to suggest to the Chinese representatives an exchange between the two countries of journalists, scholars and certain other groups of people, as well as of scientific information. Informed Washington circles expressed the cautious hope that the forthcoming meetings would open the way to new and even more productive contacts.

However, the planned meeting in Warsaw did not take place. Forty-eight hours before the meeting was to commence, a representative of the Minister of Foreign Affairs of the People's Republic of China issued a statement concerning the Chinese-American negotiations in Warsaw. "The Chinese government," the statement said, "considers that it is inadvisable at this time to hold the 135th session of the Chinese-American talks at the ambassadorial level." This decision was motivated by an existing "anti-Chinese atmosphere" which had arisen because "the United States government had inspired the treachery of Liao Ho-shu, a former Chinese diplomat in Holland who was subsequently sent to the United States."

A State Department representative, Robert McCloskey, announced to representatives of the press that China had informed the U.S. Ambassador in Warsaw of its decision before its radio announcement. McCloskey also stated that the United States was continuing its efforts, through Hong Kong and other governments, to establish contacts with authorities of the People's Republic of China. American journalists wrote frankly that U.S. officials "were less surprised by Peking's refusal to participate in the meeting than by its original proposal to hold it."

Officials in Washington, as well as experienced observers in other capitals of the world, did not trust Peking's official explanation for the postponement of the talks. Certain press organs implied that the whole affair hinged upon Peking's recognition that there was at that time no hope of reaching its desired goals at the negotiations. *The New York Times* noted in this regard that Washington's agreement to discuss the principles of peaceful coexistence with the People's Republic of China constituted a "minimal response" to Peking's proposal. "The Nixon Administration has given no indications of new initiatives" toward the People's Republic of China, the *Times* said in an editorial. The Polish newspaper *Dziennik Ludowy* noted that Peking's cancellation could be explained either by China's domestic conflicts or by its effort to strengthen its "bargaining" position. The well-informed American journalist C. L. Sulzberger bluntly stated that "surely Peking is percipient enough to know that it stands little chance of achieving its immediate objective—frustrating improvement in Soviet-American relationships—unless China itself shows signs of yielding."

The world press emphasized at the same time that despite cancellation of the talks, both the People's Republic of China and the United States were striving for contacts with each other. The well-known French journalist Geneviève Tabouis, writing for the newspaper *Paris Jour,* commented: "The weighty reasons which caused both Washington and Peking to desire these meetings remain, as before, in effect."

As is well known, the leaders of the People's Republic of China staged military provocations at the beginning of March 1969 on the Soviet-Chinese border, and these continued intermittently during the first half of 1969. This diversion, broadly planned by Peking, not only escalated the tension in Soviet-Chinese relations, but also created new difficulties in the international Communist and workers' movements, and affected the interests of all peace-loving peoples. The blatant armed provocations by the Chinese authorities stirred the deep anger and the justified indignation of the entire Soviet people. Progressive public opinion throughout the world condemned the aggressive aspirations and actions of the Chinese authorities.

Imperialist circles, on the other hand, did not try to hide their satisfaction with Peking's actions, and speculated about the advantages which might be derived for world imperialism. *The Washington Post* noted that the United States was weighing with much interest the possibility of changes in the attitude of the People's Republic of China toward Taiwan, since, under the given circumstances, Peking's concentration was not likely to be "directed toward the south." Another American newspaper, *The Christian Science Monitor,* noted with satisfaction that the hostile course of the Chinese leadership toward the Soviet Union "is accompanied by restraint toward the United States," although—quoting the newspaper—it is the United States which "maintains armed forces on the periphery of China" and is preventing the return to China of its rightful territory—the island of Taiwan.

It is significant that in those very days of March 1969, the American press devoted a great deal of space to articles on events related to China. *The New York Times* alone published at that time more than 100 stories on China, including several editorials and commentaries by prominent observers; there were 16 front page articles on China in the course of one month. The newspaper published in full the texts of the Chinese notes and statements concerning the military provocations on the Soviet-Chinese border. Readers of *The New York Times* learned from the newspaper during those days the names of the English language magazines which were being published in Peking, and the companies which were distributing these in the United States.

At first glance, it might seem odd that the largest imperialist power was so favorably disposed toward spreading Mao Tse-tung's "ideas," which reiterated his "irreconcilability" with imperialism. But such benevolence on Washington's part is easily explained. Totally disregarding the "anti-imperialist," "ultra-revolutionary" rhetorical shell of the advocates of Peking's current line, the United States ideologues facilitated the dissemination of the essence of Peking propaganda which, as is well known, has a strikingly expressed anti-socialist and anti-Soviet character. When this is taken into consideration, it does not seem strange that there are several organizations operating freely in the United States which specialize in the dissemination of Chinese publications in English translation. The largest on the West Coast of the United States is the San Francisco company "China Books and Periodicals," and, on the East Coast, the New York agency "China Publications." It is significant that some 140 titles of Chinese propaganda publications appeared in the catalogues of the San Francisco firm in 1960, and in 1969 the number exceeded 1,000. This firm alone distributes these publications to more than 500 universities, colleges, and secondary schools in the western, midwestern and southern United States.

In April 1969, many American newspapers devoted entire columns to articles on China, in connection with the Ninth Congress of the Chinese Communist Party, meeting then in Peking. On April 10, 1969, *The New York Times* published a letter from a large group of well-known American Sinologists who expressed their belief that "The leaders of Communist China have demonstrated that they are rational and intelligent statesmen."

Official Washington reacted to the Sino-Soviet confrontations along the Ussuri River with an announcement by the State Department representative Robert McCloskey that the "American government remains ready to meet with representatives of China in Warsaw." It is most significant that immediately after the events on the Ussuri River, sentiments in favor of establishing "full mutual understanding" with Peking increased noticeably. These sentiments manifested themselves with particular clarity at the first American national conference on "The United States and China: The Next Decade," which met in New York on March 20-21, 1969. The conference was organized by the National Committee on United States-China Relations, established in July 1966 with the support of big business and official circles. During the two-day session, approximately 2,500 conferees listened to speeches by the most prominent American Sinologists, major public figures, businessmen and senators. The organizers intended the conference to deal with the future—to review contemporary problems and possible alternatives for future United States actions.

Speeches by Senators Edward M. Kennedy (Democrat) and Jacob Javits (Republican) attracted the greatest attention of the American press and public. Senator Kennedy, the guest of honor at a conference dinner, noted that "For almost twenty years, the United States has pursued the same unyielding policy of military containment and diplomatic isolation toward Communist China." Kennedy pointed out that such a policy was a part of the "cold war" tradition of the Fifties, "is demonstrably false in the Sixties, and must under no circumstances continue in the Seventies." Kennedy proposed a shift to a new policy toward China, one "that abandons old slogans, embraces today's reality, and encourages tomorrow's possibility." As first steps, the Senator proposed the renewal of contacts in Warsaw, to transform these into a "more confidential" and "more significant dialogue," the removal of "restrictions on travel and non-strategic trade," and an expression of willingness to exchange consular offices with the People's Republic of China.

The Republican Senator Javits also spoke in favor of a re-examination of America's China policy, noting that "The Nixon Administration has a unique opportunity to encourage and stimulate creative, new and unorthodox thoughts about China, not only within the government, but also in the nation as a whole." In Javits' opinion, this "unique opportunity" for the Nixon government could be attributed to several circumstances. First, the Senator noted, "for all its verbal violence, China has demonstrated unmistakable military prudence" during the entire course of events in Vietnam. Second, Javits believed that China would also "exercise prudence with respect to the nuclear weapons capability." And, most important, the Chinese military provocations on the Soviet-Chinese border demonstrated, in the Senator's opinion, Peking's desire "to seek a relaxation of tension in Southeast Asia." The outcry raised by the Maoists about the northern territories, supposedly "lost" by China, should "lessen Peking's obsession about the 'recovery' of Taiwan."

With rare exceptions, the conference participants were of the general opinion that the United States must "display initiative in achieving the normalization of relations with China."

2. CURTAILING MUTUAL ISOLATION

Although many experienced Washington observers did not expect the Republican Administration to take initiatives rapidly for improving relations with the People's Republic of China, such steps were, in fact, taken by the White House in July 1969, coinciding with the declaration of the Nixon Guam Doctrine. The United States government decided to ease the trade blockade of the People's Republic of China and allowed American citizens to import into the United States souvenirs valued at up to $100, which were made in the People's Republic of China. Restrictions on travel to China by congressmen, scholars, medical doctors, students, teachers, journalists and certain other groups of Americans were simultaneously lifted. *The New York Times* emphasized that these decisions were made by the government after "thorough review of China policy by the National Security Council staff."

In the summer of 1969, both the tone and content of official statements on the government's China policy changed. As Secretary of State William Rogers then observed: "The United States is making every effort to establish better relations with Communist China," and was for its part ready to suggest specific proposals designed to establish more normal relations with the People's Republic of China. Rogers pointed out furthermore that the United States was endeavoring primarily to "remove the irritants" which were interfering with improved American-Chinese relations and to "remind the people of mainland China of our historic friendship with them."

President Richard M. Nixon, speaking at the XXIVth Session of the United Nations General Assembly on September 18, 1969, also pointed out America's readiness to begin discussions with the People's Republic of China in a "sincere and serious spirit." At the same time, Under Secretary of State Elliott Richardson disclosed the government's plans with regard to the People's Republic of China more fully, emphasizing that no collateral understandings would keep the United States "from attempting to bring China out of its angry, alienated shell."

Such an unexpected change in the views of official Washington raised questions primarily from journalists, some of whom asked outright whether these new measures with regard to Peking were prompted by the Maoist provocations on the Soviet-Chinese border. In response to these questions, Richardson stated that the United States government was not seeking "to exploit for our own advantage the hostility between the Soviet Union and Communist China." Commenting on this statement, American journalists observed that in the State Department corridors, highly placed figures were openly acknowledging that this was "easier said than done," and that Washington would obviously feel tempted to try to exploit for its own advantage Peking's anti-Sovietism.

Advocates of such actions were divided, according to the American press, into three basic groups. One group claimed that the Sino-Soviet conflict presented the United States with the most fortuitous opportunity since the beginning of the "cold war" to exert pressure upon the U.S.S.R. by "reaching an agreement" with Peking. Another favored the escalation of tension through political maneuvering—by first supporting one side, and then the other. And the third group proposed to exploit the fact that Peking's attention was "riveted on the north" by seizing the southern part of the People's Republic of China.

It was during just that period that the American press—as if on command—began intensive efforts to persuade the ordinary American that the "Chinese threat" to the countries of Asia, about which the news media had warned him for years, was not really so terrible after all. The performance of such newspapers as *The New York Times* and *The Wall Street Journal* is notable in this regard. On August 7, 1969, *The New York Times* published an article by its Hong Kong correspondent under the headline "U.S. Aides View Chinese Threat As Exaggerated." The author asserted that U.S. officials had concluded that "Communist China poses a far smaller military threat to the countries of Asia than was believed several years ago." *The Wall Street Journal,* organ of the business circles, expressed much the same opinion. "The fear of Communist Chinese expansionism, which has dominated U.S. policy for so long, may now no longer be valid," wrote the newspaper in an editorial on August 5, 1969, which noted that Peking's attention was now "too preoccupied" with its northern borders.

The American press began at the same time extensive coverage of an allegedly imminent major war between the People's Republic of China and the U.S.S.R. *The Wall Street Journal* wrote significantly in this connection that "Some of the very same authorities in the State Department and Central Intelligence Agency who a few weeks ago were strongly inclined to knock down any idea of war between the Red giants have in recent days started holding conferences and writing papers propounding the genuine possibility of assorted military blows. Any of these could escalate into mass warfare."

This theme was highly exaggerated in American newspapers and magazines throughout the entire second half of 1969. The well-known *New York Times* commentator Harrison Salisbury wrote a book, published at the end of 1969, titled *War Between Russia and China,* in which he asserted that a war was "inevitable." Even the American press was compelled to point out that Salisbury's book was not based on facts, but instead was "loaded with generalities and the kind of hemming and hawing one normally gets from a weatherman who hasn't studied his charts lately."

The problems of the future development of American-Chinese relations were of interest to others besides journalists. These problems were studied principally by special government agencies, which prepared various analyses making long-range predictions. Although all these analyses and the recommendations contained therein were usually held in strictest secrecy, certain of these were, for one reason or another, made public, thereby revealing the direction in which the specialists were working. One such document, for example, is a report prepared for the U.S. Department of Defense by the International and Social Studies Division of the Institute for Defense Analysis (Study No. P-429). This report reviews general problems related to major political decisions made by the leadership of the People's Republic of China, as well as problems of the internal power struggle in China during the "cultural revolution." The last section of the report is titled "The Future of China and U.S. Policy." The authors of the study thought it improbable that the Peking leaders would be able to organize another "cultural revolution" or a new "great leap forward," and also rejected the idea of a possible shift of power into the hands of the military in the People's Republic of China. Hopes for the collapse and fragmentation of the country were also deemed unrealistic. These same authors thought it more likely that there would be an extended transition period during which a new leadership would gradually be formed. This leadership would continue to pay lip service to the ideas of Mao Tse-tung, but would actually devote its attention to the solution of the country's real problems.

Under these circumstances, the authors of the report believed that the United States must pursue three goals. First, it must "endeavor to defend the interests of the United States and its allies against Chinese threats and pressure. This had in the past been achieved—and might still be, to a sufficient degree, in the future—by way of military containment." The report simultaneously emphasized that "there are no reasons to suppose that the United States and the People's Republic of China are on a collision course." Second, the authors of the report continued, "the United States may try to produce changes in the People's Republic of China, including changes in Chinese foreign policy." And third, the United States should, in the authors' opinion, attempt to present its policy toward the People's Republic of China in a more favorable light, thereby raising its prestige "both in the eyes of critically disposed elements of American public opinion, as well as in the eyes of foreign governments and foreign public opinion." It was recommended in this connection that the United States government take only those steps which would neither irritate the Peking leaders nor place them in a difficult position. One such step, the authors suggested, could be a "quiet lifting of control over trade in non-strategic goods between the United States and the People's Republic of China."

The end of 1969, Richard Nixon's first year in the White House, was marked by Washington's renewed efforts to improve relations with the People's Republic of China. Secretary of State Rogers asked the foreign ministers of certain countries which maintained diplomatic relations with China to inform Peking of the United States' assurance that the resumption of talks in Warsaw would be "fruitful and mutually beneficial."

At a Yugoslav Embassy fashion show at the Warsaw Palace of Culture in early December, a brief conversation was held between the American Ambassador to Poland, Walter Stoessel, and the Chargé d'Affaires of the People's Republic of China, Lei Yang. Several days later, Stoessel visited the Chinese Embassy in Warsaw, where he discussed secretly with Lei Yang the question of resuming the official American-Chinese talks at the ambassadorial level. The American press viewed this Washington initiative as part of a policy "to end the mutual isolation" which prevailed between Washington and Peking.

At the end of December 1969, the Department of State announced a new easing of restrictions on trade with the People's Republic of China. Foreign subsidiaries of American companies were given the right to sell non-strategic goods to the People's Republic of China and also to purchase Chinese goods for sale outside the United States. In addition, the import restriction on Chinese goods brought into the United States by American citizens for personal use was lifted. *The New York Times* evaluated this new Washington step as "the first basic United States initiative toward Peking" since the Korean war. Officials in Washington emphasized in private conversations that such actions demonstrated a United States attempt to make a "far-reaching overture" in relations with the People's Republic of China. It was simultaneously pointed out that there were "cautious hopes" that the Peking leaders would welcome "improvement in relations" with Washington.

The United States took simultaneous steps which were not widely publicized at that time, but were, as it subsequently turned out, among the first tangible actions demonstrating to Peking America's real desire to improve its relations with the Mao Tse-tung group. At the end of December 1969, the Japanese agency *Kyodo Tsusin,* citing "informed diplomatic sources," reported that the United States had informed Japan that, in order to "save money," American destroyers were discontinuing patrols in the Taiwan Strait. This report was published on the inside pages of the newspapers and did not attract particular attention. Peking, however, clearly understood the full significance of this step and responded very quickly by agreeing to a new meeting in Warsaw. *The New York Times* wrote frankly in an editorial that the new United States steps were "a signal to the Chinese that further bilateral talks and negotiations could lead to other similar changes in Washington's economic and political policy."

Summing up the first year of the Republican Administration in the White House, *The Wall Street Journal* wrote: "One of the most intriguing parts of the new patterns of policy is the Administration's interest in creating a basis for getting along with Communist China." In the opinion of *The New York Times,* Washington's policy toward the People's Republic of China from then on was aimed at "the establishment of formal diplomatic relations between the United States and Communist China, admission of Peking to the United Nations, and Chinese-American exchanges of scholars, journalists, businessmen and tourists."

Thus, the Republicans' first year in power had already seen fundamental changes in the direction and aims of United States policy toward the People's Republic of China. It became perfectly clear that Washington had completely abandoned the policy of "isolation without containment" and begun actively to implement a new policy—"contacts and conciliation."

3. *"FROM ESTRANGEMENT – TO DIALOGUE"*

At the beginning of 1970, the Department of State announced that the governments of the United States and the People's Republic of China had agreed to hold the next meeting between the official representatives of both Powers in Warsaw on January 20. It is significant that in making this announcement, the State Department spokesman, Robert McCloskey, referred to the government of the People's Republic of China by its official name for the first time. *The New York Times* subsequently wrote that "this was a deliberate signal to the Chinese."

The meeting took place in the Chinese Embassy and, according to the American Ambassador, was conducted in a "businesslike atmosphere." However, while Washington was, on the one hand, conducting "fully meaningful" discussions with the People's Republic of China in Warsaw, it was, on the other hand, taking steps to expand the anti-ballistic missile defense system. President Nixon, speaking at the end of January 1970, justified the necessity for such expansion primarily by the nuclear threat from China. Fears were expressed after the President's speech that Peking would use this expansion as a pretext to delay further talks. No delay occurred, however, and the next meeting was held, at Peking's suggestion, on February 20, 1970, within a month of the previous one.

The American press noted in this regard that such a short interval between the meetings was "clear evidence" that the incipient dialogue between the Nixon Administration and the Chinese Communists now promised to shift to substantive discussions. Washington emphasized that the "mere continuation of the talks is more important at this juncture than achieving specific results." But Washington, as subsequently became clear, did expect concrete results from this meeting. During the meeting, the American Ambassador to Poland, Walter Stoessel, delivered to the Chinese Chargé d'Affaires, Lei Yang, a message from President Nixon which pointed out the President's intention to send a personal emissary to Peking and inquired whether the Chinese leadership would receive such a representative. The White House was prepared to take this step, according to *The New York Times*, "as evidence of the seriousness of America's intention to improve relations with China."

Washington's proposal was prompted by those new tasks which the Republican Administration had set for itself with regard to Peking. In the report titled "U.S. Foreign Policy for the 1970's," which President Nixon submitted to the U.S. Congress in February 1972, this task was defined as follows: "With China, the task was to establish a civilized discourse on how to replace estrangement with a dialogue serving to benefit both countries." The report emphasized that the United States did not regard its principal aim as one of "containment . . . of China under cover of an American shield."

It is characteristic that the renewal of contacts between Peking and Washington was accompanied by a new wave of anti-Sovietism and war psychosis in China. The Peking propagandists tried in every way possible to incite Chinese public opinion against the socialist countries and the U.S.S.R., in order to justify the incipient turn toward American imperialism. "The true friends of China," wrote the Hungarian weekly *Magyarorszag* in this connection, "who want to see this enormous country on the healthy path of socialist development, would be glad if it ended this self-isolation. But under no circumstances should this be accomplished by means of super-secret negotiations with the largest imperialist Power, and to the accompaniment, furthermore, of despicable anti-Soviet abuse in the spirit of imperialist propaganda." American

Sinologists also observed that the Peking authorities had placed themselves in a complicated position. Professor A. Doak Barnett noted that "Those Chinese leaders who are seeking an accommodation with the United States must find ways to do so without risking charges that they are consorting with the enemy."

Washington followed approvingly the new outburst of anti-Soviet propaganda in China. According to *The New York Times,* Washington realized that the Chinese press attacks on the United States and other imperialist countries now amounted only to "a smoke-screen for internal and international consumption, the aim of which was to veil the new flexibility in China's position." In his February 1970 message to Congress, President Nixon called for an effort to achieve "improved practical relations with Peking." *The New York Times,* commenting on the President's message, wrote that "Peking policy-makers must also understand that there could be tangible economic and other benefits [for Peking] from even a partial normalization of relations with the United States."

In March 1970, the Department of State announced the virtual lifting of the ban on travel by American citizens to the People's Republic of China. At the same time, American officials expressed a desire to hold the Warsaw talks regularly, and not, as before, sporadically. The issuance of licenses was authorized in April for the export to China of some American-made goods and the required spare parts. In August 1970, Washington removed certain restrictions on the activity of American overseas oil companies, authorizing these to supply fuel to the majority of foreign ships "going or coming from mainland China ports."

The American press did not overlook a single argument in favor of more frequent discussions in Warsaw. After the first Chinese sputnik was orbited in April 1970, for example, *The New York Times* wrote in an editorial titled "Great Leap Upward": "China's first satellite only strengthens the case for more frequent Warsaw meetings and for greater efforts to normalize Peking-Washington relations."

The next meeting in Warsaw, on which Washington pinned great hopes, was scheduled for May 20, 1970. According to American journalists, it was expected that at this very meeting the Chinese would give the United States an answer to Richard Nixon's message of February 20, concerning the presidential representative's journey to Peking. At the same time, the United States ruling circles increasingly took new steps to expand their aggression in Indochina. American forces were sent into Cambodia—a decision which was made, American officials explained, because the possibility of "Chinese Communist intervention in Indochina was remote." Peking, in fact, reacted to the expansion of American aggression in Indochina by a routine cascade of verbal attacks on the United States and the cancellation of the forthcoming meeting in Warsaw. The American press, however, expressed satisfaction that Peking had simultaneously advised the United States of its readiness to resume contacts at an early date.

A widespread movement developed within the U.S. Congress during that period to repeal several resolutions which had granted to the President freedom of action "in certain military situations abroad." Initially, there was discussion of the so-called Gulf of Tonkin Resolution of 1964, but voices were soon heard on the need to repeal the 1955 resolution "Concerning the Defense of Formosa." The government at first objected to the repeal of these resolutions, but in March 1970 the Department of State announced the withdrawal of these objections. This caused alarm in Taiwan, where Chiang Kai-shek and his associates watched with anxiety the developing thaw in American-Chinese relations. Official Washington issued "appropriate explanations" from time to time, and highly placed American representatives continued to visit Taiwan. All this, however, did not reassure the Chiang Kai-shekists. Their apprehension became even more pronounced after the U.S. Department of Defense, according to *Newsweek* magazine, warned the Chiang Kai-shekists in October 1970 that they might be "completely deprived of aid" if they did not cease military raids on mainland China.

The talks in Warsaw were not renewed in 1970, despite an American proposal to that end, but close observers saw sufficient evidence that Washington and Peking remained interested in the continuation of contacts. It was clear that under the circumstances, although the United States had sharply increased its aggressive actions in Indochina, both nations preferred not to publicize their contacts and resorted to secret, behind-the-scenes diplomacy.

A report from Hong Kong indicated that the well-known author Edgar Snow returned to the People's Republic of China in mid-August 1970. During an earlier visit to China, in the winter of 1964-65, Snow had an extensive conversation with Mao Tse-tung. A detailed record of this conversation was carried in many newspapers around the world. Immediately afterwards, it was noted, the United States began to bomb the Democratic Republic of Vietnam. In 1968 Snow once again attempted to visit the People's Republic of China, but the Chinese authorities refused him a visa at the very last moment. And then, in 1970, the American journalist was allowed into Peking once more. *The International Herald Tribune* observed that "The timing of Mr. Snow's visit suggests that China is interested in continuing to develop contacts with the United States." The United States was then working with the same goal in mind. In September 1970, for example, President Nixon stated that "If there is one thing I would like to do before I die, it is to visit China." However, that statement did not attract wide press attention at the time.

It is significant that in 1970 the People's Republic of China established diplomatic relations with several nations, including Canada, Italy and Ethiopia. In 1970, for the first time in the history of the United Nations, a majority voted in favor of a resolution to admit the People's Republic of China to the United Nations (51 in favor, 49 against, with 25 abstentions). This voting result forced the Department of State to issue a statement which recognized that "a new situation had arisen" on the question of admitting the People's Republic of China to the United Nations, and that the United States government intended to take that new circumstance into consideration. Informed observers noted that Washington was significantly more concerned over the problem of keeping Taiwan's seat in the United Nations than over the possible admission of the People's Republic of China.

Thus, the Republicans' second year in power was marked by continued implementation of the "contacts and conciliation" policy toward Peking. One can conclude that, in terms of political relations, this policy found its expression in several ways: the efforts to expand official contacts with Peking, the aim being that these would lead to regular meetings; the desire to cement personal contacts between the President of the United States and the Peking leaders, through visits to Peking by personal representatives of the President; the tacit consent to Peking's establishment of diplomatic relations with third countries; and the attempts to adapt to the "new situation" in the United Nations while simultaneously preventing the expulsion of Taiwan from this international organization.

As regards economic relations, the "contacts and conciliation" policy found expression in the considerable relaxation of the embargo on trade with the People's Republic of China; the permission given subsidiaries of American firms in third countries to trade with the People's Republic of China in non-strategic goods; the admission of Chinese goods to the United States; and the lifting of certain restrictions on the activities of American oil companies.

As regards the military situation, this policy found expression in the cessation of regular patrols in the Taiwan Strait by U.S. Navy ships; the imposition of what was, in effect, a ban on Chiang Kai-shek's military raids on mainland China; and the partial curtailment of shipments of military supplies to Chiang Kai-shek's army.

At the same time, the American policy of "contacts and conciliation" by no means excluded the further expansion of the imperialist aggression in Indochina, escalation of military actions against the South Vietnamese patriots, and intensification of military pressure on the Democratic Republic of Vietnam. That the imperialists of the United States felt that they had a free hand in Indochina was the direct result of Peking's response to the new American policy.

CHAPTER IX

TREND TOWARD
RAPPROCHEMENT

It was evident by early 1971 that Washington increasingly was taking new steps toward the adjustment of relations with Peking. The President, in his annual report to the U.S. Congress on the country's foreign policy, for the first time in an official document used the full name of the People's Republic of China. In a special section titled "The Problem of China," the report discussed the necessity to draw the People's Republic of China into "a constructive relationship with the world community, and particularly with the rest of Asia." The President pointed out in his report that the United States was, as before, "prepared to establish a dialogue with Peking. . . . But neither do we wish to impose on China an international position that denies its legitimate national interests. . . . I wish to make it clear that the United States is prepared to see the People's Republic of China play a constructive role in the family of nations."

On March 15, 1971, it was announced in Washington that it was no longer mandatory for American citizens to obtain special visas for travel to mainland China. As stated subsequently, this was but one of the "carefully agreed upon public, as well as secret measures" designed to promote the establishment of further contacts between Washington and Peking. And these persistent efforts made by Washington were echoed in Peking. In April 1971, a group of American table tennis champions was invited to the People's Republic of China. The American team made a grand tour of China, and was received by Premier Chou En-lai. Within a few months, a new expression appeared on the pages of the world press—"ping-pong diplomacy."

John K. Emmerson, the former United States Minister to Japan, who visited Yenan in 1944 and talked there with Mao Tse-tung and Chou En-lai, wrote in this connection in the Japanese journal *Pacific*

Community: "In 1944, Mao was anxious to win the good will of Americans. . . . In April 1971, by inviting the American table tennis team to visit Peking, the Mao regime seemed to signal a wish for good will from the United States and a development of at least some people-to-people relations."

The White House responded to the Chinese "ping-pong diplomacy" with a whole series of measures. In May 1971, the President of the United States rescinded government control over monetary transactions with China; Peking was thus able freely to make use of dollars held in Chinese banks. American ships and aircraft were authorized to carry Chinese cargo between non-Chinese ports. American-owned freighters sailing under foreign flags were allowed to call at mainland China ports. In June 1971, Washington lifted the 21-year-old embargo on trade with the People's Republic of China, and restrictions on imports of Chinese goods into the United States were simultaneously lifted. These steps laid the groundwork for the establishment of personal contacts at the highest level between Washington and Peking.

Edgar Snow, returning from the People's Republic of China at this time, wrote a series of articles, which appeared in major American newspapers, about his trip and a new conversation he had held with Mao Tse-tung. At the end of April 1971, *Life* magazine published an article by Snow which reported a forthcoming visit to Peking by a personal representative of the U.S. President. Many were extremely skeptical about this report, but, as it turned out, they were mistaken. The visit, by Henry A. Kissinger, then the President's Special Assistant for National Security Affairs, was to prepare for the President's own journey to China. Richard Nixon subsequently commented that Snow's article in *Life* "confirmed private signals we had already received of Chinese interest in my visiting China."

Kissinger visited the People's Republic of China during July 9-11, 1971, and talked there with Premier Chou En-lai. The official report of these talks indicated that Chou En-lai, on behalf of the government of the People's Republic of China, invited President Richard M. Nixon to visit China "at an appropriate date before May 1972." President Nixon subsequently "accepted this invitation with pleasure."

It should be noted that this "unexpected Nixon diplomacy," to use the expression of the famous American journalist James Reston, was accompanied in its entirety by a widespread propaganda campaign directed from Washington. It is in this light that the publication of Edgar Snow's articles in *Life* magazine must be viewed, as well as the subsequent open hearings of the U.S. Senate Foreign Relations Committee during the summer of 1971, and the entire flood of articles on China which appeared in newspapers and magazines, including the first direct reports by American journalists from the People's Republic of China in 22 years.

It is significant that the tone and essence of what was said, both in the press and by the senators, had by now changed sharply. Here, for instance, is what Senator George McGovern, the 1972 Democratic presidential candidate, said on the floor of the Congress in the summer of 1971: "The Chinese People's Republic must take China's place in the UN, and this must not be dependent on the solution of the question of Taiwan's status by the interested parties. The United States must announce its desire to establish diplomatic relations with Peking as the only government of China."

American delegations and journalists became frequent visitors to Peking, where they were readily received by high-ranking officials, including Premier Chou En-lai. Reports from the People's Republic of China by American journalists differed strikingly from everything which these same journalists had only recently written. The reality of China was now portrayed by them as something idyllic. Reports of individuals who had managed to escape from Maoist China, whose number by then surely exceeded 250,000, almost disappeared from the pages of the American press. The American reader received instead bourgeois-respectable accounts of journeys to China, in which not a word appeared of the massive "purges" and cruel repression during the "cultural revolution" period, nor of the latest developments in the internecine struggle within the Peking leadership, nor of the serious crisis created by the internal difficulties which China was experiencing. Thus, American journalists endeavored to distort the reality of the situation in the People's Republic of China, and thereby make their contribution to the preparation for the President's visit to Peking.

During Kissinger's second visit to Peking, in October 1971, the "basic arrangement was worked out" for meetings between the President of the United States and the leaders of the People's Republic of China, and the date of arrival was set—February 21, 1972. The world press had a mixed reaction to the President's diplomatic voyage. Many newspapers and magazines emphasized the existence of serious disagreements between Peking and Washington: "Americans should not lose their heads," wrote the Japanese journal *Pacific Community*, "and naively think that their problems in relations with China are solved." The majority of commentators agreed that the most complicated problem was that of Taiwan. The position of the leadership of the People's Republic of China on this subject was repeatedly underscored during 1971 in both the official statements and articles which appeared in the journal *Jenmin Jihpao*, and especially in Chou En-lai's interview, published in August 1971, with *The New York Times* columnist James Reston.

Journalists tried to read between the lines of official statements in order to explain what was behind this or that obscure wording which was emanating from Peking. And here, once again, Edgar Snow turned out to be the best informed. In a *Life* magazine article published on July 30, 1971, Snow wrote: "China's formula for Taiwan has always been negotiable whenever American leaders so wished. As repeatedly defined, it requires two steps: first, that the U.S. and China jointly declare their intention to settle all disputes between themselves, including the Taiwan dispute, by peaceful negotiation. Second, that the U.S. recognizes Taiwan as an inalienable part of the Chinese People's Republic and agrees to withdraw its armed forces from Taiwan and the Taiwan Strait. Specific steps on how and when to withdraw would be matters for subsequent discussion. . . . Peking is likely to be found reasonable in both the procedures for the dissolution of the American position and in dealing with Taiwan itself—perhaps even granting a degree of autonomy to Chiang Kai-shek if he should wish to remain Governor there for his lifetime. . . . Mao Tse-tung has pointed out to me that peaceful assimilation of Taiwan is his aim."

As is evident, the formula set forth by Peking in 1971 for settlement of the Taiwan problem, and the proposal presented by Li Tsung-jen to the United States government in 1961 are as much alike as two peas in a pod. In 1961, however, Washington failed to react altogether to Li Tsung-jen's proposal, and responded instead to the formula expounded at the later date by Edgar Snow. The President of the United States announced in February 1972 that "the relations which will ultimately be established between Taiwan and mainland China are a problem whose solution does not depend upon the United States."

The second problem—representation of the People's Republic of China in the United Nations—was thought to be no less complex. Here, it was decided, the United States would take the initiative into its own hands. After the American Congress had on 24 occasions opposed the admission of the People's Republic of China to the United Nations, the representatives of the United States proposed in August 1971 to include the question of the "representation of China in the UN" in the agenda of the XXVIth Session of the General Assembly. Speaking this time in favor of the admission of the People's Republic of China to the UN, the United States simultaneously objected to the exclusion of the Chiang Kai-shek regime from representation in the international organization. It is common knowledge that this "two Chinas policy" did not garner any laurels for the United States. The United Nations General Assembly decided in October 1971 to restore the rights of the People's Republic of China in the United Nations and to exclude Taiwan's representatives from all UN agencies. "The U.N. vote," wrote *The New York Times*, "showed that Mr. Nixon cannot have it both ways."

It is significant that, having taken the United Nations seat which legitimately belonged to the Chinese people, the Peking representatives quickly found a common language with the envoys of the U.S. imperialist circles and joined with them in a united front on a series of important international problems. The General Secretary of the Central Committee of the Communist Party of the Soviet Union, Comrade Leonid I. Brezhnev, observed in his report "Fifty Years of the Union of Soviet Socialist Republics" that the leaders of the People's Republic of China had embarked on the road to open sabotage of the "efforts to limit the arms race, further the struggle for disarmament, and promote the relaxation of international tension."

"The behavior of the Chinese leaders toward the majority of important world problems objectively serves American imperialism," noted the French weekly *France Nouvelle*, citing as examples China's unwillingness to contribute to the conclusion of disarmament agreement, its support for the idea of expansion of the "common market," and its position on the Indochina conflict. The author of the article emphasized that the Chinese had presented American propaganda with the opportunity to create the illusion that a way out of the Vietnam conflict might be found during Nixon's visit to Peking. "It is impossible to prohibit public opinion from asking what motives drive Peking to ease Nixon's task in this direction," wrote *France Nouvelle*. *The London Times* commented that "Earlier fears that China would become a partner of the Communist bloc in the United Nations disappeared long ago. China has already ceased to be the intractable leader of the revolutionary third world." Many other world press organs wrote in the same spirit, and it is difficult not to agree with these statements.

The discernible changes in American-Chinese relations attracted considerable attention in many world capitals, especially those of the Asian countries. This is attributable to the fact that many believed, as *The London Times* wrote, that the ideological difference between Peking and Washington had in this instance been set aside in favor of the nationalist interests of both Powers. *The Washington Post* cautiously expressed doubt that the President's trip to Peking would turn out to be "more than a passing, accidental coincidence of the political needs and requirements of Nixon and Mao Tse-tung."

Washington realized that the "unexpected Nixon diplomacy" neces-sitated an explanation, and during the second half of 1971, the United States launched widespread diplomatic activity to clarify its policy. Secretary of State Rogers met with the foreign ministers of a number of countries. The President sent Secretary of the Treasury John B. Connally and California Governor Ronald Reagan as his personal representatives to several Asian nations, and he personally held a series of meetings in late 1971 and early 1972 with the leaders of numerous countries. All this activity, however, failed to satisfy very many nations. Former U.S. Assistant Secretary of State George Ball, for example, stated bitterly that Washington's actions with regard to Peking "seemed to Japan not only crude and unwise, but even of such nature as to cast doubt upon the profundity and constancy of the Japanese-American friendship." *The Times of India* observed that Richard Nixon's new policy toward China "corresponds completely with the 'cold war' psychology."

Comments on the occasion of President Nixon's forthcoming visit to Peking were published in the newspapers of many countries, and also in the American press. A number of American journalists wrote that the principal motive of the Nixon visit was to influence the sentiments of American voters during a presidential election year and to win Nixon's re-election to the Presidency. Another goal, no less important, was to increase, with Peking's assistance, the pressures upon the Democratic Republic of Vietnam in order to "arrange an acceptable settlement of the conflict in Indochina," as *U.S. News and World Report* wrote. The magazine additionally noted that "The Administration seemed to breathe more easily when the renewed U.S. bombing of North Vietnam in December 1971, which continues in 1972, evoked relatively restrained reaction from Peking."

Washington had already ceased to be content with the "tacit mutual understanding" with Peking on the question of Vietnam, for its military pressure on the South Vietnamese patriots and fierce bombings of the entire territory of Vietnam had not achieved America's desired results. For this reason, Washington was trying to shift from a "tacit mutual understanding" to the "use of Peking's influence in Hanoi" in order to further American imperialist interests. "It is clear," wrote the Polish newspaper *Zycie Warszawy* in this connection, "that certain agreements (unofficial, of course) exist between China and the United States on the problem of the war in Vietnam. There is evidence that, with regard to the American aggression, the Chinese leaders have set for themselves goals which are not always in accord with the goals of the Chinese people. . . . The Chinese leaders have continued to condemn loudly the

American aggressors and to promise aid to the Vietnamese people. Statements of this kind are being made in Peking even now, during the period of intensive preparation for President Nixon's visit. But, of course, this trip itself has much more significance than all the statements put together." The Mongolian newspaper *Unen* emphasized Peking's ever-growing servility toward Washington during the period of preparation for Nixon's trip. "One thing is clear," wrote *Unen*. "The Maoists, acting together with the United States, the main force of imperialism and aggression, against the forces of socialism and progress, are hindering the solution of the Vietnamese and other international problems by means of negotiations. The Maoists are doing everything to please the imperialists and to find a common language with them."

As for the capitalist press, it was not so much concerned with the fact of the forthcoming trip as it was with engaging in all possible speculation—about the results of the visit, about the composition of the presidential entourage, and about which correspondents would be allowed to report on the visit from Peking. The news media avidly followed the White House preparations for the trip and, having unexpectedly discovered that the "bamboo curtain" was open to them, tried to send correspondents in advance to the People's Republic of China. Large groups of journalists, photographers and Sinologists were dispatched to Peking, and all received the most cordial welcome. Many even succeeded in obtaining an interview with Premier Chou En-lai.

Thus, by the time the U.S. President began his visit, the American public already had the opportunity to read hundreds of articles, commentaries, and reports from the People's Republic of China, and to see countless photos, documentary films and a whole series of television broadcasts on China. And no one was surprised that special television broadcast units were sent to cover the President's visit to the People's Republic of China, nor that a special building was equipped for them in Peking.

The President visited the People's Republic of China from February 21-28, 1972. On the first day of his visit he met with the Chinese Communist Party Chairman Mao Tse-tung, and according to a joint communiqué, there was "a serious and frank exchange of views on Chinese-American relations and international affairs." In addition, President Nixon and the Premier of the People's Republic of China, Chou En-lai, held "extensive, earnest and frank discussions . . . on the normalization of relations between the United States of America and the People's Republic of China, as well as on other matters of interest to both sides." Discussions proceeded in the same spirit between U.S. Secretary of State William Rogers and the Chinese Minister of Foreign Affairs, Chi Peng-fei.

A joint communiqué was issued as a result of the discussions, wherein each side set forth its positions and views. Those problems on which the positions of both countries coincided were also reflected in the document. Three basic sections of the joint communiqué are readily discernible; these deal with the position of the leadership of the People's Republic of China, the position of the American leadership, and the joint views of the United States and the People's Republic of China. Furthermore, the American press emphasized that although the statements on Taiwan, Vietnam, and other "sensitive issues" contained in the joint communiqué were "presented as divergent declarations by each side," these matters had, in fact, "been subject to some intensive negotiations" between the two parties. *The New York Times* did not fail to observe cynically that each section of the joint communiqué "was to some degree adjusted by one side to obtain the acquiescence of the other side. The communiqué statements advertised as a joint position or viewpoint were negotiated in the customary fashion until each side was absolutely satisfied." Therefore, the statement in this document which details each side's "positions and views" does not represent merely a unilateral declaration; indeed, it expresses a point on which the other side tacitly agrees. Under no circumstances should this fact be overlooked in analyzing the positions taken by the respective parties, and the manner in which these are set forth in the joint American-Chinese communiqué.

After the President's visit, both American and Chinese leaders pointed out the limited significance of the journey. Thus, President Nixon, in an interview published in *Time* magazine on April 3, 1972, commented that his visit to Peking was designed "only to establish contact" and represented merely an "attempt to create a basis for future relations." Premier Chou En-lai expressed himself in the same vein when, during a conversation with the American journalist James Reston, he stated: "We do not expect a settlement of all questions at one stroke ... but by contacting each other, we may be able to find out from where we should start in solving these questions."

What, then, is this "basis for future relations," to use Richard Nixon's expression, or, to use Chou En-lai's description, the "starting point"? The answer may be found by careful examination of the joint American-Chinese communiqué. As is generally known, the aggressive actions by the United States against a sovereign state—the Democratic Republic of Vietnam—aroused the angry indignation and protests of progressive people in all countries of the world. It would be misleading, however, to look for any condemnation of the barbaric actions of the American Army, or even for simple mention thereof, in the positions set forth by the leadership of the People's Republic of China in the American-Chinese communiqué, since these were limited to obscure generalities and florid rhetoric. A comment of the *Berliner Zeitung* is significant in this regard. "It is striking," wrote the newspaper, "that on the American side, Nixon's trip was accompanied by a monstrous escalation of the bombing of South Vietnam, the Democratic Republic of Vietnam, Laos and Cambodia. During the visit, the slaughter reached almost unprecedented proportions. But those who received Nixon never mentioned these events. The government of China did not protest against the American crimes, nor did the Chinese press utter a word. This serves as the basis for certain conclusions."

World public opinion noted—not without reason—that the basic problem discussed during the American-Chinese negotiations, which was subsequently omitted from the official communiqué, was that of Indochina. *The London Morning Star* summarized the results of the talks as follows: American "smiles to China, bombs to Indochina."

In the course of the "intensive negotiations" regarding the contents of the communiqué, the American side agreed, as *The New York Times* noted, to subject the "divergent statements on Taiwan" to extensive "discussion and revision to meet one objection or another from the opposite party." As a result, it became clear from the communiqué that the United States government did not dispute that "there is but one China, and that Taiwan is a part of China." Furthermore, the U.S. government "reaffirms its interest in a peaceful settlement of the Taiwan question by the Chinese themselves. With this prospect in mind, it affirms the ultimate objective of the withdrawal of all U.S. forces and military installations on Taiwan as the tension in the area diminishes."

The press in a number of countries pointed out that the radical change in U.S. policy with regard to Taiwan could not have occurred without serious compromises and concessions by Peking. Charles W. Bray, a State Department representative, explaining the U.S. position on the Taiwan problem at a Washington press conference on March 2, 1972, said that there were 8,225 American servicemen in Taiwan, and that approximately 6,000 of these were "directly connected" with military operations in Southeast Asia—in fact, the Vietnamese theater of military operations. It was to be expected, said Bray, that as the intensity of military actions in Indochina lessened, the number of American troops in Taiwan, connected with that area, would also be reduced.

This comment by a State Department representative gives reason to surmise that an understanding had been reached in Peking to make the withdrawal of American troops from Chinese territory (Taiwan) contingent upon the successes of American forces in Vietnam—*i.e.*, in the final analysis, upon the strengthened position of American imperialism in Southeast Asia. It should be recalled in this regard that the understanding in Peking was reached at a time when this entire region of Asia—from Japan to Thailand—was literally permeated with American troops and permanent American military bases, when the U.S. Navy was cruising between the Sea of Japan, the shores of the Bay of Bengal, and the Arab countries.

At the same time, one should not overlook the aggressive acts of the other participant in the talks—the People's Republic of China, *i.e.*, Peking's aggression against India, its support of the reactionary Yahya Khan government (which had been rejected by the Pakistani people), and its subversive activity against numerous other Asian governments which it disliked.

Under these prevailing circumstances, a number of journalists interpreted the proposals of the joint American-Chinese communiqué as Great Power, hegemonic statements. Experienced international observers also called attention to the fact that the Peking discussions actually took the form of undisguised bargaining between those representing imperialist and expansionist positions, with the eventual aim of reallocating spheres of influence in this region of the globe. It was no coincidence that many diplomats and specialists on international relations, particularly from the Southeast Asian countries, noted immediately that the "basis for future relations" between the United States and the People's Republic of China, as outlined in Peking, was fraught with serious consequences for the countries located in this region. "One experienced Asian diplomat," reported *The New York Times*, described the anxiety of these countries as follows: "There are pluses and minuses for Southeast Asia in the communiqué published in China. Unfortunately, the bad news is extremely concrete, whereas the good news has been formulated very vaguely and is more difficult to discern."

The Tokyo magazine *Pacific Community*, in an article published in the April-June 1972 issue, expressed itself in this regard even more firmly: "In order to create a more stable balance of power in East Asia, the governments . . . of the smaller countries must take some part in this process. If the United States and China, by mutual agreements, attempt to impose their own order in this region, the long-term result will, in all probability, be a decrease of stability, not only as a consequence of the reaction of the governments of the smaller countries, but also, to an even greater extent, because the Soviet Union and Japan failed to participate therein."

Events which occurred in Southeast Asia after the American-Chinese discussions in Peking ended only confirmed the fears of those who viewed these sessions as a definite threat to the stability in this area. For example, soon after the completion of President Nixon's visit to the People's Republic of China, the United States escalated still more sharply the military operations against the Vietnamese people, waging a war of genocide, destroying dams in the Democratic Republic of Vietnam, and threatening the very existence of millions of people.

And how did the Peking leadership react to the new wave of American imperialist crimes? "According to earlier yardsticks, the reaction of the Chinese Communists may be called truly striking . . . ," the American commentator Joseph Alsop observed in *The Washington Post*. "Peking's moral support for Hanoi is limited, it may be said, to the conventional platitudes of family solidarity which are required by propriety at family funerals." Alsop, however, was in too much of a hurry to bury the Vietnamese patriots. Their steadfastness and bravery in defense of a just cause, supported by the entire Vietnamese people and the fraternal solidarity of the Soviet people, the people of other socialist countries and all progressive humanity, forced the United States to resort to confidential meetings with the government of the Democratic Republic of Vietnam and to begin serious peace negotiations.

The negotiations were completed on January 27, 1973, with the signing in Paris of agreements designed to end the war and restore peace to Vietnam. These agreements provided for an end to America's aggressive actions, the complete withdrawal of American and other foreign troops from Vietnamese soil, and the cessation of U.S. interference in Vietnam's internal affairs. This was an important victory in the struggle against imperialism.

During the difficult Vietnam war years, the Soviet people were always united with their Vietnamese brothers, unswervingly rendering aid and support in the struggle to repulse aggression. An important factor in achieving the Vietnam cease-fire agreement and the withdrawal of foreign troops was the combined effort of countries in the socialist alliance, Communist and workers' parties, and all peace-loving forces, which for many years had actively opposed the imperialist aggression against Vietnam and supported the selfless struggle of the Vietnamese people for their rights.

The conclusion of the agreement to end the war and restore peace in Vietnam opens the way for a final, just solution of the problems facing the Vietnamese people. It would be wrong, however, to minimize the damage done by the People's Republic of China to the cause of the

Vietnamese people's just struggle against the American invaders, as well as to the entire cause of world socialism and progress.

The actions of the Peking leaders after President Nixon's visit to the People's Republic of China are also significant in another respect. Having taken its legitimate place in the United Nations, the People's Republic of China began to participate actively in the work of this international organization. The Soviet Union, together with its fraternal states, pursues in the UN a policy designed to support the national liberation movements and strengthen peace in all regions of the globe. A proposal by the Soviet Union and a number of other states to recommend for United Nations membership the People's Republic of Bangladesh was prompted by the desire to support the struggle against imperialism and colonialism, and the effort to stabilize peace on the Asian continent. In accordance with the UN Charter, a draft resolution supporting the admission of Bangladesh was introduced for considera-tion by the UN Security Council. The Peking authorities, however, blocked a favorable decision on this important question by exercising the veto power.

"It is tragic," stated the Indian Minister of Foreign Affairs at the Security Council session, "that China, for whom the doors to the United Nations were closed for 22 years, is now itself trying to prevent the admission to this organization of a newly liberated country." The Pakistani newspaper *Dawn* commented that "by preventing the admission to the United Nations of a country with a population of 75 million, Peking is not trying to do a favor for Pakistan. It is Peking's global calculations which are primarily reflected here." The German newspaper *Die Wahrheit* also expressed the same thought, emphasizing that "China's position on the question of Bangladesh is dictated by the Great Power, chauvinistic ambitions of the Peking leadership."

At the XXVIIth Session of the UN General Assembly, which took place toward the end of 1972, the representatives of the People's Republic of China took a negative position in regard to the Soviet proposals to negate the use of force in international relations and permanently ban the use of nuclear weapons. The People's Republic of China also opposed the convocation of an international conference on disarmament. The overwhelming majority of delegations, however, approved these proposals.

It may be said with assurance that one result of the American-Chinese talks in Peking was a strengthening of the Great Power, hegemonic tendencies in the foreign policy practice of the Maoist leadership. Notwithstanding occasional peace-loving gestures and decla-rations of respect for the principles of self-determination, independence and peaceful coexistence, the Peking leadership is, in fact, pursuing a policy of betrayal of the anti-imperialist struggle, of discrediting the national liberation movements, and of opposition to the creation of a collective security system in Asia. Abandoning the united policy of the socialist countries to struggle against imperialism, the Peking leadership has substituted nationalism and Great Power chauvinism for the class struggle.

These are some practical results of the American-Chinese rapprochement. Under these conditions, world public opinion is aware that the course of China's rapprochement with the United States is accompanied in Peking by the intensification of anti-Sovietism and the fanning of war hysteria. *Ekonomicheskaya Zhizn*, the weekly newspaper of the Central Committee of the Bulgarian Communist Party, observed that "The Mao Tse-tung group is implanting in the consciousness of the Chinese people one of the most reactionary varieties of bourgeois nationalism—Great Power chauvinism. It has simultaneously rejected the class position and the class point-of-view held by the Soviet Union and other socialist countries. This attitude manifests itself in the Maoist propaganda efforts to slander the Soviet Union, its domestic and foreign policy, and thereby to shake the trust and love of the broad masses of people for that state which is the mighty bulwark of the workers in the struggle against imperialism. It expresses itself further in the attempts of the Peking leaders to knit together a world power under its hegemony. This was the purpose for launching the anti-Soviet falsehoods about the existence of two 'super-powers' pursuing an imperialist policy, and the anti-Marxist theory of the 'worldwide city' and 'worldwide country,' which are alleged to be basically opposing forces. Blinded by their anti-Sovietism and Great Power chauvinism, the Chinese leaders are prepared to take under their wing any defectors from the Communist movement and any revisionists."

The development of events confirmed the words spoken from the rostrum of the XXIVth Congress of the Communist Party of the Soviet Union by the General Secretary of the Central Committee, L. I. Brezhnev: "It is all the more absurd and harmful to sow discord between China and the U.S.S.R. at a time when the imperialists have been intensifying their acts of aggression against the freedom-loving peoples. More than ever before, the situation demands solidarity and joint action by all the anti-imperialist, revolutionary forces, instead of fanning the hostility between such nations as the U.S.S.R. and China."

AFTERWORD

President Nixon's visit to the Chinese People's Republic and his discussions with Mao Tse-tung and Chou En-lai attracted the attention of the world community. Certain members of the news media, primarily American, tried to surround this diplomatic visit with an aura of sensationalism and singularity, by exaggerating its results whenever possible. But with the passage of time, both the China visit itself and the outcome of the President's discussions with the Peking leaders are beginning to receive more sober evaluation. Noteworthy, above all else, has been the forced nature of the shift in America's China policy from one of "isolation and containment" to "contacts and conciliation." The world press has called attention in this regard to those persistent grave defeats which the aggressive policy of American imperialism has been suffering, especially in Asia. Washington is beginning to realize that its unilateral efforts to decide the fate of the world have garnered no laurels for the architects of American foreign policy. And yet, the United States remains unwilling to repudiate its notorious policy of negotiation "from a position of strength."

Under these circumstances, Nixon's trip to Peking, according to the Damascus newspaper *Al Baath*, was not prompted by "any subjective desire on the part of the President or other U.S. politicians." Instead, the purposes of the visit "stem from the totality of the political, military and social situation." The Hungarian newspaper *Nepszabadsag* wrote: "The White House has turned toward Peking not because of the strength of its realism, but because American imperialism, which grasps at anything just to cling to its position in the struggle against the forces of socialism, demands such a move to protect its interests." And the American commentator Stewart Alsop noted in *Newsweek* magazine that the most important objective of the President's visit, "in terms of immediate, concrete results, was to get help from the Chinese for a reasonably respectable exit from Vietnam."

As mentioned earlier, the joint American-Chinese communiqué on the negotiations revealed hardly anything concerning the actual content of the talks, or the substance of the understanding which the two parties reached. Moreover, the parties in the talks let it be unequivocally understood that the decision had been made to keep everything secret, and "not to discuss" anything beyond the contents of the published official communiqué. Nevertheless, many observers emphasized that, judging by certain statements made by the respective parties, one might conclude that the Peking dialogue extended beyond the subject of American-Chinese bilateral relations. Stewart Alsop wrote that "there are reasons to believe that real progress has been made in Peking toward a respectable withdrawal of the Americans from Vietnam, and that this progress would have been impossible if the President had not personally gone to Peking."

The results of the talks caused serious concern in the third world, as well as in the small countries. The Dakar weekly *Afrique Nouvelle* noted that the agreements reached during the course of the American-Chinese talks provided "documentary proof of the Maoists' betrayal of the interests of small countries, and of all that [the Maoists] had called the anti-imperialist struggle of the peoples of Asia, Africa and Latin America. . . . The parties in these talks settled, in accord with their own interests, the destiny of the small countries and agreed on the division of Asia into spheres of influence." The Mexican newspaper *El Dia* wrote in this regard that "the wordy, revolutionary fog produced by the Chinese leaders in an attempt to conceal their chauvinistic, hegemonic aspirations in Asia, has finally lifted. China's strategy coincides exactly with the American policy, which aims at the division of Asia into spheres of influence." It is impossible to disagree with such conclusions.

The published communiqué indicates that one of the main practical results of Nixon's visit to the People's Republic of China was an agreement by the respective parties to "stay in contact through various channels, including the sending of a senior U.S. representative to Peking from time to time for concrete consultations to further the normalization of relations between the two countries, and to continue an exchange of views on issues of common interest." It is well known that the first step in effectuating the understanding which had been reached was the shift of the American-Chinese talks at the ambassadorial level from Warsaw to Paris. Commenting on this decision, *The New York Times* emphasized that this change in location was evidence that the Chinese preferred Western territory for such delicate deliberations.

The first meetings between the American and Chinese Ambassadors in Paris took place in March 1972 and continued throughout the year. These meetings were conducted in even greater secrecy than the negotiations in Warsaw; it was decided not even to issue reports. When asked for an explanation, a State Department representative replied: "In our opinion, with which the Chinese People's Republic concurs, this is the best and, we hope, the most fruitful way." Other officials explained that the new approach to the talks was the result of the emergence after the Nixon visit of relations with Peking which made it possible to establish meaningful contacts.

Thus, President Nixon's visit in February 1972 to Peking, the capital of the People's Republic of China, put an end to the old, obsolete U.S. policy toward China and opened a new page in American-Chinese relations. If normalization of relations between America and China were just one part of a policy to strengthen and expand friendly relations with all countries, and, above all, with China's immediate neighbors, such a policy would have undoubtedly won the approval of the progressive world community. As the facts prove, however, the Peking leaders turned into virtual accomplices of imperialist policy. Peking's Great Power aspirations and its anti-Marxist policy promoted, according to the Polish magazine *Nove Drogi*, the aggravation of international tension and the creation of conditions for a new imperialist attack on the forces of progress and freedom.

The problems of American-Chinese relations at the present stage remain extraordinarily complex. President Nixon's visit to the People's Republic of China has not eliminated the deep and real contradictions which existed, and continue to exist between both countries. Time will reveal the true results and significance of President Nixon's China visit, as the magazine *Nove Drogi* observed. When the dust raised by the clamorous publicity settles, it will be possible to answer definitively the question of whether the journey was a step toward the relaxation or heightening of tension in Asia.

Relations between the United States and the Chinese People's Republic continue to evolve under the influence of various, often diametrically opposed factors. It should be remembered in this connection that the entire direction of U.S. policy toward the People's Republic of China is to a significant degree dependent not so much upon the Peking leadership's attitude toward America, as upon its attitude toward the world system of socialism. China's unconditional alliance with world socialism during the 1949-57 period determined the basic content of America's China policy in those years. The former U.S. President Harry Truman accurately characterized that policy as one of "limited hostility."

The subsequent departure of the Chinese Communist Party leadership from the general course of the international Communist movement, which has led to China's transformation into a force hostile to the Soviet Union and other socialist countries, strongly influenced the new trend of the U.S. ruling circles toward gradual re-examination of their policy. Under these circumstances, a determined faction within the U.S. ruling circles began persistent efforts to "build bridges" to Peking. These efforts resulted in the supplanting of the "isolation without containment" policy by the "contacts and conciliation" doctrine. Among the most striking manifestations of the latter was President Nixon's visit to China.

A development of this nature would, of course, be most welcome, if it were truly based on such constant factors as the role and significance of China's people and government in international relations. It must be said, however, that in implementing their "new strategy," certain American circles are proceeding primarily from the anti-Soviet line of Mao Tse-tung and his group, *i.e.*, from a temporary, passing policy which does not correspond to the Chinese people's fundamental interests. And under these circumstances, the "new strategy" of the U.S. imperialist circles has as its real aim not the relaxation of international tension, but a definitive alienation of the People's Republic of China from the socialist alliance. This is one further piece of evidence that Mao Tse-tung's current policy course is objectively advantageous to America's reactionary imperialist circles.

Thus, the emerging Chinese-American rapprochement is basically opportunistic in nature, and dictated to a significant degree by the hegemonic aspirations of certain circles in both countries. This rapprochement is directed by the force of objective conditions against the interests of all socialist countries, and primarily against the U.S.S.R. It does enormous harm simultaneously to the national liberation movement and the struggle against imperialism and colonialism.

It should be noted that the present trend toward rapprochement between America and China is firm in nature. This firmness will in future depend mainly upon such factors as the continuation, regularity and intensity of the political dialogue which is under way between the two countries, the expansion of the sphere of bilateral relations, and a readiness to solve those problems which still divide the two countries. The world press has noted in this regard that the political dialogue between Peking and Washington "must constitute something more than a mere ritualistic repetition of each side's positions, such as we observed during the Warsaw talks. It must constitute a serious attempt by the two parties to decrease suspicion and strengthen mutual understanding."

This American-Chinese dialogue is developing in several directions. First, the secret talks begun in Paris between the U.S. Ambassador to France, Arthur K. Watson, and Ambassador Huang Chen of the People's Republic of China are continuing. Second, highly placed American figures are traveling regularly to China. In April-May 1972, Mike Mansfield, the Democratic party majority leader in the U.S. Senate, and Senator Hugh Scott, the Republican party leader, made a 16-day visit to China. "The hospitality shown to us was profound and significant," Mansfield said. "The friendliness was obvious." He also stressed that the Chinese leaders "want rapprochement" with the United States and desire "increased exchanges between the two countries."

A succeeding Peking visit was made in June 1972 by Henry A. Kissinger, at that time the U.S. President's Special Assistant for National Security Affairs. At a Washington news conference upon his return, Kissinger said: "The main purpose of the talks was primarily to discuss American-Chinese relations and concrete measures for their further improvement, as well as a general review of the international situation."

In early July 1972, Hale Boggs, a high-ranking Democratic leader in the U.S. House of Representatives, and Gerald R. Ford, the House Republican leader, returned to Washington from a 10-day visit to the Chinese People's Republic. According to Ford, the Peking leaders were extremely interested in the American foreign policy course. The congressmen were asked specifically whether the United States intended to withdraw its troops from Southeast Asia, and Ford replied: "Among high Chinese officials, there was a great deal of interest shown in, and many questions asked about the sufficiency of our military capability. . . . They don't want the United States to withdraw from the Pacific or the world at any point. They think our presence is vital for the stability of the world, and the withdrawal of the United States would lead to instability in the world."

American officials and journalists still continue their travels to the People's Republic of China. In fact, the expansion of the sphere of bilateral relations may encompass a whole number of areas, including trade, tourism, cultural exchanges and joint participation in various international conferences and meetings. As a result of the President's visit, dramatic shifts became apparent in the expansion of trade and economic cooperation between America and China. In July 1972, the U.S. Department of Commerce announced the issuance of an export license to the largest American aviation firm, the Boeing Corporation, for delivery of passenger jets to the People's Republic of China. It was notable in this regard that the Boeing Corporation is one of the largest Pentagon contractors and, in particular, manufactured B-52 aircraft, which were used in the massive bombing of Vietnam. The American press also reported that negotiations between representatives of China's foreign trade organizations and Boeing dealt with the concrete details of a commercial transaction to furnish aircraft valued at $150 million to the People's Republic of China. Considering that the entire volume of trade between the two countries in 1971 did not exceed $4 million, it becomes clear that this was no ordinary transaction, but rather a completely new approach to the entire problem of American-Chinese trade relations. Commenting on the talks surrounding the Boeing sale, *The New York Post* expressed the hope that "the large order for planes may prove to be more than a one-time transaction, and may serve as a signal for the beginning of significant growth in trade over the next few years."

A whole group of American firms sent their representatives to the People's Republic of China in 1972 to establish contacts. Specifically, the Parker Drilling Company was exploring the possibility of oil drilling operations in mainland China, the Lockheed Aviation Company was considering the sale of turbo-prop cargo planes to China, and so forth. In November 1972, President Nixon decided to remove the People's Republic of China from the category of countries which American ships and civilian aircraft are forbidden to visit. This presidential decision opens up new prospects for the large American transportation companies.

As regards cultural cooperation, exchanges of athletic teams are taking place, and a number of American scholars and several tourist groups have visited the People's Republic of China. According to an *Agence France* news report, the well-known American Sinologist, Professor John K. Fairbank of Harvard University, stated after a 40-day tour in six Chinese provinces that the atmosphere in Peking was "very polite and full of enthusiasm for the improvement of relations between China and America."

Naturally, the location and development of areas of common interest between America and China are extremely complex matters. But here, too, the careful analysis of Peking's most recent foreign policy measures makes it possible to discern, if not common interests, then at least parallel goals. The Peking leadership, by conducting complicated foreign policy maneuvers within the framework of the Maoist course, has already brought Washington "considerable dividends," according to *The New York Times*. In particular, Peking's extremely restrained reaction to the sharp escalation of the Vietnam war helped "to stifle criticism of Washington's foreign policy, its position in the India-Pakistan conflict, and the renewal of the bombing of North Vietnam." The anti-Soviet course followed by the Maoists has thus become aligned with the policy of reaction and imperialism.

All these factors corroborate the firm nature of the trend toward rapprochement between China and the United States. This rapprochement is, as noted earlier, basically opportunistic in nature, and cannot eliminate the existing fundamental differences between the two countries, such as the conflict on the Asian continent, where both nations are striving to consolidate their positions and where their interests must inevitably clash. Nor has the dispute over Taiwan which, according to the Tokyo journal *Pacific Community*, constitutes the "central problem in relations between the United States and China," been resolved as yet. There are extremely serious disagreements between America and China over their mutual relations, as well as their policy toward other governments, primarily a whole group of Asian countries. It is not surprising that these governments are expressing concern and even alarm over the developing rapprochement between Peking and Washington.

The complex intertwining of the interests of various countries inevitably complicates the maneuvering of both Peking and Washington, and their own interests will thus collide from time to time. Under these circumstances, American imperialism is counting on Peking's anti-Sovietism and repudiation of the coordinated policy of the socialist countries against imperialism and reaction. This policy course of the Maoist leadership cannot win for it any laurels, for the anti-Leninist, adventurist policy of the Mao Tse-tung group promises nothing good for the Chinese people.

Leonid I. Brezhnev, in his speech at the XVth Congress of Trade Unions, stated: "As for our relations with the People's Republic of China, the principled position of our Party and of the Soviet state was clearly expressed in documents of the XXIVth Congress of the Communist Party of the Soviet Union. A resolution of the Congress stated that our Party stands for a position of consistent defense of the principles of Marxism-Leninism, all possible strengthening of the unity of the world Communist movement, and the defense of the interests of the socialist Fatherland.

"It further states that 'The Congress resolutely rejects the slanderous inventions of Chinese propaganda concerning the policy of our Party and our state. At the same time, our Party favors the normalization of relations between the U.S.S.R. and the People's Republic of China, and the restoration of good neighborliness and friendship between the Soviet and Chinese peoples. The improvement of relations between the Soviet Union and the Chinese People's Republic would correspond to the fundamental, long-range interests of both countries, of world socialism, and of the struggle against imperialism.' Today, as in the past, our position remains fully in force."

EPILOGUE

In both the first and second editions of *The U.S.A. and China*, which were published in Moscow in 1968 and 1973, S. Sergeichuk attempted to present a concise historical outline of U.S. policy toward the People's Republic of China, rather than a comprehensive analysis and interpretation of American-Chinese relations. The work aroused the interest of both Soviet and foreign readers for several reasons, the following being, in this writer's opinion, the most important:

First, and foremost, this book was essentially the initial effort by a Soviet author which was devoted to the "United States-China" problem. It appeared at a time when the advocates of an anti-socialist, Great Power policy within the leadership of the Communist Party of China had stepped up their activity. The publication of the first edition of the book coincided with a sharp intensification of Maoist anti-Sovietism, [1] to which many capitalist countries responded either by calls for almost open solidarity with the Maoists, or by a silence amounting to approval. Naturally, the Soviet people were not indifferent toward information about the prospects of the Peking leaders in their gamble on the anti-Soviet attitudes within the capitalist countries, and primarily in the United States.

Furthermore, America's search for new ways and means to preserve its position in the world—and this at a time when it was searching for a way out of the Vietnam impasse as well as its serious domestic political difficulties—could not fail to attract the attention of this book's readers. Those in the Soviet Union sought in the book an answer to the question of what the prospects for U.S. relations with Maoist China actually were, in light of that tacit mutual understanding which had developed between Washington and Peking during the Vietnam war, and in light of the American endeavors to find the fastest way out of the Vietnam stalemate. Sergeichuk took a bold step toward exploring the problems which had aroused the interest of the Soviet public.

In the book's first chapter, "American-Chinese Relations: A New Factor," the author discusses the circumstances preceding the withdrawal of the Chinese Communist Party leadership from the foreign policy course which had been agreed upon in conjunction with the other socialist countries. Although the Maoist group's Great Power aspirations were clearly revealed during the Sixties, these aspirations had actually already surfaced in the activity of Mao and his associates as long ago as the Thirties and Forties. The specific conditions under which the Communist Party of China was formed (the predominance of the peasant masses, the weakness of the working class, the strong position of the petit-bourgeoisie, etc.) led, in the words of V. I. Lenin, "with particular force and persistence, ... to prejudices of national egotism and national narrow-mindedness." Naturally, this was bound to be reflected in the enduring nationalism within the Chinese Communist Party.

On the other hand, there also emerged within the Chinese Communist Party a core of Communist-internationalists, formed on the principle of solidarity with the ideas of the Great October Revolution and cooperation with the international Communist movement. Thus, the dialectics of the development of the Communist Party of China reflected the struggle—at times extremely sharp and severe—between two tendencies: the Marxist-Leninist internationalist tendency, on the one hand, and, on the other, the petit-bourgeois nationalist tendency. The actions of the Chinese nationalists within the Communist Party of China exhibited qualities which were characteristic of the petit-bourgeoisie and were related, above all, to the nationalists' instability and vacillation between the petit-bourgeoisie and the proletariat. As long ago as the Forties, the Maoist practice of reciprocal relations with the U.S.S.R. and the United States demonstrated the obvious inclination of the Chinese Communist Party nationalists to try to profit by the international contradictions between the two social systems, and to exploit in their own policy the ancient Chinese principles of "sitting on a mountain to observe the fight of two tigers," "joining with the far against the near neighbor," and so forth.

There is currently a great deal of writing and discussion in various countries about the American efforts during the Forties to find avenues of cooperation with Mao Tse-tung. But perhaps no one is more enthusiastic in discussing this topic than the Americans themselves. Guided at times by absolutely conflicting motives,[2] those advocating various means and methods to implement America's China policy have published numerous books and articles on the history of American contacts with the Maoist circles.[3] Attempts have often been made to give to the American reader the impression that the Washington Administration had erred in not establishing closer relations with the Maoists during that hectic period on a basis acceptable to the United States, including an anti-Soviet basis. In this regard, reference is often made to Mao Tse-tung's discussions with the participants in the "Dixie Mission," during which the leader of the Chinese Communist Party described, in rosy terms, the prospects for Sino-American cooperation in the post-war world. From the historian's vantage point, I would like to challenge the validity of this kind of retrospective interpretation of the American experience in China.

During World War II, many Americans who had established contacts with China's "special regions," which were controlled by the Communist Party of China, proceeded from the existing realities and, in their efforts to mobilize China's resources against Japanese militarism, took into account (or were forced to do so) the vital tasks of the anti-fascist coalition. One such American, John K. Emmerson, in an October 1974 conversation with this writer, cited numerous examples from his own past activity which dealt with American efforts to activate an anti-Japanese front in China. Among U.S. diplomats, however, there were also those who pinned greater hopes on the Maoists' anti-Sovietism, which they regarded as an important means to achieve long-term imperialistic goals; to this end, they gambled (as, for example, the diplomat John Paton Davies had proposed) on a split between the Soviet Union and the Communist Party of China. However, this latter course ran counter to the interest of the nations' struggle against the common enemy, as well as to that of strengthening Soviet-American cooperation. America's active gamble on the Maoists' anti-Sovietism could lead only to the growth of suspicion and mutual distrust among the allies and, thus, prove detrimental to the cause of the anti-fascist coalition.

Mao Tse-tung felt compelled during the Forties to limit his flirtation with the United States to top-secret negotiations, so that (in this writer's opinion) his advances toward the Americans would appear to be tactical measures. The Maoist foreign policy program, which envisioned a dialogue with the United States, could not go beyond the bounds imposed by both the anti-feudal and anti-imperialist nature of the Chinese revolution.

S. Sergeichuk correctly writes that the Soviet Union's active role in the crushing defeat of Hitler's Germany and imperialist Japan was the most important international factor in determining the success of the Chinese revolution. It resulted in the significant strengthening of the internationalist forces within the Communist Party of China, and the transformation of Manchuria, liberated by Soviet troops, into an outpost for the Chinese Communists in the struggle against the Kuomintang regime. From this outpost, units of the Chinese People's Liberation Army launched a broad offensive against the Kuomintang and, by the summer of 1949, liberated the most important economic and political areas of China. Faced with this situation, Washington appeared ready to take steps toward a change in its China policy.

The U.S. government, which had decided to justify the failure of its China policy and explore the possibilities for a new approach to China, took an important step in 1949 by publishing the "China White Paper." That Sergeichuk begins the second chapter of his book with a sub-chapter titled "China White Paper" is not coincidental. The documents published in the "White Paper," highly critical of the Kuomintang government, were designed to prepare American public opinion for the inevitable defeat of Chiang Kai-shek and, at the same time, to establish favorable conditions for a possible dialogue with the nationalist leaders of the Communist Party of China. The publication of the "White Paper," as well as Washington's other foreign policy propaganda actions, were all designed to drive a wedge between the leadership of the Communist Party of China and the Soviet Union, and were prompted (as is noted in the book) by the desire to find a basis for mutual understanding with the nationalist elements within the Chinese Communist Party leadership. Mao Tse-tung, however, could not respond at that time to the Washington advances. "The slogan 'Prepare for the Struggle,' " said Mao in 1949, when the "China White Paper" was published, "is aimed at those who are still nurturing definite illusions about the relations between China and the capitalist countries, and especially between China and the United States." [4]

On the eve of the Chinese revolutionary victory, Mao, undoubtedly fearing the loss of his own position in the Party, was forced to come to terms with the position of the Communist-internationalists. This, however, can scarcely justify the references to the alleged "miscalculations" of the American Administration in formulating U.S. policies toward the Communist Party of China during the war and the early post-war years. The Maoist flirtation with the United States during the Forties could hardly (and, most likely, not at all) lead to any substantive improvements in Chinese-American relations. This statement becomes more persuasive when one analyzes the events in China at that time.

The People's Republic of China, established as the result of an anti-feudal, anti-imperialist revolution, and acting in the international arena in concert with other socialist camp countries, has achieved considerable successes in both its domestic and foreign policies. The authors of the report prepared by the "Conlon Associates" organization—which Sergeichuk cites in his book—reached, for instance, the conclusion that friendly relations between the People's Republic of China and the Soviet Union had "increased her [5] world prestige within as well as without the Communist orbit."

The joint participation of the People's Republic of China with other socialist countries in the solution of the most pressing current problems did not, of course, signify a unity of views among the Chinese leadership on all foreign policy questions, including relations with the United States both prior to and during the early Sixties. At the end of the Fifties, when questions of peaceful coexistence among countries with differing social systems and the prevention of general nuclear war acquired special urgency in world politics, articles had already appeared in the Chinese press which were obviously designed to undermine the trend toward a relaxation of international tension. The calls for a war against imperialism "by sword against sword" were aimed toward that end, as was the thesis, for example, that "American imperialists will not be able to discard the butcher-knife and become living Buddhas." [6] During the same month when the government of the People's Republic of China supported a Soviet disarmament proposal, the Chairman of the All-China Federation of Trade Unions, Liu Chan-shen, issued a statement on June 28, 1960, which essentially disavowed the Chinese government's official position. "Some people now believe," he said, "that proposals for a general disarmament can be realized while imperialism exists, and that the danger of war can be averted by means of these proposals. This is an unrealistic illusion." [7]

The Maoists were compelled to reconcile themselves to the necessity of proclaiming the importance of unity among the socialist countries in the world political arena. Unable to launch an open attack upon the Soviet Union, they were searching for an appropriate tactic to assure the success of their Great Power, chauvinistic policy course. They considered the creation of their own nuclear arsenal one of the most important features of this plan. Even then, the accomplishment of this plan was linked to Peking's desire to stand up to the United States independently, and its intention to use the atomic bomb as an important lever for influencing the situation in Asia. At that time the Maoists were attempting publicly to adapt their nuclear program to their declared foreign policy aims. [8] The Maoists' Great Power aspirations influenced Peking to use anti-Americanism as a particularly nationalistic doctrine, designed to serve as an important means to strengthen the domestic position of Mao's supporters. This situation became especially clear in the efforts to discredit the Soviet-American negotiations, primarily as related to disarmament, and to pressure the United States in order to gain recognition for the People's Republic of China as a Great Power.

At the beginning of the Sixties, the Maoist leadership made virtually an open break with the general policy of the international Communist movement—a policy which had been developed in 1957, with the Communist Party of China itself participating, at the Moscow Conference of Communist and Workers' Parties. In extremely sharp tones, the Maoist leadership began to proclaim its anti-Marxist-Leninist platform of Great Power chauvinism, hegemony and anti-Sovietism. The Maoists at the same time endeavored to split the world Communist movement, and started down the path of active rapprochement with certain capitalist countries, pinning special hopes in that regard on the so-called "buffer zone" countries in Europe. The "buffer zone theory" was also used to accomplish on a global level the Chinese leaders' anti-Soviet and anti-socialist policy. Later, the Maoist leadership, asserting that the U.S.S.R. had entered into an agreement with the United States, also employed the "buffer zone theory" against the Soviet Union, making that theory the foundation for its concept of the struggle against the "super-powers," *i.e.*, against the U.S.S.R. and the United States.

The Maoists proved wrong in their calculations that an anti-Marxist, pragmatic platform, filled with anti-Soviet and anti-American slogans, could be exploited to attract economic and political resources from the capitalist West. The Chinese leadership's Great Power chauvinism, coupled with adventurism and militarism, put a brake upon the intentions of the capitalist world's ruling circles to improve relations with the People's Republic of China. It can now be said without doubt that the extremism in Peking's foreign policy objectively contributed to the strengthened position of the most militaristic American circles, which had fought to expand the power of the military complex that opposes the socialist countries, including China. The American Administration, significantly influenced by these forces, toughened its aggressive policy in Indochina, as well as its military-political pressure upon the national liberation movement, and stirred up those circles which relied on subversive actions in Indonesia, Burma and Ceylon.

The foreign policy-makers in the capitalist West remained briefly uncertain about the validity of the Maoists' resolution to split with the socialist countries; they believed that those viewing the Maoists' anti-Sovietism as a factor of long-term significance lacked sufficient evidence to support their theory. Toward the end of the Sixties, however, Peking's anti-American course, specifically reflected in the theory of "peoples' wars," essentially lost its efficacy as a means to exert pressure upon Washington for accepting conditions of a Chinese-American settlement which would be most favorable to Peking. A further turn in the foreign policy of the People's Republic of China made anti-Sovietism, rather than anti-Americanism, the most important means for the Maoists to realize their Great Power policy. Immediately thereafter, calls began to be heard—at first timid, but later increasingly persistent—for a reassessment of U. S. policy toward China. S. Sergeichuk dwells in his narrative on the evolution of the position of the American "China Lobby," which actively promoted in earlier years Washington's implementation of a pro-Chiang Kai-shek policy, and was compelled in the Sixties to adjust to the new trends in America's China policy.

If it were merely a question of the normal development of relations between two countries, there would be little reason to search for anything unusual in the accelerated development of political and economic-trade contacts between the United States and People's Republic of China in the late Sixties and early Seventies. After all, peaceful coexistence and cooperation between countries with differing social systems is completely natural. For more than two decades the Soviet Union has been advocating the establishment of normal diplomatic relations between the Chinese People's Republic and the United States, as well as the other capitalist world Powers. It was another question, however, which disturbed the Soviet people and public opinion throughout the world: Were not those measures which had been directed toward normalization of Sino-American relations detrimental to the interests of other countries, and contrary to the interests of the entire world? For example, could the fact that the Chinese-American rapprochement commenced soon after the IXth Congress of the Chinese Communist Party, on the eve of which Maoist anti-Sovietism manifested itself in the form of blatant adventurist actions along the Soviet borders, escape notice by the Soviet and peace-loving public?

It is well known that in 1970-71, during the preparation for the reception of the American President in Peking, the population of the People's Republic of China was subjected to intense propaganda treatment. The Chinese citizen was reminded of the necessity to distinguish between his "primary" and "secondary" enemy. The Peking leaders turned to the directive of the Central Committee of the Chinese Communist Party ("On Our Policy"), prepared by Mao Tse-tung as far back as December 25, 1940, which included a call to "exploit conflicts, win over the majority, fight against the minority, smash the opponents one by one." Based on such a thesis, Maoist propaganda was attempting to inculcate in the Chinese population the belief that, in exploiting the conflicts between the Soviet Union and the United States, one should first rail against the U.S.S.R., and then denounce the United States as well.

The material published in the Hong Kong press indicates that the Chinese leadership viewed the U.S. President's visit to the People's Republic of China as a maneuver aimed at isolating the Soviet Union. The concluding chapter of Sergeichuk's book is devoted to this truly important event in American-Chinese relations—the President's visit to the People's Republic of China. And the author, in commenting upon that event, reaches the justified conclusion that world public opinion is well aware of the heightened anti-Sovietism and the fanning of military hysteria within China, which have accompanied the policy of rapprochement with the United States.

The basis upon which normalization between Peking and Washington is established, now and in the future, is extremely important for the fate of peace, as well as for that of Soviet-American and Soviet-Chinese relations. Will this basis serve to strengthen international security, or will it be directed against the interests of other countries, including the countries of the socialist alliance? In evaluating the results of the American President's visit to China, the General Secretary of the Central Committee of the Soviet Communist Party, L. I. Brezhnev, in his address to the Xth Congress of Trade Unions, said: "Regarding the Peking meeting, it must be said, in general, that many widely varied opinions and conjectures are being expressed. However, opinions are opinions, and the final word will come, I reiterate, after all the facts become known. Thus, we are in no hurry to make a final evaluation. The future, possibly the near future, will show the reality of the situation. And we will draw from this the appropriate practical conclusions."[9]

The new situation in American-Chinese relations, predetermined by the Shanghai communiqué of 1972, demonstrated that the Maoists' hopes for playing the American card to further their Great Power policy were not realized to any significant degree. The new trends in international relations which are developing during the Seventies, and the ideas of peaceful, mutually advantageous cooperation and respect for the independence and territorial integrity of states (regardless of the social system to which they belong) are gaining increased popularity among nations. Under these conditions, any adventurist actions by the Peking leaders in the international arena, even if intended for the

Maoists' domestic political needs, are not and will not be excused by all those who are concerned over the fate of the world. And for this very reason, a realistic consideration of the limits within which the Chinese factor can be exploited in an anti-socialist strategy has become the criterion for sober thinking by the American policy-makers. Furthermore, credit is due, in my opinion, to those political figures in the United States who perceive the danger—both to international and American interests—of gambling upon the Maoists' anti-Sovietism.

The development of new trends in international relations, which signifies an improvement in the political climate of our planet, was bound to influence the internal political struggle within the Chinese leadership and produce conflicts in Peking over the problem of relations with the United States. The definite downward turn in the relations between the People's Republic of China and the capitalist countries, including the United States, which occurred from late 1973 to mid-1974, must be regarded as a result of the intensification of this type of struggle. Above all, the Chinese leaders, as the events of 1974 proved, are continuing to work with unrestrained energy toward the subversion of the trend toward relaxation of international tension, and are endeavoring to use their relations with the United States to that end. The discussions between the Peking leaders and the American congressmen who visited the People's Republic of China during the first half of September 1974 are characteristic of this plan. The published interview with J. William Fulbright, the leader of the congressional delegation, indicates that the Chinese discussed at length their position with regards to the Soviet Union. ("They spoke extremely openly about Russia," Fulbright said.)

It can hardly be considered coincidental that during the very period when the American congressmen were visiting the People's Republic of China, the Maoist press distinguished itself by its particularly aggressive vilification of the Soviet Union. Peking clearly demonstrated its alignment with the opponents of detente. This Maoist position does not, of course, serve the cause of peace, the alternative to which may only be a general nuclear catastrophe. Those American politicians who categorically think in a rational manner and consider the existing realities of the modern world recognize the danger inherent to such a position. It was not without reason that J. W. Fulbright, in sharing his impressions of his trip to China, expressed his disappointment that the Chinese leaders do not understand, as he asserted, the necessity of finding a new approach for solving international problems, which would take into account the destructive power of nuclear weapons.

The recent development of American-Chinese relations has shown that the two sides are unable to find fundamental solutions for settling the conflicts which exist between them. The Vietnam ceasefire somewhat lessened the inflammatory nature of these conflicts, but could not completely clear the way for their removal. The differing socio-political structures, the clash of interests in Asia, the problem of Taiwan—these and other factors will continue to exert a restraining influence on the development of American-Chinese relations. With the increasing relaxation of international tension, and with Peking standing firm in its earlier position, further steps along the path to American-Chinese normalization will meet with ever greater difficulties.

American policy toward the People's Republic of China, as well as toward the U.S.S.R., Western Europe and Japan, is not, of course, limited by regional boundaries. American policy clashes or accords with the interests and policy of these countries in practically every corner of the globe and on the most varied international problems. The degree of success in the solution of problems which have significant priority for the fate of all humanity—problems such as disarmament, trade, aid to the developing countries, environmental protection, etc.—depends upon the pace at which positive tendencies (from the perspective of world peace) develop in the entire system of international relations, wherein Soviet-American, Soviet-Chinese and American-Chinese relations all occupy an important place.

The Soviet Union's interests are linked to the interests of world peace and the further strengthening in the world arena of the principles of mutually advantageous, active cooperation, without any detriment whatsoever to the interests of other countries. Our country's efforts are directed toward the restoration of friendly ties between the U.S.S.R. and the People's Republic of China, which the Maoists bear responsibility for rupturing. Comrade A. A. Gromyko, at the gala meeting held at the Kremlin on November 6, 1974, which was dedicated to the 57th anniversary of the Great October Socialist Revolution, emphasized: "The present leadership of China has joined forces with the opponents of world detente. Its policy, which is one of struggle against the Soviet Union and the socialist alliance, endeavors to obstruct the improvement of peaceful international cooperation. Our Party has repulsed, and will continue to repulse those actions by Peking which aim at an alignment with the extreme imperialist reactionaries. At the same time, we shall strive, as in the past, for the normalization of Soviet-Chinese relations, and we shall do everything we can to restore friendly relations between the Soviet Union and the People's Republic of China. We proceed from the same premise that this corresponds to the fundamental interests of both the Soviet and Chinese peoples."[10]

The Soviet Union today firmly advocates the creation of a structure for international relations which will completely exclude the threat of war, as well as suspicion and mistrust among nations. A structure of this nature truly responds to the long-term interests of the world nations and of the citizens of the Soviet Union, the United States and the People's Republic of China.

VLADILEN B. VORONTSOV
Professor, Far East Institute
U.S.S.R. Academy of Sciences

November 1974

FOOTNOTES

1. It is common knowledge that the Maoists' provocations along the U.S.S.R. borders took place in 1969. (*Author's note*)

2. It is difficult to feel both sympathy for Chiang Kai-shek and good-will toward Mao Tse-tung. (*Author's note*)

3. No small effort was made in this connection by Professor Anthony Kubek, John Stewart Service, John Paton Davies, Barbara Tuchman and many others. (*Author's note*)

4. Mao Tse-tung, *On the U.S. White Paper*, Foreign Languages Press, Peking, 1961, p. 7.

5. *i.e.*, the People's Republic of China (*Author's note*)

6. *Mezhdunarodnaia Zhizn (International Life)*, No. 1, 1974, p. 37.

7. M. S. Kapitsa, *Two Decades–Two Policies*, Moscow, 1969, p. 180.

8. "When China has atomic bombs," stated Chen Yi on October 2, 1961, "the possibility of the outbreak of war will be lessened." (*Author's note*)

9. *Pravda*, March 22, 1972.

10. *Pravda*, Nov. 7, 1974.

INDEX